AF813223

Institute of Consumer Financial Education

Certified Identity Theft Risk Management Specialist – CITRMS® XV Independent Study Guide

Textbook and Desk Reference

By Yan Ross, J.D., CITRMS®

ICFE Certified Identity Theft Risk Management Specialist - CITRMS® XV
by the Institute of Consumer Financial Education
ISBN-13: 978-0692683880 (Institute of Consumer Financial Education)
ISBN-10: 0692683887

Written by: Yan Ross, J.D., CITRMS®
Publication Design by: P. William Zivanchev

Published and made available in English worldwide by the
Institute of Consumer Financial Education (ICFE)

Administrative Headquarters Mailing Address:
ICFE Permissions Section
U. S. PO Box 34070
San Diego, CA 92163-4070 (USA)
619-239-1401
Email: icfe@twc.com
Web Site http://www.icfe.org

DISCLAIMER
The 2015 CITRMS® XV Independent Study Guide, like the original course, includes reference to and language from various federal and State laws and regulations, but is not intended to provide legal opinions or advice. The Institute of Consumer Financial Education and the Author strongly advise participants in this program to seek any required legal advice from qualified legal counsel.

Special note: Due to the nature of the internet and/or current social media, it is possible for internet links or Uniform Resource Locators (URLs) to become invalid, inactive, redirected, or otherwise unusable. This is the nature of the internet and The ICFE can accept no responsibility for changed, redirected, or otherwise expired URLs and web-based documentation from organizations or government entities resourced herein. Should a URL become invalid please use the topic "title" to search the internet via your PCs embedded search engine of choice. We encourage feedback and input on all our programs and any information shared will be held in confidence to be used with the intent of benefitting our certification peers, through course improvements.

Institute of Consumer Financial Education

Certified Identity Theft Risk Management Specialist - CITRMS® XV

Textbook and Desk Reference

ICFE – P.O. Box 34070, San Diego, CA 92163 - USA

Othello, by William Shakespeare (Act 3, Scene 3)

(Image from the Wikimedia Commons. Commons is a freely licensed media file repository.)

IAGO *

Good name in man and woman, dear my lord, is the immediate jewel of their souls.

Who steals my purse steals trash. 'Tis something, nothing:
'Twas mine, 'tis his, and has been slave to thousands.

But he that filches from me my good name robs me of that which not enriches him and makes me poor indeed.

** Iago is the villain who plants the seeds of the destruction of his General, Othello. Although he does show an understanding of the damage that's done by one who steals our good names, which we'd refer to in modern times as "Identity Theft," it's clear he lived in an age without the Internet, credit reports, or consumer protections.*

Introduction by Paul S. Richard, ICFE President

Welcome to the Textbook and Desk Reference version of ICFE's Certified Identity Theft Risk Management Specialist CITRMS® XV Independent Study Guide (ISG). In response to many requests from professionals and consumers, for the first time, ICFE is publishing the CITRMS® XV ISG as a separate textbook.

The ICFE CITRMS® XV ISG is a new and improved document, providing a new overview, current information on specific technological and demographic developments, and a current perspective on the phenomenon of identity theft. Extensive End Notes are included with many hyper-links to online sources.

Many changes and new challenges have occurred in the world of identity theft since the original CITRMS® study program was first introduced in 2006 by the ICFE. Consequently, CITRMS® XV undertakes a completely new approach to recognizing and dealing with these developments, with particular emphasis on two groups of specialized concerns: divided into technology and demographic/activity categories.

The focus remains the same; ID theft risk management; however many of the details have been updated and expanded, including a variety of developments in criminal methods and trends, plus new approaches to identifying and managing the risk.

Due to the proliferation of data breaches, requirements for organizations that have suffered such breaches have expanded as well, notably the requirement to make prompt notification to all individuals who may be at risk of identity theft due to the compromise of the security of their personally sensitive information.

In the past eight years, over seven thousand professionals have successfully completed the CITRMS® program and have been ICFE certified. They include people who work with consumers and small businesses, credit and debt counselors, legal assistants, military counselors, the financial services industry, private investigators, law enforcement, both investigative and prosecutorial, and an entire entitlement oversight department in one mid-western state, among numerous others.

For those readers who wish to earn the CITRMS XV ® or become ICFE Certified for the first time, ICFE is pleased to offer a credit toward enrollment in the CITRMS® XV course in the amount of the purchase price of this book.

It is my hope you will take the next step in developing your ability to help consumers manage their risk of identity theft and help small businesses with their compliance procedures.

Yours truly,

Paul

Institute of Consumer Financial Education

"Helping families solve the financial puzzle for over 25 years."

A non-profit organization

ABOUT THE AUTHOR:

Yan Ross is an accredited educator, recognized authority, and actively practiced law for over 30 years, including 10 years in government positions and 20+ years in private practice. He is a graduate of Princeton University and Yale Law School.

His accredited courses include a wide array of subjects, such as identity theft, alternative dispute resolution, and ethics, for numerous disciplines, such as attorneys, Certified Financial Planners, and Certified Public Accountants.

For over 15 years, he has addressed Identity Theft Risk Assessment and management for consumers, organizations holding personally identifiable information, and professionals who work with individuals and organizations who are at risk of falling victim to identity thieves.

As Director of Special Projects for the Institute of Consumer Financial Education, Mr. Ross participated in the Identity Theft Standards Panel, a national initiative of the American National Standards Institute, and also conducted a comprehensive survey of providers of identity theft services and risk management solutions.

He was a contributing editor of the original CITRMS® course, among the first to earn the CITRMS® credential, and has written this new CITRMS® XV course for 2015 and beyond.

AUTHOR'S NOTE

ACKNOWLEDGEMENTS AND INVITATION

The author has many individuals and organizations to thank, for their support and contributions over the past years this work has been in progress. It's not practical to attempt to name them all, but it's appropriate to single out for special thanks Paul Richard, President of the Institute of Consumer Financial Education, publisher and certifying authority of the CITRMS® and CITRMS® XV credentials.

The author has included extensive footnotes with substantial identification of the original sources for much of the material in this independent study guide. In most cases, the information comes from public entity web sites; in others, wide-ranging news and other publications constitute the sources of identity theft information; in some cases, information was supplied by sources preferring to maintain their anonymity.
Wherever possible, the footnotes include specific reference to the actual sources of the material, with hyper-links included to facilitate access to the original publications. The phenomenon of identity theft is quickly and continuously developing, and it's our hope that this facility will help CITRMS® XV professionals to stay current.

As the CITRMS® XV Independent Study Guide will also be made available in .pdf format, the author wishes to invite all parties to submit information and updates for consideration to be published in the ongoing update of the online version and in subsequent *errata* lists.

Please direct comments and suggestions for course improvements to the author, via the ICFE at
van.ross@icfe.info

Overview re CITRMS® XV Learning Goals and Objectives:

1. Be familiar with the principal laws defining identity theft and setting requirements for holders of identity theft related information
2. Know the common identity theft terms and define key differences
3. Understand the magnitude and trends of reported incidents of identity theft
4. Be able to list the various types of information vulnerable to identity theft and where it is held
5. Know the main ways identity thieves gain access to sensitive information and how they misuse it
6. Be familiar with the currently identified "Specialized Areas of Concern," including technological developments and those listed by demographic and activity categories

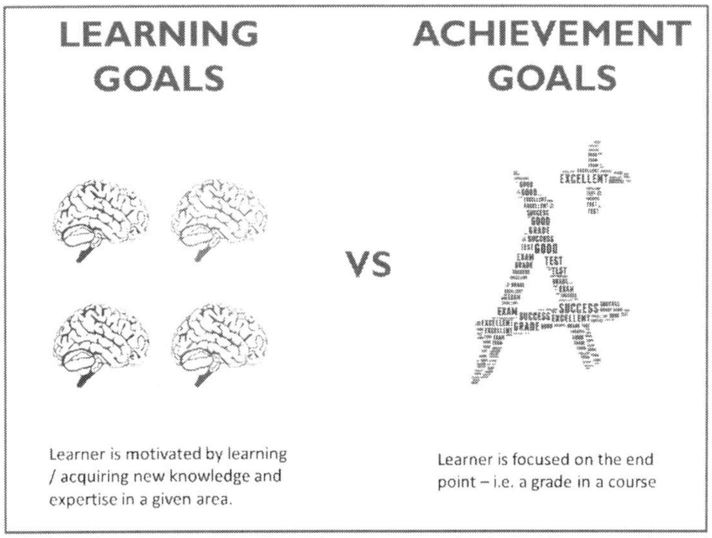

7. Understand the roles of the principal federal agencies responsible for administering identity theft related laws and regulations
8. Know which agencies to contact in the event of identity theft, and how to contact them
9. Know the steps consumers can take to minimize the risk of identity theft, and what to do if a consumer learns his/her information has been compromised in an identity theft incident
10. Identify methods of access to credit reports and credit scores, free and otherwise
11. Know the types of identity theft that usually do NOT show up in credit reports
12. Be familiar with the main requirements for businesses to protect sensitive customer information, to comply with applicable laws and regulations
13. Understand the requirements to notify affected individuals in the event of a data breach, and know the most common means of helping them minimize the adverse effects of such a breach.
14. Understand the types and features of identity theft prevention and resolution services for consumers and businesses
15. Be familiar with the considerations in deciding how to utilize third party services to help manage the threat of identity theft

SUMMARY TABLE OF CONTENTS

There are NINE areas of study and testing:

Appendix:
The 2015 CITRMS® XV ISG includes information on public and private agencies, with points of contact and basic applicable forms to report and follow up identity theft incidents.

ENDNOTES: Sources, Resources, and Acknowledgements
The endnotes include many hyper-links to online sources in the .pdf format, to facilitate further study.

Table of Contents

General Course Overview

At the time the Institute of Consumer Financial Education initiated the Certified Identity Theft Risk Management Specialist CITRMS® program, the name was selected with great care. While identity theft was a well-documented and statistically measured challenge, the responses tended to be held out as "prevention" or "protection."

However, it became clear that the means used by identity thieves were too broad and pervasive to be subject to counter-measures promising definitive results. Since nearly everyone is to some degree at risk to experience identity theft, ICFE decided to treat it as a risk, and to create the course to respond by preparing consumers and professionals who work with them to manage that risk. Nonetheless, since common usage continues to rely on "prevention" or "protection" to describe steps that can be taken for such purposes, they also are used colloquially in this Guide.[1]

For the CITRMS® XV Independent Study Guide, use of the word "victim" is treated as a term of art, and is distinguished from the popular usage connoting the victim mentality (blaming others or not accepting responsibility), since there are concrete steps to be taken to manage the risk of identity theft.

Since the CITRMS® course was initiated in 2006, there have been many changes in the size and shape of the Identity Theft phenomenon. While the basic definitions and principles have remained relatively constant, there have also been major developments in the methods and magnitude of the capture, storage, transmission, and protection of identity theft related information.

The ISG itself has also benefitted from technological advances, in particular the available publication in .pdf format, which includes both textual and End Note hyper-links to online sources, to facilitate further study.

It is not surprising, then, that identity thieves have responded to these technological changes with new capabilities of their own. It is also to be expected that the industry that has grown up around the prevention and remediation of identity theft has grown apace. Finally, further actions by the government sector have followed in turn, responding to this growing threat by collecting information, holding hearings, passing laws and implementing regulations to require protective actions by the holders of sensitive information. Future projections are for more and more sophisticated means of exploiting vulnerable information, followed by more and more sophisticated means of protecting it.

Use of the internet and other technological platforms for all kinds of financial and personal transactions have become the daily norm for the vast majority of our population. With the advent of such social networking sites, accessibility of a broad range of transactional services, and electronic record keeping for all types of customer/client relationships, the activities of identity thieves now follow the ever-growing technological and demographic fields of opportunity.

There have been vast and swift developments in the field of identity theft prone technologies. There is no doubt that this trend will continue, and new technologies will offer future challenges to professionals working to help clients and consumers manage the risk of identity theft.

No discussion of developments in identity theft would be complete without mention of privacy issues. The history of identity theft is firmly rooted in privacy issues. It is notable that concerns about maintaining confidentiality and privacy of personal information were expressed by individuals and consumer groups well before the identity theft phenomenon became apparent.

Historically, privacy concerns came from the desire to exercise the *right to privacy*, with the intention of preventing known and unknown parties' access to personal information. Initially, privacy constituted an end in itself. For many years, there has been a major movement devoted to maintaining the individual's own control over access to and use of personal information.

As the misuse of such information has grown over the intervening years, the need to control and protect such personal information has expanded from, the desire to exercise the *right to privacy* to the need to control and protect against identity thieves. Identity thieves, who use such information for a broad variety of illicit uses, wreak financial and personal damage to the person whose identifying information has been stolen. Today, the right to privacy and management of the risk of identity theft are inextricably intertwined.

In the past, the pattern of government action was based on a centralized organizational focus, mainly placing responsibility in the hands of the Federal Trade Commission. In the CITRMS® XV course, it is important to note the proliferation of the means of identity theft, and the resulting response involving several more specialized federal entities to oversee compliance with law and regulation. The Federal Trade Commission remains the principal federal agency for dealing with identity theft issues, including the collection and publication of statistical information and the promulgation and administration of the Red Flags Rules (covered in detail in Section 6).

One of the most notable changes, in terms of governmental oversight, is the establishment in 2010 of the Consumer Financial Protection Bureau (CPFB) which was given broad oversight authority of the credit, credit reporting, identity theft safeguards and collection industry, among many other relevant business groups. Despite past legal challenges to the Board's authority, as of this date, the CFPB is in full operation, with executives and staff carrying out its statutory duties. Nonetheless, even with certain overlapping activities, the full extent of the CFPB's authority in promulgating and enforcing identity theft standards, and its position in relation to other federal agencies is still developing.

The role of the U. S. Department of Health and Human Services ("HHS") has also grown considerably, especially in discharging its responsibilities for the administration of HIPAA and HITECH laws that include provisions for the protection of personal health information ("PHI"). Statistically and financially, the cost of data breaches involving personal health information has grown considerably in recent years, and has presented a major challenge to the integrity of both the health care delivery systems and the payment mechanisms involved, both private and public.

Since California's enactment (effective July 1, 2003) of the first law requiring notification to consumers in the event of a breach of their personally identifiable information, nearly every State has adopted some form of notification requirement for such events that could result in identity theft. As of the date of this writing, no federal law has been enacted to require notification to consumers in the event of a data breach. [2]

In response to the destructive nature of identity theft, a major industry has grown up, to educate professionals and consumers, undertake preventive measures, and perform restoration and remediation services for victims of identity theft. Holders of protected personally identifiable information are also subject to a growing body of law and regulation, as well as receiving support services from trained and equipped professionals who assist in compliance and preventive actions to forestall data breaches that can result in financial liability and loss of reputation.

For the CITRMS® XV course, the author has employed certain features to make the material most accessible and enable use of this Independent Study Guide as a reference volume. In particular, in addition to this General Course Overview, each of the nine substantive sections includes an overview as well. Where citations of law and regulation warrant, portions of the text may be found in more than one location, for convenience of reference.

Identification and management of the risks of identity theft embody the concept and approach of the CITRMS® XV course. Accordingly, it will be helpful to the CITRMS® XV student to review the course Table of Contents above, as well as the Section Overviews, in order to appreciate the flow of study.

For those renewing the CITRMS® credential, you will note both continuity and an in-depth approach to understanding and dealing with the subject, one that we hope and trust will enable you to integrate what you have learned in the past and improve your ability to serve your clients, the consumers whose identities are at risk.

Section 1 -- Identity Theft Basics and Concepts

SECTION OVERVIEW

This section outlines the basic building blocks of understanding identity theft. It includes definitions from statutory, regulatory, and commonly used sources. There are many basic concepts used in the study of identity theft, as well as numerous useful acronyms. Note that further elaboration of the legal and regulatory foundations appear in Section 6.

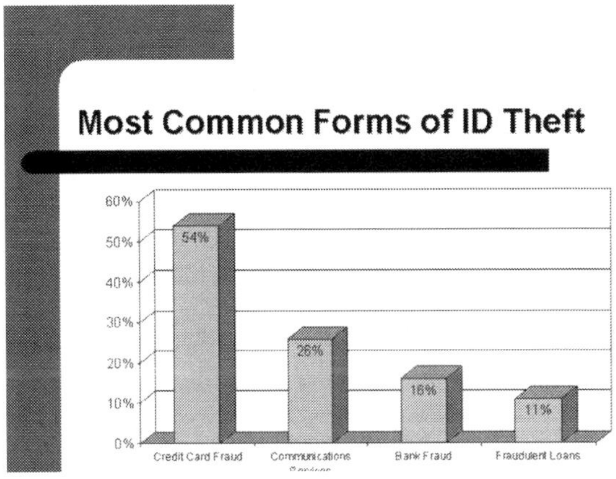

http://www.identitytheftpreventiontips.com/how-identity-theft-happens/

In addition to the definition sources and applications, three additional issues are introduced here: privacy, data breaches, and the notification and remediation steps commonly taken to mitigate the adverse effects of data breaches. Beyond the basics, detailed discussion of these topics is provided in Sections 6, 8 and 9.
Basic Concepts of Identity Theft.

The history of "identity theft" as a discrete phenomenon, as distinct from prior forms of invasion of privacy, financial and related fraud, or other unauthorized use of personal information, goes back over 25 years. In the early 1990's, the Social Security Administration was reported to offer a new number to anyone who needed to stop an existing case of "identity theft" through fraudulent use of the victim's Social Security number. According to common sources, the term had been used as far back as the 1960's, but with less specific reference to the widespread phenomenon, we see today.

There are, in fact, numerous accepted definitions of "identity theft." Some are rooted in statutory language, others in State and federal regulations, and still others by vernacular usage. For purposes of this course, a brief elaboration is useful, as well as a review of related terms that are sometimes used in conjunction with or in place of "identity theft." It's important to recognize that "identity theft" is a dynamic, not static, phenomenon, and the definitions and concepts will continue to change in the future.

The most basic statutory definition comes from the Identity Theft and Assumption Deterrence Act, signed into law in October 30, 1998. This Act makes it a crime when someone:

"knowingly transfers or uses, without lawful authority, a means of identification of another person with the intent to commit, or to aid or abet, any unlawful activity that constitutes a violation of federal law, or that constitutes a felony under any applicable state or local law."

The Fair and Accurate Credit Transactions Act of 2003 (abbreviated *FACT Act* or FACTA) was signed into law on December 4, 2003. Portions of the Act amend the *Fair Credit Reporting Act (FCRA)* to enhance consumers' ability to resolve problems caused by identity theft. Section 111 of the Act adds several new definitions to the FCRA, including "identity theft" and "identity theft report." The Act permits the Federal Trade Commission (FTC) to further define the term "identity theft," and requires the Commission to determine the meaning of the term "identity theft report," although the Act does provide a minimum definition. Section 111 of the Act defines the term "identity theft" as:

"a fraud committed using the identifying information of another person, subject to such further definition as the Commission may prescribe, by regulation."

FTC's working definition: *Identity theft happens when someone uses your Social Security number or other personal information to open new accounts, make purchases, or get a tax refund.* [3]

It should be noted that the empowering language of FACTA gives the FTC broad authority to modify or amend this definition, generally through the regulatory process of promulgating, publishing, receiving comment, and adopting a new or amended rule. For instance, a broader description has also come from the FTC: Identity theft occurs when someone uses your personally identifying information, like your name, Social Security number, or credit card number, without your permission, to commit fraud or other crimes.

Other definitions are used by other organizations, in different contexts, though for purposes of this course, the FTC's definition is the standard. In order to provide a broader perspective, however, it's useful to note some of the other definitions and their uses:

- United States Department of Justice (DoJ) - Identity theft and identity fraud are terms used to refer to all types of crime in which someone wrongfully obtains and uses another person's personal data in some way that involves fraud or deception, typically for economic gain.[4]

- Consumer Financial Protection Bureau (CFPB) - Identity theft occurs when someone steals your financial identity to commit fraud. [5]

- Stealing your identity could mean using personal information without your permission, such as:
    - Your name
    - Social Security number
    - Credit card number

- Wikipedia - Identity theft is a form of stealing someone's identity which someone pretends to be someone else by assuming that person's identity, typically in order to access resources or obtain credit and other benefits in that person's name… [6]

In a formal sense, "identity theft" refers to stealing the information, and "identity fraud" refers to using the stolen information for unauthorized or criminal purposes. In practice, the terms "identity theft" and "identity fraud" are often used interchangeably. Due to the manner in which reporting and statistical analysis are managed by the relevant government agencies, for the purposes of this course, they will be referred to collectively as "identity theft." Any departure from this rule, based on practical distinctions, will be noted and emphasized.

What is protected information?

"Protected" information is any information or data element specified in a variety of federal and state laws, and by regulations based on those laws. The specific laws and regulations that apply depend on the kind of information, and on by whom and how the information is being collected, stored, or distributed. Many governing bodies for professional licensing and certifications also address protection of personal information. It is usually covered by the organization's internal policies, which integrate the requirements of relevant government entities as well as the organization's own requirements about what should be protected.

What is sensitive information?

Common usage may also to refer to "sensitive" information, but this is not primarily a legal determination. Some kinds of information that do not immediately appear to be sensitive, such as a person's name or address, may be subject to legal, regulatory, or organizational protections, depending on what other information may be attached to it. [7]

Personally Identifiable Information ("PII")

There are various definitions in federal & state statutes; nearly all have selected an exact or similar formulation of the phrase "Personally Identifiable Information" (abbreviated "PII").

An internet search of the term "Personally Identifiable Information," using any of the standard search engines, will produce a broad array of sources and uses of this term. It is interesting to note that many of them are posted by organizations that are selling services to assist consumers and businesses in responding to identity theft threats.

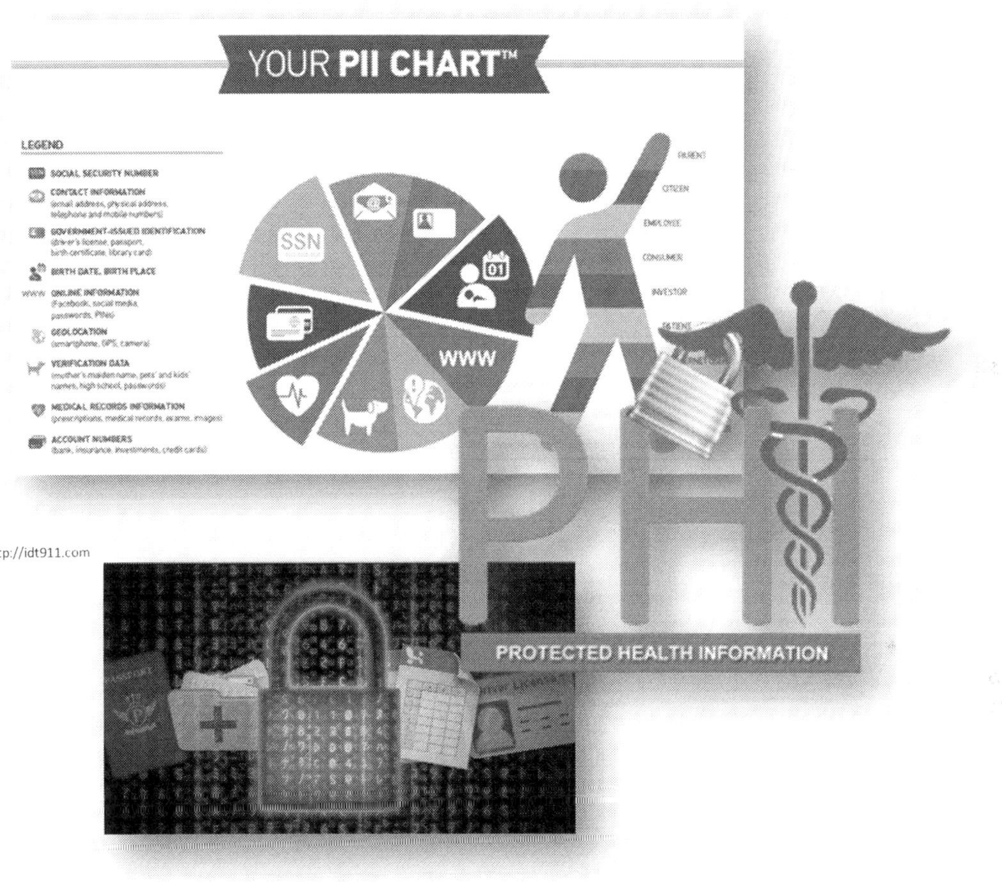

http://idt911.com

For purposes of this course, the following working definition of PII is brief and broad:

Personally, identifiable information (PII) is any data that could potentially identify a specific individual. A more elaborate formulation is also useful to note:

PII is any information or data element which can be used to determine an individual's identity, such as the name, social security number, biometric records, etc. alone, or when combined with other personal or identifying information which is identifiable to a specific individual, such as date and place of birth, mother's maiden name, etc.

In its broadest form, personally identifiable information (PII) is any data that could potentially identify a specific individual.

Definitions vary, based on legal and regulatory requirements, as well as common usage. They generally include several individual components of a person's identity, either separately or in the aggregate. To support both analysis and preventive measures, elements of PII are often categorized as sensitive (only one or two elements can be used together to commit identity theft) or less sensitive, or non-sensitive (more than one of the data elements would be required to assemble information sufficient to commit identity theft).

Among the principal elements of PII are the following; (NOTE this list should not be considered to be exhaustive):

Examples of sensitive PII elements include, but are not limited to:

- First name, last name, and other names used
- Social Security number, full and last four digits
- Driver's license and other identification document numbers
- Citizenship, legal status, gender, race/ethnicity, such as passport or green card
- Birth date, place of birth
- Home and personal cell telephone numbers
- Personal email address, mailing and home address
- Religious preference
- Security clearance
- Mother's middle and maiden names
- Spouse information, marital status, child information, emergency contact information
- Biometrics
- Financial account information
- Medical information, disability information
- Law enforcement information
- Employment information
- Educational information
- Military records
- Log-In or Access Credentials
- Insurance (life, health, liability, real estate & auto)
- Passport information
- Home ownership & mortgage info (Public Records about details of mortgage often results in blind mailings for re-financing)

Examples of less sensitive PII elements include, but are not limited to:

- Office location
- Business telephone number
- Business email address
- Employee identification

"PII" is the foundation for protective provisions in identity theft law and regulation. Regardless of the relationship, business, service, or activity subject to the particular law or regulation, the common thread is requiring the treatment of PII in a manner that avoids disclosure that could lead to identity theft.

The regulations tend to follow the function of the relationship, whether it be financial, medical, employment, or even government program or benefit.

In practice, the concept of PII has tended to concentrate on financial information in first instance. This is the reason why credit reports were first area of concentration in monitoring exercises to prevent or begin the process of resolving identity theft. However, as identity thieves have broadened their access to non-financial information, and developed a market for such PII, the breadth of types of information they steal, sell, and abuse has also grown. This trend is shown in the reports on identity theft covered in Section 2.

Consumers and their advisers should be cautioned that even elements of apparently non-sensitive PII can be collected and cross-referenced by would-be identity thieves, then used to aggregate and capture other elements that may be used to perpetrate identity theft.
Even the "re-identification" process may be utilized to re-construct various elements of PII into a viable profile that can then be used for illicit purposes. It has been observed that "Any information that distinguishes one person from another can be used for re-identifying data." [8]

Protected Health Information ("PHI")

At the outset of this section, it's important to mention that an in-depth treatment of by the U. S. Department of Health and Human Services ("HHS") and its administration of the Health Insurance Portability and Accountability Act ("HIPAA") would be worthy of an entire course on its own.

For our purposes, this section is limited to the principal definitions involve in the HHS requirements in dealing with identity theft-prone aspects of medical and health information. In Section 6, there is further elaboration of the rules HHS imposes on covered entities and their business associates, which hold PHI.
The term Protected Health Information (PHI) is applied specifically to medical and health-related data, and has been established by the U. S. Department of Health and Human Services ("HHS"). In discharging its responsibilities under the Health Insurance Portability and Accountability Act (HIPAA), the Health Information Technology for Economic and Clinical Health (HITECH) Act, and the Privacy Rule as promulgated under that authority. Under the regulation published at 45 CFR § 160.103, PHI is defined as follows:

- Individually identifiable health information transmitted or maintained in any form or medium by a Covered Entity or its Business Associate [9]

"Individually identifiable health information" closely tracks the PII definition, though is focused on health and medical data. Specifically, HHS refers here to health information, including demographic information, which relates to an individual's physical or mental health or the provision of or payment for health care, and identifies the individual.

HHS also carves out some examples of what is NOT covered, such as the employment records of the covered entity, and also records under the Family Educational Rights and Privacy Act ("FERPA").

It is worth noting that HHS does provide a means of gaining an exception to the rules for treating PHI, based on the concept of "De-Identification" of the PHI, pursuant to the regulation published at 45 CFR § 164.514(a)(b). This entails removal of certain identifiers so that the individual who is subject of the PHI may no longer be identified.[10] Successful de-identification requires stripping of listed identifiers such as:

- Names
    - Geographic subdivisions
    - All elements of dates
    - Social Security Numbers

Parsing out this definition requires some additional study, principally what it means to be a Covered Entity or its Business Associate. HHS provides helpful guidance here as well. [11]

"Covered Entities" for purposes of application of HIPAA rules on PHI are generally divided into three groups: Health Care Providers, Health Plans, and Health Care Clearinghouses.

- Health Care Providers*
    - Doctors
    - Clinics
    - Psychologists
    - Dentists
    - Chiropractors
    - Nursing Homes
    - Pharmacies *only if they transmit any information in an electronic form in connection with a transaction for which HHS has adopted a standard.

- Health Plans
    - Health insurance companies
    - HMOs
    - Company health plans
    - Government programs that pay for health care, such as Medicare, Medicaid, and the military and veterans' health care programs

- Health Care Clearinghouses
    - This includes entities that process nonstandard health information they receive from another entity into a standard (i.e., standard electronic format or data content), or vice versa.

"Business Associate" of "Covered Entities" for purposes of application of HIPAA rules on PHI is defined as follows:
A "business associate" is a person or entity that performs certain functions or activities that involve the use or disclosure of protected health information on behalf of, or provides services to, a covered entity. [12]

Additional Concepts and Definitions

"Synthetic identity theft"

A form of identity theft that goes beyond stealing and using elements of a real person's identity is *synthetic identity theft*, in which identities are completely or partially based on authentic information and then constructed into a whole other person.

One common technique involves combining an existing Social Security number or other PII with a name and birthdate other than the ones associated with the number. Synthetic identity theft is more difficult to track as it doesn't show on either person's credit report directly, but may appear as an entirely new file in the credit bureau or as an account on one of the victim's credit reports. Synthetic identity theft primarily harms the creditors who unwittingly grant the identity thieves credit. Individual victims can be affected if their names become confused with the synthetic identities, or if negative information in their account information negatively impacts their credit ratings.

The impact on the person whose PII has been misused to create a synthetic identity can be minimal or overwhelming, depending on which elements of the victim's PII have been used. The greatest financial harm can come to a business that has hired, or extended credit to, or formed another dependent relationship with the identity thief who uses a synthetic identity to gain access to these resources. [13]

Privacy

Much has been written about individual privacy, both as it relates to identity theft and in its own right. For our purposes, the interplay of privacy protection and managing the risk of identity theft centers on two aspects, which are discussed in depth below: (1) How identity thieves gain access to personally identifiable information ("PII"), and (2) Actions consumers can take to minimize the risk of identity theft.

It is clear that individuals who take steps to safeguard their privacy are also acting in ways that impede would-be identity thieves in their attempts to gain access to and misuse PII. It's axiomatic that the less information that is distributed to vulnerable locations, the fewer opportunities identity thieves have to take advantage of it.

Although the following observation is anecdotal, not statistical, in the experience of the author in teaching many courses on identity theft, people tend to say that their privacy is important, but fail to take steps to restrict the sharing of personal information by businesses of which they are customers. Two illustrative examples of this phenomenon are participation in "loyalty" programs, and failure to "opt out" of information sharing by financial institutions.

A frequent question to course participants has been: "Do you value your privacy and take steps to protect it?" The vast majority of participants answer in the affirmative. However, the follow-up questions and responses indicate that there is a disconnect between stated preferences and behavior, as demonstrated by these follow-up lines of questioning.

- "How many of you participate in retail loyalty programs?" (Keychain is held up, showing a variety of bar-coded key tags from various stores.) Response: Almost everyone.
- "Why?" Response: Because they receive discounts on prices.
- "What do you trade in exchange for the discounts?" Generally, people don't realize that their purchasing patterns are collected, shared with vendors and other interested parties, result in the generation of coupons that print out with the register tape, and promote either the products they are buying, or competing products.
- In signing up for such loyalty programs, the consumer also provides a variety of PII. Responding to the "survey" request on the register tape (usually entering a drawing for a prepaid card or credit for products) also results in answering questions about the household profile, age, income, home ownership, and other elements valuable to potential identity thieves.

Another example of the disconnect is elicited by showing the course participants a notification from a bank or other credit card issuer. These "Gramm-Leach-Bliley" opt-out notices, which are usually included in mailings of financial statements for deposit, loan, or credit card accounts, disclose the various other parties with which the PII of the customer is shared – with an opportunity to write back and require restrictions on sharing such information with non-affiliated parties. Again, almost no-one bothers to write to express such a preference for limiting the distribution of their PII.

In addition to the privacy implications, these implicit permissions for holders of such information to proliferate its dissemination to other, sometimes vulnerable, data bases can have profound negative impact on the vulnerability of consumers to identity theft.

"The Right to be Forgotten"

This concept is a sub-set of privacy concerns of the individual. The issue centers on the practices of internet search engine companies and other web site owners to capture and sell information about the individuals who search for or access information and go from there to the subject web sites.

Capturing the information may be accomplished by simply logging the search term, or sending "cookies" to the computer used for the search, or more sophisticated means of identifying the internet protocol ("IP") address of the user (which may enable personal identification of the individual and connect this information to other available elements of PII.

While this practice is usually designated as being permitted, in favor of the search engine provider, in the "Terms of Use" and "Privacy Policy" documents to which the consumer must agree in order to use the facility, the dispute arises in the context of who owns the information.

As might be expected, the term "Right to be Forgotten" has been promoted by privacy advocates, not internet companies. The other side of the story is that the use and sale of the information collected enables the search engine companies to provide their services at no financial cost to the consumer.

At the time of this writing, there has been no clear resolution of the overall issue. It is worth mentioning that outside the United States, in the European Union for instance, the "Right to be Forgotten" has been adopted in favor of consumers. In the United States, at this point, if a consumer wishes to conduct an internet search without having the results tracked, it is necessary to use a search engine that operates under Terms and Privacy Policies that include this right.

More information appears in the discussion of "Big Data" item of Section 5.
For an advocate's point of view, see http://www.righttobeforgotten.org/ [14]

Data Breaches

What is a "data breach"?

As the term implies, for our purposes, a data breach is the unauthorized access to information that can be used to perpetrate identity theft. The data consists of any element of PII, and the breach is any unauthorized access to such information.

Typically, a data breach involves all or a major portion of the PII in records maintained by an organization, either in hard copy or (more often) in digitized format. The data breach may occur because of physical access to files or a portable computer or from a remote location by use of a program designed to gain unauthorized access to the target files.

In depth, discussion of how data breaches occurs, how the unauthorized access to the information is misused, and attendant requirements for the breached organization appear in Sections 4 and 8 below. [15]

Breach Notification

What is "breach notification"?

Upon learning of a data breach, the organization whose security has been compromised is required to notify all of the individuals whose information was involved.

The laws of nearly every State impose notification requirements. Currently, legislation is pending in the U. S. Congress to enact a nationwide requirement for such notification.

For our purposes, "breach notification" is the communication, usually by letter, to the individual at the address listed as the contact point in the relationship between the breached organization and the potentially affected individual.

In most cases, the notification letter must advise the recipient of the date of the breach, the nature of the data involved in the breach, a general description of the breach incident, and contact phone numbers for more information. In addition, the breached organization may provide information on measures that have been taken to protect individuals whose information has been breached, and advice on steps the individual can take to mitigate any damage.

Specific provisions and applications are discussed in detail in Section 8.

Data Breach Remediation

What is "data breach remediation"?

The responsibility of the organization whose security has been compromised by a data breach goes beyond merely notifying the individuals who may be affected.

Both for legal and business reasons, the breached organization generally undertakes to provide the potentially affected individuals with some form of third-party service to mitigate the adverse effects of the data breach.

The terms "remediation," "restoration," and "recovery" are often used interchangeably, depending on the nomenclature used by the company that provides the service.

For our purposes, any of these terms may be used to describe the service to assist consumers in mitigating the adverse effects of a data breach or other identity theft event.

It should be noted that the offer of such a service almost always requires the individual receiving the notification and offer to take positive action to register with the provider of the remediation service.

Specific provisions and applications are discussed in detail in Section 8.

Section 2. Magnitude, Classifications, and Trends in Identity Theft

SECTION OVERVIEW

The principal repository for reported identity theft incidents is the Federal Trade Commission (FTC). The FTC maintains a data base of complaints filed by or on behalf of consumers who have learned that they are victims of identity theft. Approximately once a year, the FTC publishes a report of these complaints. It is instructive to examine the information in these FTC reports, to learn more about the size and shape of the identity theft phenomenon. It is also useful to examine public-source statistics and other anecdotal evidence to learn about cases that are either unreported or substantially delayed in being discovered. Emerging trends in the activities of identity thieves and classifications of misuse of personal information help understand future actions to be taken to manage the risk of identity theft. Identity theft topped the Federal Trade Commission's national ranking of consumer complaints for the 15th consecutive year. https://www.ftc.gov/news-events/press-releases/2015/02/identity-theft-tops-ftcs-consumer-complaint-categories-again-2014

In terms of gross numbers of individuals potentially affected by identity theft incidents, the FTC report of complaints is dwarfed by the potential impact on consumers whose PII is compromised in data breach events. Millions of records at a time, including various elements of PII and PHI, have been subject to unauthorized access by identity thieves. The affected individuals are referred to as being "potentially" affected due to the uncertainty of how the information is misused, and the difficulty in evaluating exact damage inflicted.

The most commonly cited sources for information on identity theft involving data breaches are two non-governmental organizations. The Privacy Rights Clearinghouse ("PRC"), for over 10 years has maintained and published a Chronology of Data Breaches. Online at http://www.privacyrights.org/data-breach the PRC provides up-to-date information on reported incidents of data breaches. The Identity Theft Resource Center (ITRC) also maintains and publishes a similar chronology, posted online at http://www.idtheftcenter.org/ITRC-Surveys-Studies/2014databreaches.html . More detail is listed below in the Subsection on Data Breaches.

Basic Statistics

Periodically, approximately once per year, the Federal Trade Commission publishes a report on identity theft for the prior calendar year. The current version is called the Consumer Sentinel Network (CSN) Data Book. As described in the Executive Summary of the current Data Book:

Begun in 1997 to collect fraud and identity theft complaints, the CSN now has more than 10 million complaints, including those about credit reports, debt collection and mortgage assistance scams, among other subjects. The CSN has a five-year data retention policy; complaints older than five years are purged biannually. Between January and December 2014, the CSN received more than 2.5 million consumer complaints, which the FTC has sorted into 30 complaint categories. Some organizations transfer their complaints to the CSN after the end of the calendar year, and new data providers, added to the system each year, are contributing complaints from prior years. As a result, the total number of complaints for 2014 will increase during the next few months, and totals from previous years may differ from prior CSN annual reports.

NOTE: The 2014 Consumer Sentinel Network Data Book is based on unverified complaints reported by consumers. The data is not based on a consumer survey.

* It's worth noting that such officially reported cases omit a likely significant number of identity thefts which have not yet been discovered by the victim or which the victims simply don't report. A familiar example might be a case in which an unauthorized charge is made to a credit card by an identity thief, and duly reported by the consumer to the card issuer, so the victim does not bear the cost – nor report the incident.

The Federal Trade Commission at the agency's web site posts current updated information on Identity Theft. Current articles and comments can be found at: http://www.consumer.ftc.gov/search/site/identity%20theft%20survey

In addition to participating law enforcement organizations, in 2014, for the first time, the U.S. Departments of Defense, Education and Veterans Affairs began contributing educational institution and student lending complaints from military members and their dependents.

While the individual complaint data is available only to participating law enforcement organizations, the aggregate data is reported in detail, and broken out in a variety of ways that are useful for examination and interpretation to help understand the trends and challenges in identity theft and other fraud-related developments.

At the time of this writing, the most recent report is from 2014, and carries "apples to apples" comparisons with the findings for the years 2010 to the present. The following may be supplemented with additional information found on the web site of the Federal Trade Commission at www.ftc.gov and by searching for "identity theft" using the internal search engine.

Further detail is available in the online report. For current purposes, the following represents essential information from the Executive Summary of the most recent 2014 report.

- The CSN received over 2.5 million complaints (excluding do-not-call) during calendar year 2014: 60% fraud complaints; 13% identity theft complaints; and 27% other types of complaints.

- Identity Theft was the number one complaint category in the CSN for calendar year 2014 with 13% of the overall complaints. The complete ranking of all 30-complaint categories is listed within the report.

- Government documents\benefits fraud (39%) was the most common form of reported identity theft, followed by credit card fraud (17%), phone or utilities fraud (13%), and bank fraud (8%). Other significant categories of identity theft reported by victims were employment-related fraud (5%) and loan fraud (4%).

- Thirty-two percent of identity theft complainants reported they contacted law enforcement. Of those victims, 88% indicated a report was taken.

- Florida is the state with the highest per capita rate of reported identity theft complaints, followed by Washington and Oregon.

Drilling deeper into the details of the report, there are additional notable developments in the reporting of Identity Theft complaints.

- Since 2003, the number of complaints has fluctuated within a range of 215,240 in 2003 to 369,143 in 2012.

- The highest number of complaints was reported in 2012 (369,143)

- A substantial decrease reported complaints occurred in 2013 (290,0999)

- For 2014, the reported complaints again rose by over 10% (332,646)

[Note that the complaint counts from years prior to 2010 represent historical figures as per the Consumer Sentinel Network's five-year data retention policy. These complaint figures exclude National Do Not Call Registry complaints.]

Basic Statistics

Consumer Sentinel Network Identity Theft Complaints
How Victims' Information is Misused[1]
Calendar Years 2012 through 2014

Government Documents or Benefits Fraud

Theft Subtype	Percentages CY-2012	Percentages CY-2013	Percentages CY-2014
Tax- or Wage-Related Fraud	43.4%	30.0%	32.8%
Government Benefits Applied For \ Received	1.6%	2.4%	4.1%
Other Government Documents Issued \ Forged	0.8%	1.0%	1.3%
Driver's License Issued \ Forged	0.6%	0.6%	0.5%
Total	**46.4%**	**34.0%**	**38.7%**

Credit Card Fraud

Theft Subtype	Percentages CY-2012	Percentages CY-2013	Percentages CY-2014
New Accounts	8.9%	11.2%	12.5%
Existing Account	4.7%	5.7%	4.9%
Total	**13.6%**	**16.9%**	**17.4%**

Phone or Utilities Fraud

Theft Subtype	Percentages CY-2012	Percentages CY-2013	Percentages CY-2014
Utilities - New Accounts	6.2%	8.9%	7.6%
Wireless - New Accounts	2.5%	3.5%	3.5%
Unauthorized Charges to Existing Accounts	0.4%	0.6%	0.7%
Telephone - New Accounts	0.6%	0.6%	0.7%
Total	**9.7%**	**13.6%**	**12.5%**

Bank Fraud

Theft Subtype	Percentages CY-2012	Percentages CY-2013	Percentages CY-2014
Electronic Fund Transfer	3.0%	3.7%	3.3%
New Accounts	1.9%	2.2%	2.8%
Existing Accounts	1.5%	1.8%	1.5%
Other Deposit Accounts[2]	-	-	0.6%
Total	**6.4%**	**7.7%**	**8.2%**

Employment-Related Fraud

Theft Subtype	Percentages CY-2012	Percentages CY-2013	Percentages CY-2014
Employment-Related Fraud	**5.4%**	**5.6%**	**4.8%**

Loan Fraud

Theft Subtype	Percentages CY-2012	Percentages CY-2013	Percentages CY-2014
Business \ Personal \ Student Loan	1.3%	2.1%	2.6%
Auto Loan \ Lease	0.6%	1.1%	1.1%
Real Estate Loan	0.5%	0.8%	0.7%
Total	**2.4%**	**4.0%**	**4.4%**

Other Identity Theft

Theft Subtype	Percentages CY-2012	Percentages CY-2013	Percentages CY-2014
Uncertain	6.1%	8.5%	11.2%
Miscellaneous	7.6%	8.7%	3.3%
Data Breach	1.1%	1.3%	2.1%
Internet \ Email	1.2%	1.7%	1.5%
Medical	0.7%	1.0%	1.0%
Evading the Law	0.8%	1.0%	0.9%
Apartment or House Rented	0.4%	0.5%	0.6%
Insurance	0.2%	0.3%	0.4%
Prepaid Debit Cards[3]	-	-	0.3%
Bankruptcy	0.1%	0.1%	0.2%
Securities \ Other Investments	0.1%	0.2%	0.1%
Property Rental Fraud	0.1%	0.1%	0.1%
Child Support	0.1%	0.1%	0.1%
Magazines	0.1%	0.1%	<0.1%
Total	**18.6%**	**23.6%**	**21.8%**

Attempted Identity Theft

Theft Subtype	Percentages CY-2012	Percentages CY-2013	Percentages CY-2014
Attempted Identity Theft	**6.6%**	**7.2%**	**4.8%**

[1]Percentages are based on the total number of CSN identity theft complaints for each calendar year: CY-2012 = 369,143; CY-2013 = 290,099; and CY-2014 = 332,646. Note that 17% of identity theft complaints include more than one type of identity theft in CY-2014, 16% in CY-2013; and 11% in CY-2012.

[2]Theft Subtype "Other Deposit Accounts" was added to the database in CY-2014.

[3]Theft Subtype "Prepaid Debit Cards" was added to the database in CY-2014.

Federal Trade Commission | *Page 12 of 102* | *Released February 2015*

Beyond the Statistics of the Federal Trade Commission/Sentinel Report

While reviewing the statistical figures and analyzing the various categories of identity theft and misuse of the illegally obtained information is useful in understanding the size and shape of the challenge, there are several factors that are not apparent from the numbers alone.

Among these are such aspects as how the victim learns of the unauthorized access to and use of the PII, how long it takes the victim to discover the theft of his identity, and even the unintended effects of legislation and regulation intended to protect the consumer.

It's obvious that before registering a complaint with the FTC, to be counted in the annual report, the consumer must find out that there has been an identity theft event. The principal ways this occurs are closely related to the type of identity theft that has happened. The following represent the most likely ways that each of the major types of identity theft come to the attention of the affected party.

Government/Benefits Fraud:

Notice of a change in status of benefits or address or account information from the agency; automatic deposit missing; other change not initiated by the victim.

NOTE: Such notices are NEVER communicated by telephone or e-mail; any receipt of this type of communication should be viewed as suspicious and should be reported to the agency using the official points of communication, usually listed at the agency web site.

Credit Card Fraud:

Card issuer may decline authorization for a transaction; communicate by text or phone (as provided in the card agreement); statement may show an unauthorized transaction.

NOTE: If in any doubt as to the origin of a phone call or text from the card issuer, the cardholder should call the toll-free number listed on the back of the credit card.

Phone or Utilities Fraud:

Statement may not arrive at the usual time of the month, or may have a change in the address or method of payment usually used; consumer may learn of a fraudulent new account by receiving a demand for payment on an account with a different number.

NOTE: There has been a telephone scam in which the caller claims to be from the utility company and demands immediate payment to avoid an interruption in service; payment is usually demanded in the form of a credit card or money order transaction. Consumers are warned that utilities never make such communications by phone, and never to threaten immediate shut-off unless payment is made in some manner other than the usual one.

Bank Fraud and Loan Fraud:

As in the case of credit card fraud, the consumer usually learns from the financial institution of an unauthorized transaction. This may be on the monthly statement, or through online access to account information. Application for a new loan or credit card may also disclose the misuse of a consumer's financial information, especially in situations that require checking the credit report or credit score.

Employment Related Fraud:

This can be very difficult for the consumer to learn about, since the information flow tends to occur either during a job search or with the filing or receipt of tax and Social Security-related documents. In any case, there is usually a substantial lag time from the incident to the discovery.

It is worthy of note regarding the less-frequent types of identity theft that a small but growing component is "Data Breach," which is covered in more detail in Section 5. The FTC Report shows that this type has grown from 1.1% in 2012 to 1.3% in 2013, to 2.1% in 2014. The most likely way the affected consumer learns of his PII being compromised in a data breach is by letter from the organization that has suffered the breach, or even from news media.

The other categories, such as "Uncertain" and "Miscellaneous" are not sufficiently specific to be able to determine with any accuracy the way in which the victim learned of the incident.

How long it takes for the victim to discover the identity theft incident similarly is relate to the type of identity theft and the relationship with the other party to the occurrence. Reviewing the above listing, it is apparent that organizations like credit card issuers are most timely in making the cardholder aware of possible unauthorized use by text or phone. This may well be a function of who bears the loss, as the card issuer (not the cardholder) generally ends up paying for fraudulent transactions if they cannot be reversed. Notifications by mail or in periodic mailed statements tend to take longer, and make it more difficult to unwind unauthorized transactions. In sum, the range of time for discovery of an identity theft incident may be from almost immediate to several months or more.

There may be cases in which there may be a delay in finding out or even missing an incident of identity theft. One is discussed in more detail in Section 5, regarding medical debt. Under a fairly recently enacted law on credit reporting, a six-month delay is now required in reporting delinquent medical debt. The provision was intended to protect the consumer against adverse credit effects of insurance claims being held up in processing, resulting in the insured portion of the debt being prematurely added to the consumer's personal obligation. In practice, in the event of medical services being provided not to the consumer but to an identity thief, this may postpone the discovery of the incident.

HOW Victims' Information is Used to Perpetrate Identity Theft

It is instructive to review the information reported for the years 2012-2014, since there is some indication that the trends in the distribution of types of identity theft cases may help determine where the threats are growing, and where responses to the challenge of identity theft may be most effective.

What does all this mean about how identity theft victims' information is used?

Interpretations and Trends

- As in the statistics on consumer complaints during the period 2012-2014, there was a decrease in 2013, then a further increase in 2014
- Government Documents or Benefits Fraud was the highest percentage of reported identity theft incidents
- Credit Card Fraud continued to grow as a percentage of reported incidents
- Phone or Utilities Fraud continues to be the third most reported category
- Bank Fraud (mainly on deposit accounts as distinct from Credit Card Fraud) has increased slowly but steadily
- Employment Related Fraud continues to represent a small but significant factor
- Loan Fraud is concentrated in Business, Personal, and Student Loan activity, and continues to grow slowly but steadily
- "Uncertain" is the largest and fastest growing sub-category of Other Identity Theft, representing 11.2% of all reported cases in 2014
- Data Breach Fraud appears to be growing in percentage terms, but at 2.1% of reported cases in 2014 is still quite small overall; this is notable because of the major press coverage devoted to large-scale data breaches, but the FTC/Sentinel figures only include cases in which the consumer is actually damaged and files a complaint
- The category of Attempted Identity Theft appears to be decreasing, but there is no clear reason given for this occurrence
- There is a growing trend for identity theft complaints to be included in more than one category
- Many of the reported types of identity theft are of a nature that do not appear in the credit reports of the victims; this has an impact on the ways in which identity theft prevention and protection programs are modifying their operations (More details are covered in Section 9)

Data Breaches

The burgeoning phenomenon of data breaches has dominated news coverage of identity theft incidents, largely due to the huge number of people potentially affected. In addition to the FTC's Sentinel compilation of identity theft complaints, there are other, non-governmental sources of information on the larger events of data breaches. For our purposes, the two sources of published reports available are from the Privacy Rights Clearinghouse ("PRC") and the Identity Theft Resource Center ("ITRC").

It should be noted that the methodologies of the two organizations differ for accessing, confirming, and reporting the data breaches. Based on their respective descriptions, the criteria they employ has resulted in a larger number of breaches being reported by ITRC than PRC. While their statistics may differ, each is important for consideration in recognizing and dealing with the risks of identity theft. [16]

The Chronology of Data Breaches maintained and published online by the Privacy Rights Clearinghouse is a very informative and useful tool in tracking the magnitude and cost of data breaches. The chronology is searchable by time frame and also by the types of data breach reported. The following information is from the PRC web site.

In gross numbers, during 2014, the Chronology lists 296 breach incidents involving 67,876,246 records. To date in 2015, the corresponding numbers are only 56 breaches, but with a much larger total of 91,319,845 records affected. A brief comparison of the trend over the 10 years this report has been kept, it appears that the number of breaches may be decreasing, but the number of records affected is growing -- overall, the number of records compromised on average in each data breach has grown considerably. As further discussed in Section 5, regarding "Big Data" and "Cyber-Warfare," this trend may be due to the means and purposes involved in such data breaches.

For purposes of analysis, it is instructive to note the categories of data breach listed.

- Unintended disclosure - Sensitive information posted publicly on a website, mishandled or sent to the wrong party via email, fax or mail.
- Hacking or malware - Electronic entry by an outside party, malware and spyware.
- Payment Card Fraud - Fraud involving debit and credit cards that is not accomplished via hacking. For example, skimming devices at point-of-sale terminals or through the use of Radio Frequency Information Device (RFID) readers.

- Insider - Someone with legitimate access intentionally breaches information - such as an employee or contractor.
- Physical loss - Lost, discarded or stolen non-electronic records, such as paper documents
- Portable device - Lost, discarded or stolen laptop, PDA, smartphone, portable memory device, CD, hard drive, data tape, etc.
- Stationary device - Lost, discarded or stolen stationary electronic device such as a computer or server not designed for mobility
- Unknown or other [17]

In contrast, the ITRC reports that the number of U.S. data breaches tracked in 2014 hit a record high of 783 in 2014. The number of records compromised is reported at 85,611,528. Compared to the PRC report, it is a much larger number of breaches, involving a substantially larger number of records, but a somewhat smaller average number of records per breach.

As reflected on the ITRC web site, breaches are broken down into five categories, as follows:

- Business
- Financial/credit/banking
- Educational
- Governmental/military
- Medical/healthcare.

ITRC also breaks out seven types of data breaches (not counting "Unknown").

- Insider Theft
- Hacking
- Data on the Move
- Subcontractor/Third Party
- Employee error/negligence
- Accidental web/Internet Exposure
- Physical Theft

The ITRC breach list also tracks four types of information compromised:

- Social Security number
- Credit/Debit Card number
- Email/Password/User Name
- Protected Health Information (PHI) [18]

Selected Illustrative Cases of Data Breaches

While the aggregate numbers are instructive in understanding the overall nature of data breaches, it is also helpful to look at some of the specific cases. Selected illustrative cases of data breaches that have received prominent media attention include the following:

Organization	Number of Records	Breach Type	Information Type
Anthem, Inc.	80 Million	Criminal Hackers	Broad PII & PHI
Home Depot	56 Million	Card Readers	Credit Cards
Evernote	50 Million	Criminal Hackers	Passwords & Email
Sony Pictures	50,000 (employees)	Ransom Hack	Internal Corporate Information
JPM Chase	76 Million	Criminal Hackers	Customer PII
US Internal Revenue Service	100,000	Criminal Hackers	Tax Refund Fraud
Office of Personnel Management (US Federal)*	4-20 Million	Cyber War (China?)	Broad PII, Security Background Checks

* The OPM breach is discussed in greater detail in the "Cyberwar" part of section 5

How much is the cost of the damage caused by incidents of identity theft?

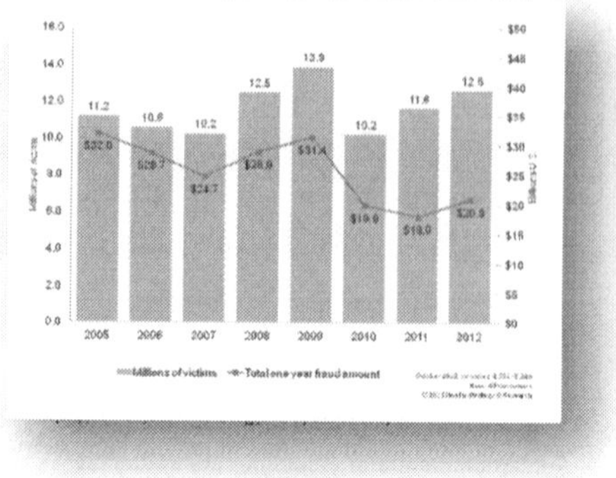

What is the magnitude of the losses and damage to consumers and the businesses that are affected by the reported incidents of identity theft? There are several categories of parties affected by identity theft incidents; in general they may be divided into these groups for purposes of our analysis:

- Consumers whose PII has been misused by identity thieves
- Companies and other organizations that maintain consumer PII and have experienced a data breach
- Lenders, including credit card issuers, depositories, and others with financial ties to the affected consumers
- Providers of other services, such as medical and health services and insurance companies
- Other affected parties who may be secondarily affected by identity theft involving either a direct consumer event or a data breach by another holder of the consumer's PII.

While there is an abundance of statistical information, gathered by law enforcement agencies, the FTC and State agencies, and private concerns, it tends to concentrate on numbers of complaints, or reported data breach events, or other measures that are easily and reliably accessed. The "dollar" cost is a less precise concept, due to many intangible factors, especially in the context of business operations and ongoing relationships with consumers. The following information and related sources represent current reports from various organizations that have collected a variety of statistics and analyzed them to estimate a "dollar" cost suffered by the affected parties. Note that they are illustrative, and should not be considered as either definitive or necessarily subject to being projected onto other financial or economic situations. One size definitely does not fit all in this exercise.

Consumers

To get an idea of the magnitude of the cost of identity theft to consumers, it is possible to establish an amount of losses in the aggregate from representative surveys, and then calculate an average based on those numbers. While it may not be an elegant or accurate means of weighing the exact cost, at least this provides a range that can be used for purposes of analyzing how identity theft fits into the consumer's financial and economic life. This analysis helps to answer the question of whether it's worthwhile for the consumer to take actions to minimize the risk of identity theft.

The following report is from Javelin Strategies, and shows prominently that identity thieves stole $16 billion from 12.7 million U.S. consumers last year. Simple mathematical division indicates that the average loss per consumer in this survey was approximately $1260. This figure is based on dollar losses only, and does not account for the time lost by the individual victim. Relevant portions of the press release report of the study appears below:

The 2015 Identity Fraud Study, released in March 2015 *by Javelin Strategy & Research*, revealed that 2014 was a mixed year in the fight against identity fraud, with some advances and some setbacks. The study found that fraudsters stole $16 billion from 12.7 million U.S. consumers last year. With a new identity fraud victim every two seconds, there is still significant risk to consumers, particularly students. Encouragingly, new account fraud – when someone opens an account in your name that you are not aware of – hit a record low in 2014, but continues to be one on the most damaging types of fraud. Data breaches were a big headline in 2014, and they had a significant impact on identity fraud. The study found that two-thirds of identity fraud victims in 2014 had previously received a data breach notification in the same year, with many indicating their wariness about shopping at merchants, including big box retailers.

The annual 2015 Identity Fraud Study is a comprehensive analysis of identity fraud trends, independently produced by Javelin Strategy & Research and made possible by LifeLock, Inc., a leading provider of proactive identity theft protection services for consumers, and fraud and risk management solutions for enterprises. Now in its twelfth consecutive year, it is the nation's longest-running study of identity fraud, with 58,800 respondents surveyed since 2003.

Identity fraud

Identity fraud is defined as the unauthorized use of another person's personal information to achieve illicit financial gain. Identity fraud can range from simply using a stolen payment card account, to making a fraudulent purchase, to taking control of existing accounts or opening new accounts. The 2015 Identity Fraud Study found several significant trends, including:

- Incremental decrease in victims doesn't tell the whole story – The number of victims of identity fraud decreased by 3 percent from 13.1 million in 2013 to 12.7 million in 2014. But progress has been made with total fraud losses declining to $16 billion in 2014, a decrease of 11 percent from 2013 ($18 billion). This decrease is attributable to the combined efforts of industry, consumers, and monitoring and protection systems that are catching fraud more quickly.

- Students are least concerned yet are most severely impacted by fraud – Among several demographic segments analyzed, students indicated the least amount of concern about fraud occurring, with more than 64 percent saying they were not very concerned about fraud. Yet, this same group is more likely to perceive significant effects due to the occurrence of fraud (15 percent experiencing moderate or severe impact). Students are also the least likely to detect identity fraud themselves. In fact, 22 percent of students were notified that they were a victim of identity fraud either by a debt collector or when they were denied credit, three times higher than average fraud victims. Students are also four times more likely to be victims of "familiar" fraud, versus all other consumers.

- Fraud victims avoiding retailers – 2014 saw a significant amount of data breaches, most notably from retailers Neiman Marcus, Home Depot, Staples and Michael's, as well as financial institution JPMorgan Chase. These breaches had a great impact on consumer purchasing decisions, with 28 percent of fraud victims saying they avoided merchants post-fraud. Notably, individuals whose credit or debit cards were breached in the past year were nearly three times more likely to be an identity fraud victim. This highlights the need for increased security, vigilance and quick response by retailers.

- New account fraud going undetected – New account fraud reached record lows in 2014, yet the study showed that victims of new account fraud are three times more likely to take a year or more to discover that their identities were misused compared to other types of fraud, such as existing non-card accounts. This can open the door for fraudsters to be able to use the victim's identity for illicit behavior for a long period of time, which can result in greater harm to consumers in the form of financial losses, and problems with their credit history and scores. These findings reinforce the need for consumers to actively monitor their identities and accounts.

"Despite the headlines, the occurrence of identity fraud hasn't changed much over the past year, and it is still a significant problem," said Al Pascual, director of fraud & security, Javelin Strategy & Research. "Consumers, financial institutions and retailers are all taking aggressive steps, yet we must remain vigilant. The criminals will continue to find new ways to commit fraud, so taking advantage of available technology and services to protect against, detect and resolve identity fraud is a must for all individuals and corporations."

Methodology

In October 2014, Javelin Strategy & Research conducted an address-based survey of 5,000 U.S. consumers to assess the impact of fraud, uncover where fraudsters are making progress, explore consumers' actions and behaviors, and identify segments of consumers most affected by fraud. [19]

Data Breached Organizations

Even more challenging than calculating the cost to an individual consumer of an identity theft event is the task of estimating the dollar cost to an organization that suffers a data breach. However, there are indicators that can help see such a loss in a financial perspective. Chief among them are the immediate cost of plugging the gap in security that permitted the breach to occur, notifying the potentially affected consumers whose PII was compromised, and providing them with a remediation or identity restoration program (usually from a third party service provider).

The breached organization may also be subject to regulatory penalties and fines, as well as longer term costs of overhauling an entire data management system to include state-of-the-art security measures to avoid a repeat of such an event.

Ultimately, however, the most costly part of a data breach to an organization may be the impact on customer relationships. As reported above in the Javelin study: "These breaches had a great impact on consumer purchasing decisions, with 28 percent of fraud victims saying they avoided merchants post-fraud." Businesses operate in a competitive environment, and it's generally easy for a disaffected consumer to find another provider of most products and services.

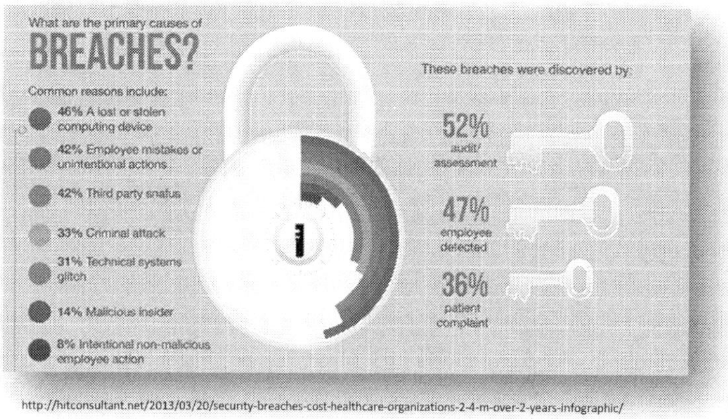

http://hitconsultant.net/2013/03/20/security-breaches-cost-healthcare-organizations-2-4-m-over-2-years-infographic/

Lost customers result in lost revenue, diminished profits, decrease in the value of the company (including, in the case of public companies, decrease in the stock price), and other impediments, both financial and non-financial. In sum, taking steps to avoid a data breach is a worthwhile endeavor, similar to risk management efforts in any other part of the business process.
In addition, depending on the jurisdiction and applicable laws, there may be additional legal claims by affected customers. In this regard, it should be noted that federal identity theft laws do not provide a "private right of action" enabling affected consumers to sue the organization that failed to protect their PII against a data breach. However, such liability is a recognized threat, and is often covered by "cyber-insurance." A more detailed discussion of this kind of liability and coverage appears below in Section 8.

One further observation in this regard comes from the prior year's Javelin study, as reported by the Consumer Reports organization: "...22.5 percent of consumers who received notice of a security breach, like the one that occurred at Target, subsequently became victims of identity theft" according to a survey of 5,000 consumers by Javelin Strategy and Research. Javelin Strategy and Research is a California consulting firm that has studied this crime for more than 10 years. It was also noted in that article, "Breach victims are 8 times more likely to become (a) victim of identity theft." Whether or not the incident of identity theft is a result of the breach, it can certainly do nothing to the advantage of the breached organization for the consumer to believe that the two are related.

http://www.consumerreports.org/cro/news/2013/12/protect-your-identity-from-target-security-breach/index.htm

What is the cost to large organizations for large data breaches?

Public reports of the immediate and overall recognized financial costs to the organization suffering a data breach vary widely. Examples of large data breaches that have been analyzed in the media have featured Target, Home Depot, Sony, and Anthem as examples.

On one hand, the "gross costs" including notifications, remediation programs, settlements with consumers and government agencies, information technology and security upgrades, and other related expenses written off for accounting purposes appear to be quite large. Target reported in its SEC filings some $160 million as the gross cost of the 2013 data breach involving about 40 million Target payment cards and about 70 million other customer accounts. However, after insurance reimbursements and deduction of losses from taxable income, the figure is approximately $105 million, a number that represents 0.1% of Target's sales for the year 2014. Home Depot's similar report, involving the breach of 50 million credit card holders in 2014, showed $43 million as the gross cost, with about $15 million of recoverable expenses, for a net loss of $28 million, representing only 0.01% of Home Depot's sales for the year 2014.

And Sony's breach in 2014, of about 47,000 files (many including Social Security Numbers) was much smaller in scale, but still cost a reported $15 million in "investigation and remediation" costs, and a further expected $35 million in restoring financial and information technology systems. The company reported that these amounts were not considered "material" for accounting and disclosure purposes. However, it has also been observed that there is no practical way to evaluate the cost to the company and its officers and employees the adverse effects of the compromise of personal and sensitive information, even internal e-mails about confidential company information.

A recent court ruling may result in additional costs to Sony. While most claims involving data breaches are subject to a requirement that the affected party sustain demonstrable economic loss, in the current claims against Sony, Judge Klausner ruled that by requiring employees' PII, Sony created a "special relationship that provides an exception to the economic loss doctrine." At the time of this writing, the matter remains unresolved. [20]

In the health care and medical sector, the 2015 Anthem data breach involving the health records of 80 million people has resulted in a reported loss in excess of the $100 million covered by insurance provisions. That amount has been estimated to pay for notification, and credit monitoring and remediation programs. Additional costs have not yet been reported at the time of this writing.

On a more generalized basis, the 2015 Ponemon Institute Cost of Data Breach Study reported that the average consolidated total cost of a data breach is $3.8 million representing a 23% increase since 2013. The study also reports that the cost incurred for each lost or stolen record containing sensitive and confidential information increased six percent from a consolidated average of $145 to $154. [21]

What does this analysis of costs mean, or how does this information translate to exemplify the costs of smaller breaches, especially for smaller businesses and other organizations?

A brief review of the two Chronologies of Data Breaches, mentioned above, indicates that the magnitude of breaches covers a wide range of incidents; they are not primarily breaches of huge data bases. In that context, it should be noted that the PRC does not report breaches involving the records of fewer than 10 people, and the ITRC's report methodology results in the designation of a large number of records compromised as "Unknown."

In practice, this means that many of the smaller breaches may go unreported, or at least may not be reported in meaningful detail. One aspect of this gap may be that smaller companies, with few employees or customers, may not be subject to notification laws, and are not required to report breaches or implement notification or remediation procedures.

In terms of prevention, or advance risk management, many small organizations may not have the resources to devote to security testing, software updates, and in consequence fail to take measures to avoid data breaches and other compromise of information that is by its nature vulnerable to identity theft. [22]

Further discussion of the developing trend to hold small businesses liable for credit card fraud is included in Section 5 under Credit Cards and "liability shift."

Note that an adversely affected company in this light may not be a business at all, but a community or other non-profit organization. They are, after all, subject to the same threats to their continued existence or effectiveness in providing for recipients of its services as a for-profit business.

The method of evaluating the cost of data breaches to a small organization is less transparent than for a large business. First, the direct costs are very difficult to assess, as the financial statements of small organizations tend to be less detailed than large ones, especially if they are not accompanied by an unqualified opinion of a Certified Public Accountant.

Second, it is difficult if not impossible to calculate the value of loss of business, reputation, or a silent departure of existing customers (or those who are dissuaded from doing business with a company that has lost public confidence).

There have been surveys based on the experiences of small businesses that participate in national trade associations. One such survey, carried out in 2013 by the National Small Business Association reported that 44% of the 843 participating small businesses had suffered a cyber attack, and that the average cost was nearly $9,000. Average losses from bank accounts due to cyber attacks on the participating businesses amounted to nearly $7000; it should be noted that business accounts do not enjoy the same level of protection as consumer accounts. [23]

Lenders/Credit Card Issuers

Several factors are at play in analyzing the impact of identity theft incidents on credit card issuers and other lenders. They reflect the roles of the parties to a credit transaction, and the nature of the identity theft and identity fraud. For our purposes, the three main parties are the consumer (in this section, this term is interchangeably used with "borrower" or "cardholder"), the lender (credit card issuer), and the merchant (or other party receiving payment from a credit transaction).

Nearly as long as credit cards have been in widespread use, federal law has limited cardholder liability for an unauthorized transaction to $50.00. The Fair Credit Billing Act (FCBA) and the Electronic Fund Transfer Act (EFTA) offer protection if the consumer's credit, ATM, or debit cards are lost or stolen.

In Section 7, this ISG XV provides specific steps recommended for the cardholder in the event of loss.

Credit Cards vs. Debit Cards

It is important to distinguish between the effect on the cardholder of a lost or stolen or misused debit card and credit card. The most obvious difference is this:

- With a credit card, once the report of unauthorized use has been made, the consumer is under no obligation to pay the disputed charge, unless and until the dispute is resolved against the consumer.
- With a debit card, the funds have already been deducted from the cardholder's account; once the unauthorized use has been reported, there is a lag time during which the financial institution must confirm the consumer's claim before the funds are restored to the account and made available to the consumer.

There is no practical means of determining or even approximating the financial costs to the consumer of these types of identity theft incidents. Individual cases will vary so greatly that even the immediate inconvenience of funds and credit being made unavailable may not reflect the actual cost, which will in most instances include loss of time in replacing or re-arranging cash availability and credit lines. It is easy to recognize, but hard to quantify potentially costly effects such as these:

- Missed payments lead to penalties due to blocked checking account funds
- Over-limit fees on credit cards caused by unauthorized charges
- Replacement cards and account numbers will require numerous phone calls and online updates for auto-pay accounts
- Interruption of timely payments of any account may result in negative information being sent to credit reporting agencies and decrease in credit scores
- Failure by the consumer to take appropriate action to report and follow up potentially may subject the consumer to further liability
- Under developing practices by banks and other card issuers, claims of liability may be made against the merchant that accepts a credit or debit card in an unauthorized transaction, this can have an adverse effect on the relationship between the merchant and the consumer
- In assessing liability for such claims, the Red Flags Rules of the FTC may come into play; more information on this rule and its application is covered in Section 6

Medical Identity Theft

Currently, the Ponemon Institute conducts the most comprehensive report on medical identity theft.

According to the "Fifth Annual Study on Medical Identity Theft" by the Ponemon Institute, medical ID theft in 2014 was up 21.7 percent from the prior year. Some 2.3 million Americans adults, averaging 6,300 each day, were medical identity theft victims in 2014. See www.ponemon.org.

"Medical identity theft occurs when someone uses an individual's name and personal identity to fraudulently receive medical services, prescription drugs and/or goods, including attempts to commit fraudulent billing," according to Ponemon's "Fifth Annual Study on Medical Identity Theft."

In addition to out-of-pocket expenses, victims often suffer serious risks related to their health care as a result of medical identity theft. As a result of abuse of Protected Health Information, (PHI) the identity thief's medical record may appear in the file of the victim, potentially resulting in a misdiagnosis, erroneous, delayed or harmful treatment, and even rejected insurance claims.

Medical identity theft is costly to consumers.

Unlike credit-card fraud, victims of medical identity theft can suffer significant financial consequences. Sixty-five percent of medical identity theft victims had to pay an average of $13,500 to resolve the crime. In some cases, they paid the health care provider, repaid the insurer for services obtained by the thief, or they engaged an identity-service provider or legal counsel to help resolve the incident and prevent fraud.

Those who have resolved the crime spent, on average, more than 200 hours on such activities as working with their insurer or health-care provider.

Medical identity theft can have a negative impact on reputation.

Forty-five percent of respondents said medical identity theft affected their reputation mainly because of embarrassment due to disclosure of sensitive personal health conditions; 19 percent of respondents believed the theft caused them to miss out on career opportunities. Three percent said it resulted in the loss of employment.

Medical identity theft is a complicated crime to resolve.

The health-care provider or insurer seldom informs the victim about the theft. In general, victims learn about the theft of their credentials more than three months after the crime and do not know when they became a victim.

Resolution of medical identity theft is time-consuming.

Because of federal privacy regulations, victims must be involved in the resolution of the crime. In many cases, victims struggle to reach resolution. Only Ten percent of respondents in the Ponemon study reported achieving a completely satisfactory conclusion of the incident. [24]

The Medical Identity Fraud Alliance ("MIFA") is a 501(c)(6) organization working with industry members to reduce medical identity fraud through collaboration and partnership. MIFA provides leadership, education and awareness to drive the development of best-in-class technologies and influences changes to regulation, policies and law regarding Personally Identifiable Information (PII) and Protected Health Information (PHI). [25]

Additional commentary from MIFA on Medical Identity Theft indicates the trends present a growing threat to consumers, health care providers and insurers, and nearly every other party involved in the maintenance and protection of medical and health records. The following news article reflects this concern and points out some of the steps being taken by the industry.

The lion's share of medical identity theft victims can expect to pay upwards of $13,500 to resolve the crime. What's more, about 50 percent of consumers say they would find another healthcare provider if they were concerned about the security of their medical records. How's that for a business case to take security a little more seriously?

As Ann Patterson, senior vice president and program director for MIFA, emphasized, the reputational impacts of medical identity theft for both consumer and provider organizations are huge. Patterson pointed to some concerning numbers found in the MIFA-sponsored annual medical identity theft study. Conducted by researchers at the Ponemon Institute, the study underscored a staggering 22 percent increase in medical identity thefts from just last year (2013).

And if you're looking at it from a business case point-of-view, shirking one's security duties is just bad news. First off, it's not like having your credit card number stolen where you can make a quick call to your bank, cancel the charge and have them issue you a new card. This is personal medical data that can't be tracked by credit monitoring services.

"As humans, we're more concerned about whether or not a credit card number has been stolen," said Kevin Johnson, CEO of security consulting firm Secure Ideas, in an interview with *Healthcare IT News* earlier this year. "And there's such a lack of concern about my medical records, my personal data." And there is also the fact that "tomorrow Bank of America will ship me a new credit card."

In the February 2015 Ponemon study, 89 percent of victims said the identity theft "affected their reputation mainly because of embarrassments due to disclosure of sensitive personal health conditions." What's more, nearly 20 percent said it caused them to miss out on career opportunities.

"Take the average cost most medical identity theft victims have to pay out, and consider their collective impact on your healthcare organization. Half of respondents say they'll go to another provider if they had concerns over it.

"There are things, though, healthcare organizations can do, and are doing, that are helping," Patterson added.

MIFA's members, for instance which include giants like Kaiser Permanente, Aetna, the U.S. Department of Veterans Affairs and Henry Ford Health System, among others – are making significant strides.

There is huge interest for some members in developing technologies that would address the notification, alerts and monitoring specifically for medical identities, similar to what credit monitoring does for those affected by financial identity theft.

"We do see healthcare organizations and health plans making moves for instance to do things like remove the Social Security number as part of the patient identifier," said Patterson. They have also seen a considerable uptick in biometrics and investing in technologies that would help with accurate reconciliation. [26]

SUMMARY

It will always be a challenge to consumers, businesses, and regulators to learn about and stay ahead of the predations of identity thieves. For every method of foreseeing and preventing identity theft incidents, the unauthorized users of sensitive information will continue to develop and employ new means to avoid detection and perpetrate their crimes.

Understanding the trends and methods involved can lay a foundation for the successful management of the risk of identity theft and the associated losses, both financial and indirect. To this end, the task is ongoing, and requires unceasing attention to news and other reports in order to stay current on the subject.

In this endeavor, we are fortunate to have the facility of news feeds and related means of receiving updated information on nearly any topic of interest. It is recommended CITRMS® XV professionals utilize this type of news retrieval capability in order to keep up to date on developments and trends in Identity Theft Risk Management.

Section 3. What Information is Involved and Who Holds It

SECTION OVERVIEW

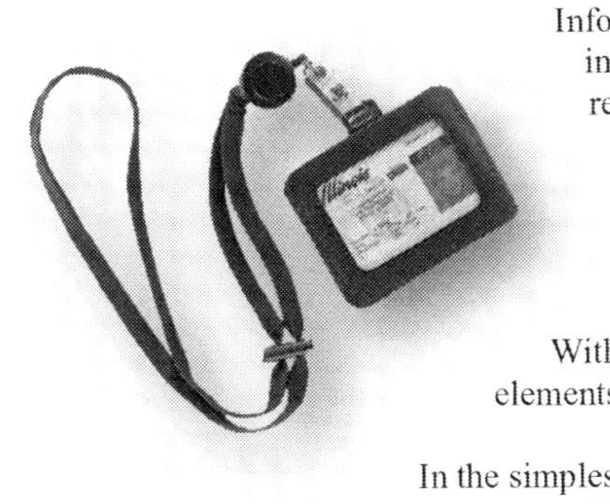

Information used by identity thieves is generally divided into two broad areas: information controlled by the consumer and information held by others (generally referred to as "Holders"). There is a further division among the Holders, those subject to specific law and regulation and those that are exempt (by either deliberate omission or oversight). This section delves into the specific types of information that is vulnerable to identity thieves, and how to help consumers become aware of the huge and growing range of accessible information that can lead to becoming a victim.

With the understanding of what Personally Identifiable Information is, and what its elements are, the question arises as to WHERE it is and WHO holds it.

In the simplest terms there are two places: Consumers & Everyone Else (generally referred to for this purpose as "Holders" of PII).

Consumers

Consumers hold and control information that is vulnerable to identity theft in a broad variety of locations and forms. Just taking a look around the home, automobile, and personal items can provide a lengthy list of types of such information and the places it is held. It is important to note that control and protection of this information is primarily the responsibility of the consumer, even though there are many circumstances in which other parties who may hold it may compromise this same information.

At home, consumers keep such sensitive information as bank and investment account statements, credit card and other types of loan files, tax-related documents, and tax preparation lists, and a broad array of similar documents. They are generally too voluminous to fit into a safe or other secure facility; besides, it is too inconvenient to require opening a safe every time the consumer needs to review an account or pay a bill.

At a minimum, the current bills are likely to be found near the computer (for online payments) or near the desk with the checkbook (which carries the bank's routing number and customer account number, items very convenient for identity thieves to abuse).

In the automobile or other vehicles (boats or licensed ATVs, for instance), there is the potential identity thief will find registration and insurance cards. These reveal the home address, identifying information about the vehicle and insurance accounts, and other information that can be used either directly or as part of a scheme to aggregate elements of identity information to perpetrate various forms of identity theft.

Another vulnerability created in the automobile is the remote garage door opener. With the home address listed on the registration and insurance cards, an identity thief knows just where to go to gain access to the garage. Anecdotally, it is common practice to leave an unlocked door from the garage into the utility room or other area in the main floor of the home, for convenient access upon arrival at home. After all, the garage door is locked, and why bother with two locks?

In addition to a wallet with all manner of identification and credit cards, the consumer is likely to be carrying a smart phone. The burgeoning functionality of this device is covered in more detail below, but suffice to say at this point there is generally a wealth of sensitive information within the smart phone, and identity thieves are always developing new ways to penetrate the security features of these devices, both by gaining physical access to the phone and also remotely.

Consumers also transmit, store, and maintain a great deal of sensitive information online, typically for data back-up and other computer purposes. Both the information content and the means of accessing it, usually a user name, password, and other authentication device, constitute opportunities for identity thieves to perpetrate their crimes. This kind of information management is within the control of the consumer, and must be carried out in an informed manner.

Passwords and other authentication routines present a particular challenge. It may be viewed as another application of the Security-Convenience Spectrum analysis. The more convenient a password is, the less secure, and *vice versa*. Various "solutions" to the problem of how to remember passwords range from writing them down in a secret place to storing them online in a "password vault." A more detailed discussion of passwords and password use appears in Section 7.

Everyone Else

Sensitive, identity-theft prone information is held in such a wide variety of places that it would be difficult to list them all. There are official records held by various government agencies, from birth to death and everything in between. Everyone with whom the consumer has a business or social relationship likely possesses numerous elements of PII. For purposes of this discussion, the following are the categories for more detailed consideration.

- Government, at all levels, which is divided into (1) public and (2) confidential files.
- Financial and Economic Relationships, which is divided into (1) publicly available and (2) protected information, either by law or regulation; regardless of whether the information is open to the public, the data in this category is provided by the consumer.
- Many elements of PII are held by friends, family, social connections, and others, and may be published or otherwise made public or available with or without the consumer's permission.

Government

Before entering into the discussion of PII and other identity-theft prone information held by government agencies, it should be noted there is no current way for the consumer to know or control in a comprehensive way in which this information is collected, stored, or utilized. The issues involved are being played out in the public and legislative arenas, but it appears that at least federal government agencies have accessed and stored vast amounts of data about the communications of people inside and outside the U.S. Whether PII is involved is not clear, as the primary target of the information gathering is claimed to be *meta-data*, or the time, place, and means of the monitored communications, rather than their content.

The government agencies holding consumer PII are at all levels: federal, State, and municipal (local). Any government entity with which the consumer has a relationship of any kind holds records reflecting the nature of the relationship, and supporting data about the individual consumer. Many governmental and official functions require consumers to file their personal information. In addition, much of this information is available to the public, either openly or upon application for access. For our purposes, there is an important distinction to be made between information that is readily available to the public, upon request, and information that is maintained as confidential.

For instance, the Freedom of Information Act ("FOIA") permits almost anyone to gain access to public files that do not include information considered by the government to be among the specific FOIA exemptions. It is beyond the scope of this ISG to discuss in depth the details of FOIA's disclosure requirements, procedures, and exemptions.

However, it is worth noting that most information not specifically protected from disclosure may easily be obtained by anyone who makes a formal request for it. In the following listing and discussion, patterns emerge demonstrating the wide range and availability of PII for those with appropriate and illicit purposes to obtain and utilize it.

Examples of exempt (not subject to disclosure under FOIA) material tend to be specific to the agency and its functions. There is no comprehensive list of such exemptions, as they are regularly being challenged and defended in the regulatory and judicial processes. In general, exempt categories include those involving national security, personal and company financial and tax data, investigation details, proprietary information relating to the operations of the agency, and other confidential information vital to the interests of the public, as determined by the government. [27]

Government – Publicly Available Records

From birth to death and everything in between, many common life events and activities are recorded and maintained in public data bases, accessible without regard to whether it is for legitimate or illicit purposes, either in person or more and more often online. With few exceptions, the consumer has no choice in limiting collection of or access to such records. In most cases, the person seeking the information does not have to pay for it or reveal his or her own identity. It is easy to see that this vulnerability can give rise to identity thieves taking advantage of the accessibility of sensitive elements of personally identifiable information.

The following are some of the major categories of government records that are available to the public, identity thieves included. Note that the specific offices in which these records are held will differ from jurisdiction to jurisdiction.

Personal or "Vital" Records

Information on all types of "Life Events" is recorded and filed in public data bases, either in hard copy or digital format, or both. The major categories include the following:

- <u>Birth Records</u> include information on the parents, the location of the birth, details on the physical attributes of the newborn, and other personal data.

- <u>Marriage Records</u> contain the names of the parties being married, date and location of the issuance of the license, officiant performing the wedding, witnesses and other parties to the wedding certificate, and other PII, depending on the jurisdiction.

- Divorce Records can be succinct or very detailed, usually depending on the nature of the divorce (contested or uncontested), and may include specifics on custody and financial arrangements; they may be sealed by court order if so requested by one or more of the parties, usually for reasons of personal privacy or the protection of sensitive information.

- Death Certificates in most jurisdictions carry very detailed information not only on the decedent, but also other family members. Examples of specific data vulnerable to identity theft may include the decedent's Social Security number, dates of birth and death, birth names of parents and children (who are often the ones who have reported the death), cause of death, whether there was an autopsy, funeral home making the arrangements, and the certifying physician. The death certificate and all this information is distributed to numerous other organizations, as part of the process in transferring financial accounts, modifying benefits, and other required steps, resulting in the proliferation of sources identity thieves can access to get sensitive information.

- Adoption Records are treated differently, since in many cases the birth parents (usually the mother) and the adoptive parents may wish to keep the records confidential for various personal reasons. Usually, this is to make it difficult for the adopted child to find the birth parents, at least without obtaining permission from both birth and adoptive parents. At the same time, such confidential treatment may make it more difficult for the potential identity thief to gain access to these records.

People who are interested in learning more about family genealogy routinely utilize all of these "Life Event" records. Whether the research is conducted directly by the individual or through one of the genealogy services that have become prevalent, online access to these types of records is relatively easy. Several web-based genealogy research services offer inexpensive, even free trial, access to their programs to facilitate this kind of research.

Moreover, arcane information on deceased persons, their families, and related facts may be learned by searching for their burial sites, using a free service such as the one online at the URL www.findagrave.com . While intended for the benefit of survivors among family and friends, this is just one more example of how sensitive information with its original source in official files can become subject to abuse.

Both genealogy and related research is often pursued using census data. At least in this area, there is a substantial delay in the release of information by the Census Bureau: **Decennial census records are confidential for 72 years to protect respondents' privacy.** [28]

Real Estate Records

Usually available either in person or online through county offices of the Recorder and Assessor, or other similar office designation, much personally identifiable information is included about the following aspects of the property and transaction, among others:

- Deed specifics
- Purchase price
- The title in which real estate is held (Name, Address, etc.)
- Trust information if held in a trust, such as a family trust
- Mortgages recorded (including the name and contact information of the lender, loan number, and amount of the original loan)
- Tax records and liens, and other related information
- Names of the sellers and buyers of properties
- The price paid
- Street address and other parcel identifiers
- Size and value of the improvements
- Easements or rights of way (and who holds them)
- Building Code and Compliance with Zoning Restrictions

Title insurance companies usually conduct a search of all relevant filings and documents regarding a property when it is under contract of sale; all such information is obtained from public sources. The findings of the title search may be made available to other parties with (or claiming to have) interests in the subject property.

In addition to the information on file on the real property purchase and sale, other records are maintained in files open to the public. An illustrative list would include:

- Applications for building permits, including the architectural plans
- Building permits and restrictions on property improvement
- Violations of building codes and zoning restrictions
- Mechanics' liens and liens for materials
- Tax assessments and taxes owed and paid
- Changes in mortgage lender
- Changes in title in which the property is held
- Changes in easements or rights-of-way

Court Records

Nearly all types of litigation filings and court orders are generally open to public view, unless some overriding reason is accepted by the court to seal such records from the public. Some examples of the types of court records that are open and available:

- Litigation (civil lawsuits of all types in courts of general jurisdiction)
- Criminal prosecutions
- Small claims, which are heard in a less formal setting
- Alternative dispute resolution
- Bankruptcy
- Probate of wills and estates
- Separation and divorce
- Protective orders against family members or others
- Cases on appeal in higher courts
- Case Dockets (list of all filings in the case)

These documents may include a wealth of personally identifiable information about consumers, their businesses, accounts, and other sensitive information. Especially vulnerable is information available in transcripts of hearings and attachments to filings. Note that courts may, upon the request of one or more parties, seal or hold confidential certain filings and transcripts, for reasons such as national security, unwarranted invasions of privacy, intellectual property and trade secrets, and other similar attributes.

Professional Licenses

While each State has its own list of professions and specialties for which a license is required, the purpose is to regulate activities for the safety and protection of consumers. The data in filings for professional licenses typically include the name of the applicant or registered licensee, contact information, education and experience to qualify for the license, and other information pertinent to the individual or business seeking the license. In many cases, very sensitive data, such as the Social Security number, may be included in these files.

Complaints filed or disciplinary and enforcement actions taken against the licensee are also maintained in the files of the regulatory agency. These files may include the name and contact information of the complainant (usually the consumer). It should be noted, however, that complaints still in the investigative stage may not be subject to public release prior to a decision being made and action taken against the licensee; if no action is taken by the agency, such files may never be released or identifying information may be deleted from the publicly disclosed file.

The following represent some of the more common activities for which most States (the list is of necessity illustrative, not exhaustive) requires a license:

- Lawyers and law firms
- Accountants and accounting firms
- General contractor
- Specialty trade contractors (electricians, plumbers, etc.)
- Beautician/Barber
- Architect
- Medical Services (doctor, nurse, dentist, chiropractor, podiatrist, etc.)
- Shorthand reporter
- Civil Engineer
- Land Surveyor
- Massage Therapist
- Midwife
- Athletic Trainer
- Interior Designer
- Occupational Therapist
- Pharmacist
- Optometrist
- Social Worker
- Veterinarian & veterinary tech
- Auctioneer
- Funeral Director
- Real Estate Broker/Agent
- Mortgage Broker

The relevant point for Identity Theft Risk Management purpose is that a vast amount of PII is included in the application and administration of professional licenses, much of which may be disclosed to the public – and therefore may be at risk to misuse by identity thieves.

Corporate Filings

The authority of one of the States charters most corporations, limited liability companies, and other entities used for business or financial purposes. Usually, it is the State Secretary of State or Corporations Commission or other similar agency that issues such charters.

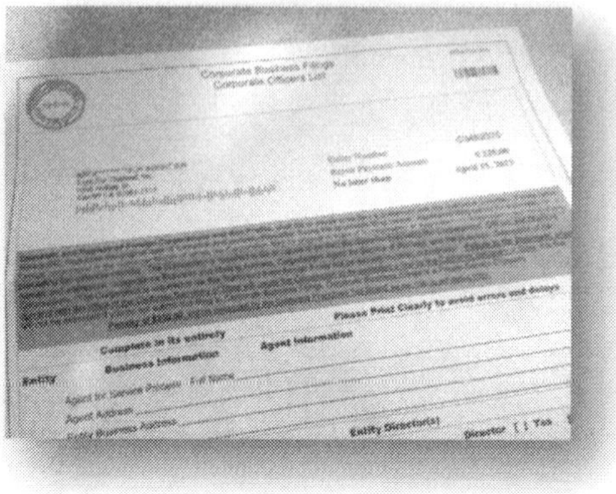

The public information easily available usually includes the following data;

- Name of the corporate entity
- Who incorporated it
- Names and addresses of the members of the board of directors of a corporation or the members of a limited liability company
- Date of formation
- Articles of incorporation and any amendments
- Address and contact information
- Registered agent for legal purposes (such as service of process)
- Status (good standing, inactive, expired, etc.), and other basic facts

In this digital age, the vast majority of corporate filings are accessible online either free of charge or for a nominal fee. In the case of free access, the person seeking corporate information need not disclose his or her identity or purpose. For paid access, a credit card is normally required (although an identity thief seeking this kind of corporate information might well employ unauthorized use of a stolen credit card or an entirely bogus one).

Searches of Public Records

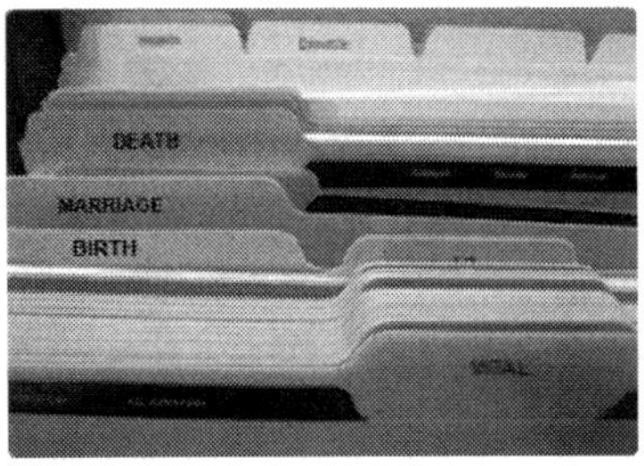

Most of the popular internet search engines facilitate searching for the name of an individual, a business, or other entity. Paid advertisers are usually included in the search results, with links to use their services. Among these are fee-based services that will perform searches of public records on any individual or entity. These services tend not to inquire as to the purpose of the search or if the search is for a legitimate reasons. The important takeaway is that anything in a public data file can (and usually will) be accessible to identity thieves - -whether they perform the search themselves, or pay someone else to do it. [29]

Government – Confidential or Non-Public Records

With the foregoing as a foundation for the content and accessibility of public government records, the next category is government-held confidential information.

As suggested earlier regarding the sealing of certain court and related records, there are many reasons for maintaining confidentiality – generally for the security and protection of government functions or established privacy or other rights of the parties involved (such as national security, unwarranted invasions of privacy, intellectual property and trade secrets, and other similar attributes).

It is not surprising, even more than for public records, that there is no comprehensive list of confidential databases. The following lists and discussion cover representative, not exhaustive, locations and circumstances under which PII may be stored and maintained for government purposes. Recent occurrences have led to assurances that vulnerabilities and security systems are continuously being evaluated, but the commentary is not encouraging; see more in the discussion of data breaches in Section 5.

Federal Records

- *Security clearance background check*
    - In many cases, such as in the intelligence services, even the existence of such checks is secret, not only the results.

- *Social Security – Personal Earnings and Benefit Estimate Statement*
    - Earnings history
    - What your Full Retirement Age is
    - Retirement benefits at the retirement ages of 62, your Full Retirement Age and 70
    - Disability benefits if you become disabled now
    - Various survivor benefits

- *Military Service – Active*
    - Military Serial Number
    - Rank
    - Posting
    - Specialty training
    - Family members
    - Other distinguishing characteristics

- *Veterans*
    - Years of service
    - Separation date and reason
    - Nature of Discharge
    - Disabilities if any
    - Benefits
    - Health records

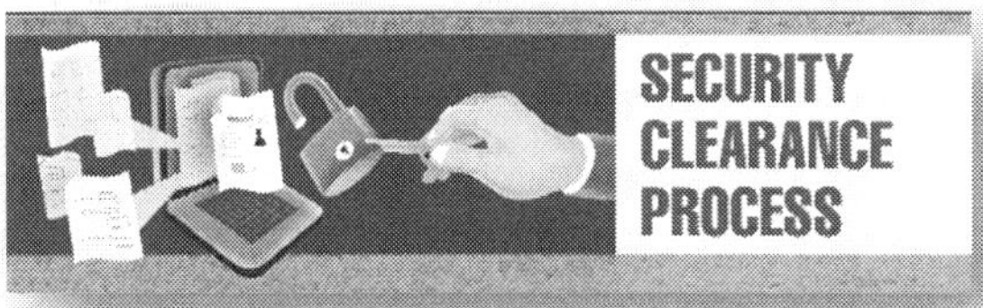

- *Courts*
    - In general, court records may be sealed for specific reasons, especially homeland security, intelligence activities, and other sensitive economic and personnel reasons
    - Foreign Intelligence Surveillance Court (FISA) -- This Court entertains applications made by the United States Government for approval of electronic surveillance, physical search, and certain other forms of investigative actions for foreign intelligence purposes

- *Internal Revenue Service (IRS)*
    - Tax Records of all individuals, families, and filing entities
    - NOTE: IRS acknowledged a breach compromising substantial information on over 100,000 taxpayers in 2015; the consequences are not yet known

- *Academic Institutions and Grants*
    - Individual records of students at military academies
    - Records involving scholarships and grants to individuals in official educational institutions and private institutions
    - Application files
    - Specialized training for U. S. citizens and members of foreign military groups

- *Office of Personnel Management (OPM)*
    - Comprehensive personnel records for all
    - NOTE: In 2014-2015, OPM suffered a breach compromising detailed information on at least four million current and former government employees; the actual number has been estimated in the range of 18 million to 32 million; the consequences are not yet known

Based on a report from the Government Accountability Office, the vulnerability of federal government data files is more widespread and prone to breaches than has previously been reported.

"For fiscal year 2014, 19 of 24 major federal agencies reported that deficiencies in information security controls constituted either a material weakness or significant deficiency in internal controls over their financial reporting," GAO reported in April. "In addition, inspectors general at 23 of these agencies cited information security as a major management challenge for their agency." [30]

State and Local Records

Similar to the federal level, massive amounts of PII are included in non-public or confidential files held at State and municipal offices. There are various reasons these individual files are not subject to public access, although the gross numbers may be made public for analytical and statistical reasons. The breadth of these files mirrors governmental functions, as the following list demonstrates.

- *Employment-related*
    - Personnel files of public employees at all levels
    - Individual files on individual employees and their employers, by function
        - Unemployment
        - Workers Compensation
        - Immigration Status
        - Pension Fund participation and benefit calculations

- *Law Enforcement*
    - Matters under investigation
    - Personnel files
    - Confidential informants and undercover assignments
    - Training and specialty capabilities

- *Child Protective Services and Victim Services*
    - Very closely guarded information about the names and other personal information of children under CPS service and victims of violent crimes
    - Unless and until criminal charges are brought, very limited information is released identifying the alleged perpetrator
    - Location of individuals who may be under threat of harm by others, whether family or unrelated persons

- *State Attorneys General and County/Municipal Attorneys*
    - Grand jury activities, including names of grand jurors
    - Matters under investigation and under consideration for prosecution
    - Personnel files
    - Communications subject to attorney-client privilege (usually with outside law firms)

- *Courts*
    - As discussed above, records may be sealed for specific reasons
    - Court personnel files
    - Other confidential treatment of internal and case matters

- *Grey Areas of Public/Non-Public Official Government*

Demonstrating these issues tend to be dynamic, rather than cut-and-dried, there are several government activities selected for further comment, due to the fact they are subject to numerous factors that impinge on the way they are either made public or kept under confidential treatment. Two illustrative areas have been selected for this purpose: Academic Institutions and Motor Vehicle Divisions (may be called by other names, depending on the State).

- *Academic Institutions*
    - Principally covered by federal law, under the Family Educational Rights and Privacy Act of 1974 (FERPA), regarding access to academic records
    - Primary and Secondary Schools, usually records are also subject to additional State or local (School Board) policies and procedures
    - Colleges and Universities ("Higher Education" both public and private) often have their own policies and procedures for granting, denying, or limiting access to student information
    - Bullying and harassment issues have come into sharp focus, but issues remain regarding verification of incidents and the circumstances under which they may have occurred; typically, such investigations are under confidential seal until conclusions are reached
    - These are subject to review and change as new facts come to light regarding the use and misuse of the records of both students and faculty.

- *Motor Vehicle Department ("DMV") –*
    - States designate this office in differing ways, but for our purposes, "DMV" is used for this ISG. In almost all instances, the responsibilities of the DMV include testing for and issuance of driver licenses, registration of motor vehicles (and boats, in many cases), documenting liens and loan information on titles, and confirming proof of insurance in States that require minimum liability coverage.

    - Immigration issues may also be disclosed in DMV records in some States, as there may be notations in the files on whether the licensee has citizenship, permanent resident status, or other situations that could lead to identity thieves taking advantage of the consumer.

    - Many States use the driver license issuance process to enroll consumers in other programs, like organ donation & voter registration. In practice, this means the consumer's PII will appear in other data bases, such as the entity that administers the program in which the consumer has enrolled. The additional data base may be a government or private entity, so the rules that apply to confidentiality may differ and make the subject PII even more vulnerable than with the DMV.

    - The DMV is included in this discussion due to ancillary data collection and potential deliberate or inadvertent authorization to disclose PII. The practice of the Arizona DMV is illustrative for this purpose. In particular, attention is drawn to the following "Optional" Consent for Release of information:

    - The Federal Driver's Privacy Protection Act 18 U.S.C. 2721-2725, as well as Title 28, Chapter 2, Article 5 of the Arizona Revised Statutes, regulates the disclosure of personal information from driver license and vehicle records, such as name, address and medical/disability information. Unless an individual or entity has a permissible use under these statutes to obtain your personal information, your permission or consent is required for its release to all requesters and can be accomplished by checking the box below.

This consent is optional.

I consent to the release of personal information contained in my driver license and vehicle record. I understand that this is not a one-time consent that applies only to a specific individual or organization, but is instead a general consent that applies to all requests from any and all individuals or organizations for any purpose, until revoked by me in writing. Consent for a vehicle record applies to all owners. [31]

The consumer's immediate reaction is often to check the box, since it's an official request. But consent is not required, and a careful reading of the permission shows that it is very broad and authorized the DMV to share this information with anyone who requests it, regardless of purpose or intent.

While making no judgment about the purpose or intent of facilitating the release of the PII by the DMV, it is recommended to deny the requested permission, especially as it is a one-time election, with no apparent limitation of time or scope.

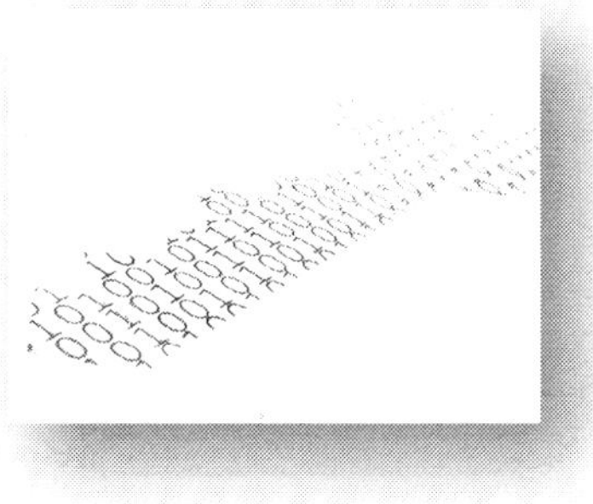

Non-Government (Private Sector) Consumer Records

The consumer chooses the vast majority of private-sector holders of such information and it is the consumer who furnishes the information to them. The focus of this section is on the nature and location of the information and elements of identity theft prone data rather than how it is protected or gets into the hands of identity thieves.

At the same time, it is instructive to take note of the categories of such holders and degree to which they are regulated. Typically, the formality of such responsibilities follows the nature of the relationship. The particular activity on which the relationship is based also defines the law or regulation, jurisdiction, and administering agency that controls these responsibilities. Legal and regulatory requirements at discussed Section 5. As holders of PII, these organizations are generally subject to regulations, and possibly legal liability to maintain confidentiality in the collection, transmission, storage, and distribution of PII. However, it should also be noted that not everyone holding such PII is subject to rules and regulations regarding their responsibilities in protecting it from abuse by identity thieves.

In general, the most highly regulated groups of holders of potentially vulnerable identity theft information are the following:

- Financial institutions and other creditors
- Consumer credit bureaus "Credit Reporting Agencies" or "CRAs")
- Specialty reports data bases (such as insurance claims and tenant history)
- Providers of medical services (including administration of accounts and records)
- Other business relationships may also fall into the more general group of holders of protected information with extensive legal and regulatory requirements to take steps to avoid its compromise and abuse

Financial Institutions and Creditors

Whether the consumer relationship is based on a checking or other deposit account, personal loan, home mortgage, business loan, credit card, or other debt instrument, the institution taking the deposit or extending the credit has, by the nature of the transaction, received and holds a great deal of information on the consumer. The consumer file often includes such detailed and sensitive information as:

- Name
- Address
- Social Security Number
- Assets of all types, including identifying information

Real Estate

- Home and mortgage
- Vacation home and mortgage
- Investment properties and loans, tenants and rents

Financial Investments

- Securities accounts
- Retirement accounts
- Other banking relationships
- Loan of all types, including lender and loan number, interest rate & payment schedule
- Employment information
- Income and tax returns
- Marital Status
- Children and other Dependents
- Credit report, credit score, and any credit or payment history or other information that may bear on creditworthiness or the ability to repay loans.

In the case of financial institutions and creditors, there are two sets of legal requirements discussed in more detail in Section 6. One is the Gramm-Leach-Bliley Act, which provides consumers with an opportunity to limit some, but not all, sharing of information by financial institutions. The other is referred to as the "Red Flags Rules," which sets out a process that must be implemented to protect sensitive information against exploitation by identity thieves.

The information collected by these organizations is regularly shared with intermediaries, so potential lenders can evaluate applications for credit by consumers. This leads to the next group of holders of sensitive PII: credit-reporting agencies.

Consumer Credit Bureaus -- "Credit Reporting Agencies" or "CRAs")

Credit Reporting Agencies collect information from various sources and provide consumer credit information ("credit reports") on individual consumers to lenders. Lenders use this information to help them make decisions on applications for credit, including amounts and terms, based on the applicant's credit and payment history. Many of the elements in credit reports are included in the list above, and in fact often comes from other lenders that have extended credit to the applicant.

There are three principal consumer credit reporting agencies with generalized consumer credit files. In addition, many more operate in more areas that are specialized. These three are Equifax, Experian, and TransUnion; for each, basic contact information for identity theft issues and a hyperlink is provided below, to facilitate getting more detailed information on each of them. Section 7 contains a full discussion of actions consumers can take with the CRAs in the event of actual or suspected identity theft.

- Equifax http://www.equifax.com/
  - Equifax Credit Information Services, Inc.
    P.O. Box 740241
    Atlanta, GA 30374
  - 800-525-6285
- Experian http://www.experian.com/
  - Preferred contact is online.
  - 888-397-3742
- TransUnion http://www.transunion.com/
  - TransUnion LLC
    P.O. Box 2000
    Chester, PA 19022-2000
  - 800-680-7289

A visit to each of their web sites will demonstrate they are oriented toward the consumer, as well as the lenders who purchase their reports. Prominent on each web site is the offer of some form of identity theft protection, beginning with credit report monitoring, and also advice on steps to take in the event the consumer has experienced a situation that appears to be identity theft. The pricing for these programs varies, and the field has become very competitive. More on this subject is discussed in Section 9.

NOTE: When a consumer finds an error or omission in the credit report at one of the three major credit reporting agencies, and notifies the credit reporting agency of the mistake, it is common practice for the one receiving the notification to share this information with the other two.

CITRMS® XV Exercise – Get Your Own Credit Reports

Log on to www.annualcreditreport.com -- the national web site set up for consumers to get free copies of their own credit reports, pursuant to the provisions of the Fair and Accurate Credit Transactions Act of 2003. Every consumer is entitled to receive one free credit report annually from each of the three major credit reporting agencies. It is generally desirable to obtain one of the three CRA credit reports each four-month period, on a rolling basis. Select which of the three you want to obtain – or all if desired. Note the substantial verification process required to prove the authenticity of the requester – and how much information the CRA has already to be able to confirm responses. Then note the detail in the credit report and how much PII is on file. Finally, see how many additional services are on offer, such as access to the credit score and identity theft prevention/protection programs – for an additional price.

In addition to the three "major" CRAs, there are other credit reporting agencies which collect and report on various aspects of consumer and business credit. They may be referred to as "supplementary or alternative" credit reporting agencies. Among the more prominent are the following:

- Innovis https://www.innovis.com/
    - Provides supplementary credit reports to lenders. Provides ID verification data to assist with fraud detection and prevention.

NOTE: Although Innovis may be considered a credit-reporting agency, notifications to the "three major CRAs" are not automatically shared with Innovis. However, a "freeze" (see Section 7) for Innovis credit files can also be initiated online.

CoreLogic

- CreditIQ Credit Report by CoreLogic Credco https://www.credco.com/
    - Collects data such as property ownership and home loan obligation records; property legal filings and tax payment status; rental applications and collection accounts; consumer bankruptcies, liens, judgments, and child support obligations.

- LexisNexis Risk Solutions Bureau,LLC https://personalreports.lexisnexis.com/
    - Collects information from public records and multiple proprietary data sources. The company will provide one free report every 12 months upon request.

SageStream

- SageStream, LLC http://www.sagestreamllc.com/
    - Formerly known as IDA, Inc., this CRA collects information from, and provides supplementary credit reports to: auto lenders, credit card issuers, retailers, utilities, wireless telephone service providers among other service providers.
    - SageStream is a subsidiary of ID Analytics, Inc.

Specialty Reports [32]

NOTE: Additional information on these specialty reporting agencies and how consumers can contact them to receive copies of their reports, correct errors, and use these resources to respond to identity theft incidents appear in Section 7.

The Fair Credit Reporting Act (FCRA) defines any company that issues non-credit reports as a "nationwide specialty consumer reporting agency" (NSCRA).

The operations of NSCRAs are similar to credit reporting agencies. The information they collect comes from a variety of sources, such as:

- Credit history
- Financial institutions, including insurance companies and banks
- Bankruptcy filings
- Medical information
- Driving records
- Real estate records
- Public records of criminal or civil court cases

NSCRAs use this data to create reports based on the requirements of their customers such as insurance companies, employers, and landlords.

Although there is no official or complete list of the companies meeting the definition of NSCRA, the following is a representative listing of prominent companies operating in each of the respective activities identified by the federal agencies.

Check and Bank Screening

- Certegy Check Services, Inc. www.askcertegy.com
    - Collects check-writing histories and provides check-screening services primarily for retail merchants and gaming establishments who accept checks as payment.
    - Certegy is affiliated with Fidelity National Information Services, Inc. (FNIS)
    - The company will provide one free report every 12 months upon request.
- Chex Systems www.consumerdebit.com
    - Provides account verification services primarily for financial institutions.
    - Chex Systems is affiliated with Fidelity National Information Services, Inc. (FNIS)
    - The company will provide one free report every 12 months upon request.
- Early Warning Services, LLC www.earlywarning.com
    - Assists financial institutions, check acceptance companies such as retail merchants, payment processors and other financial entities in detecting and preventing fraud associated with bank accounts and payment transactions.
    - Early Warning Services is owned by Bank of America, BB&T, Capital One, JPM Chase, and Wells Fargo Bank.
    - The company will provide one free report every 12 months upon request.

- TeleCheck Services, Inc. www.firstdata.com/telecheck
    - Assists financial institutions and check acceptance companies such as retail merchants in detecting and preventing fraud associated with check writing.
    - Telecheck Services is a wholly owned subsidiary of First Data Corporation
    - The company will provide one free report every 12 months upon request.

Auto and Property Insurance

- C.L.U.E. Inc.
  https://personalreports.lexisnexis.com/
    - The Reed Elsevier (now RELX Group)/Lexis-Nexis subsidiary, the former independent company ChoicePoint, has conducted data aggregation services in the insurance industry since the 1990's, and provides insurance carriers with historical reports on insurance claims. C.L.U.E. (Comprehensive Loss Underwriting Experience) is the trade name under which the company provides these reports. In addition to the substance of the reports, information on how to dispute the statements in the report are provided to the consumer upon request.
    - The C.L.U.E. Personal Property report provides a seven year history of losses associated with an individual and his/her personal property. The following data will be identified for each loss: date of loss, loss type, and amount paid along with general information such as policy number, claim number and insurance company name.
    - The C.L.U.E. Auto report provides a seven year history of automobile insurance losses associated with an individual. The following data will be identified for each loss: date of loss, loss type, and amount paid along with general information such as policy number, claim number and insurance company name.
    - C.L.U.E Inc. is affiliated with LexisNexis Risk Solutions Bureau LLC.
    - The company will provide one free report every 12 months upon request.

- Insurance Information Exchange (IIX) www.iix.com
    - Collects and reports motor vehicle records, including traffic violation data, to insurance providers and prospective employers.
    - Insurance Information Exchange is affiliated with ISO (see below).
    - IIX is a subsidiary of Verisk Analytics www.verisk.com

- Insurance Services Office, Inc. (ISO) www.iso.com
  - ISO is a source of information about risks of many kinds. For purposes of this study guide, the company's relevant service is the proprietary claims information product named ISO ClaimSearch. According to the Verisk online information at http://www.verisk.com/products-and-services/product-category/claims-information-and-services/improve-claims-processing-and-prevent-fraud-with-iso-claimsearch.html
  - ISO ClaimSearch® is the property/casualty insurance industry's first and only comprehensive system for improving claims processing and fighting fraud.
  - The ISO ClaimSearch system furnishes essential data for researching prior-loss histories, identifying claims patterns, and detecting suspect claims. ISO's Internet interface lets users conduct broad and flexible searches of the data.
  - Participation in ISO ClaimSearch is open to insurers, self-insured organizations, and claims administrators.
  - Collects insurance claims and loss information associated with homes and commercial buildings. Consumers are entitled to full disclosure of any data regarding their own claims that may be in the A-PLUS data base. [A-PLUS™ Property provides details on past insurance claims filed by policyholders and claims filed at the property insurers consider for underwriting.]
  - ISO is a subsidiary of Verisk Analytics www.verisk.com

Tenant History (includes certain Employment Verification services)

- Contemporary Information Corporation www.CICreports.com
  - Conducts background screening services for landlords and residential real estate management companies. Information includes eviction and criminal background data.
- CoreLogic SafeRent www.residentscreening.com
  - Collects information for tenant and employment screening, including landlord-tenant actions and court judgments.
  - The company will provide one free report every 12 months upon request.
- Experian RentBureau www.experian.com/rentbureau
  - Collects rent payment history from property owners and property management firms, electronic rent payment services and collection companies, and makes that information available to the multifamily housing industry through tenant screening CRAs.
  - The company will provide one free report every 12 months upon request.
- First Advantage Corporation Resident History Report www.fadv.com
  - Provides background-screening services.
  - The company will provide one free report every 12 months upon request.
  - Leasing Desk (RealPage) www.realpage.com
  - Provides data for tenant screening.

- Screening Reports, Inc. www.screeningreports.com
  - Provides background-screening reports nationally to the multifamily housing industry. Includes previous rental verification, employment verification, consumer credit reports, landlord, tenant and eviction actions, criminal and sex offender reports, and foreign asset compliance.
  - Tenant Data Services www.tenantdata.com
  - Provides rental performance history such as data on damages, unauthorized pets, lease violations, and missed payments.

TransUnion Rental Screening Solutions. Inc. www.mysmartmove.com

- Provides tenant screening and verification data for independent landlords and residential real estate management companies. Also provides pro-active pre-screening service for prospective renters.

Employment

Note that this group of consumer reporting agencies specialize in screening in support of employment decisions. While there may be some duplication in the screens performed for landlord/tenant services, the focus here is entirely on potential employment issues.

Note that many employment-screening companies do not maintain files on individuals unless and until the employee or potential employee authorizes the potential or actual employer to obtain an employment background screening report.

All of the listed companies describe their services as "background screening services," so there is no additional commentary, other than those offering a free annual report to the consumer.

- Accurate Background www.accuratebackground.com
- American DataBank www.americandatabank.com
- EmployeeScreenIQ www.employeescreen.com
  - The company will provide one free report every 12 months upon request.
- First Advantage Corporation www.fadv.com
  - The company will provide one free report every 12 months upon request.
- General Information Services, Inc. (GIS) www.geninfo.com

- Hirease www.hirease.com
    - Hirease has been acquired by Accurate Background.
    - The company will provide one free report every 12 months upon request.
- HireRight Solutions, Inc. www.hireright.com
    - The company will provide one free report every 12 months upon request.
- Info Cubic www.infocubic.com
- IntelliCorp www.intellicorp.net
    - Provides employment and criminal histories.
    - IntelliCorp is a subsidiary of Verisk Analytics.
- Pre-employ.com www.pre-employ.com
- Professional Screening & Information, Inc. www.psibackgroundcheck.com
- Sterling BackCheck www.sterlingbackcheck.com
    - Legally known as Sterling Infosystems, Inc.
- The company will provide one free report every 12 months upon request.
- Trak 1 Technology www.trak-1.com
- Verifications, Inc. www.verificationsinc.com
    - Verifications has been combined with First Advantage Corporation.
    - The company will provide one free report every 12 months upon request.
- The Work Number www.theworknumber.com
    - The company is operated by Equifax Workforce Solutions, also known as TALX Corporation; TALX is a wholly owned subsidiary of Equifax.

National Association of Professional Background Screeners (NAPBS)

In addition to the listed information on the individual background screening companies, there is valuable material posted on the web site of the National Association of Professional Background Screeners (NAPBS) at www.napbs.com. The purposes and services of NAPBS are described as covering consumer reporting agencies, businesses, and individual consumers in their interface with the background screening process. While a full search of background screening providers is available only to members, there is a facility for individuals to request a search and receive the results.

Low Income and Subprime Lending

- Clarity Services www.clarityservices.com
  - Provides information on payday loans, installment loans, auto loans, check cashing services, rent-to-own transactions, telecommunication account openings, and financial services with an emphasis on low income and subprime market segments.
  - The company will provide one free report every 12 months upon request.
- DataX, Ltd. www.dataxltd.com
  - Provides payment history of subprime consumers.
  - The company will provide one free report every 12 months upon request.
- FactorTrust, Inc. www.factortrust.com
  - Provides loan payment and bankruptcy data on low income and subprime focused consumers to providers of payday, short term and installment loans, credit and prepaid cards, auto loans, retailers, wireless services, and collection agencies.
  - The company will provide one free report every 12 months upon request.
- PRBC/MicroBilt www.microbilt.com
  - Provides credit information, bill payment information, employment information, bank account data, property records, court judgments, address and phone information.
  - The company will provide one free report every 12 months upon request.
- Teletrack www.teletrack.com
  - Collects consumer information about, and provides data to, payday lenders, rent-to-own businesses, furniture stores that offer financing, auto finance companies, high risk consumer finance businesses, subprime home lending businesses, subprime credit card issuers, banks, credit unions, cable/telecom companies, and debt buyers/collectors.
  - Teletrack is affiliated with CoreLogic.
  - The company will provide one free report every 12 months upon request.

- *Consumer Data Industry Association (CDIA)* http://www.cdiaonline.org/about

In addition to the many listed individual providers of consumer credit and specialty reports, CDIA gives a focal point for this type of activity in general, not only for the businesses that use the report products, but also for all parties involved. CDIA is an international trade association with more than 140 corporate members. CDIA describes its purposes and services as educating consumers, media, legislators, and regulators about the benefits of the responsible use of consumer data. CDIA members provide businesses with the information and analytical tools necessary to manage risk and help ensure fair and safe transactions for consumers and facilitate competition to create opportunities for customers and the economy. CDIA member products are used in more than nine billion transactions each year, expanding consumers' access to a market, which is innovative and focused on their needs.

MEDICAL

- MIB, Inc. www.mib.com
  - Collects information about medical conditions and hazardous avocations – with the consumer's authorization. Individuals will not have an MIB report unless they have applied for individually underwritten life or health insurance at a MIB member insurance company within the last seven years.
  - An MIB Consumer File includes:
    - Any medical and personal information that MIB maintains in its database about you, if any, in the form of translated MIB codes; and
    - The name(s) of the MIB member companies, if any, that:
    - Reported information to MIB, along with the dates such information was reported;
    - Received a copy of your MIB Consumer File during the three (3) year period preceding your request for disclosure and the dates the companies received your file; and,
    - Made an inquiry to MIB about you within the past two (2) years, along with the dates of such inquiries.
  - The company will provide one free report every 12 months upon request.
  - MIB, Inc. is a subsidiary of MIB Group, Inc.

- Milliman InteliScript www.rxhistories.com
  - Collects information on prescription drug purchase histories. The individual may have a prescription report on file here if he/she has authorized the release of medical records to an insurance company and that company submitted a request to Milliman.

- Optum 360 (formerly OptumInsight MedPoint) www.optum360.com

    - Ingenix, Inc. delivers its reports to consumers through a separate online facility operated by Ingenix, Inc., a wholly owned subsidiary of United Health Group, Inc. Consumers should be aware that Ingenix, Inc. has contractual relationships to acquire data from Pharmacy Benefit Managers ("PBM"), which maintain records of individuals' prescription drug histories. Ingenix, through MedPoint, obtains an insurance applicant's five-year prescription drug history from the PBMs, creates a prescription medical profile on the applicant for the insurance company, and sells the MedPoint prescription profiling data product.
    - The medical profile generated by MedPoint includes, but is not limited to, prescription drugs, including dosage and number of refills filled by the insurance applicant for the previous five years. It also includes for each drug, the name and address of the dispensing pharmacy, as well as the name and address of the prescribing doctor, including specialty medical practice. The medical profile generated by MedPoint analyzes the individual's prescription drug history, and provides, based on that analysis, potential medical conditions that may be present and predictive scores for the individual.[33]

Utilities

- National Consumer Telecom & Utilities Exchange www.nctue.com

    - Collects information on new connect requests, account and payment histories, defaults, and fraudulent accounts associated with telecommunications, pay TV, and utilities (electric, gas, water) services.
    - The company will provide one free report every 12 months upon request.

PII collected through Relationships – Business and Consumer

Anyone or any organization with which the consumer has a payment relationship receives detailed information on payment method, account specifics, and other PII. Consider for a consumer with ordinary life style and activities some of the following places sensitive PII is held:

- Employer
  - Holds file copies of employment background checks, credit checks, etc.
  - Social Security Numbers
  - Both W-2 (employees) and 1099 (independent contractors) are affected. ANYONE sending the consumer a W-2 or 1099 is in this group; includes payment for work as an employee and as an independent contractor

- Newspaper & Magazine Subscriptions
  - Hard copy with delivery
  - Online paid access

- Club Memberships and Volunteer Organizations
  - Social Clubs
  - Community Organizations
  - National and International Non-Governmental Organizations ("NGOs")

- Cell Phone Provider, Phone Company & Cable Provider
  - Communications providers are not required to telecommunication consumers when they have been subpoenaed in criminal or homeland security investigations

- Veterinary Services

- House Accounts

  - DIY Hardware & Lumber Stores and other retailers may offer credit (though proprietary credit cards are used by larger stores)

- Amazon / Netflix   other online vendors

  - Convenience of having a credit card on file may make this information vulnerable to hackers or other potential identity thieves.
  - "Remember me" option when signing in weakens authentication and security routine in any situation where account information is on file.
  - Potentially, a stolen computer could give the thief access to the vendor account and payment method all in one event.

- Insurance Company

    - Auto.
    - Home.
    - Liability (personal and business).
    - Specialty, such as flood or earthquake coverage.
    - Medical (see below) .

- Medical & Health

    - Medical services providers.
    - Insurers.
    - Third party administrators & claims processors.

- Municipal Utility (water, sewer)
- Condominium/Homeowners' Association/Property Manager
- AARP and other Senior-Related Organizations
- AAA & Service Club Memberships
- Loyalty programs, usually with retailers, travel and hospitality companies, and others who collect personal information about buying and travel habits, as well as payment patterns, may provide valuable data to potential identity thieves.

Note that many of these organizations may be on an auto-pay arrangement, in which regular credit card charges or bank draws are set up for the convenience of the consumer and the business. These arrangements, of course, give rise to another direct opportunity for identity thieves.

Business and Social Networking Web Sites

In today's fast-moving online society, it may be tempting to post as much detail as possible on personal developments, including professional and family activities. Reading the "terms of use", "privacy policy" and EULA – End user license agreements, found with the website used can provide a better understanding in which ways information is used. Inclusive or the website owner and those third parties that such information is shared with.

It is not unusual for third parties, to whom the consumer may be connected or not, to acquire and post data, images, and other forms of information to publicly accessible web sites, without the permission or even knowledge of the affected individual.

The CITRMS® XV professional should take into consideration the needs and vulnerabilities of the consumer in keeping these vulnerabilities in balance with the advantages of participating in such networking activities. The key is guiding consumers to make mindful decisions on what to share and what to keep private.

Further discussion of this "Specialized Area of Concern" appears in Section 5, and steps consumers can take are in Section 7.

FURTHER COMMENT:

It's worth noting that the foregoing lists where PII may be located consist of many parties and places, some obvious and some not-so-obvious. In any case, such a list can never be considered complete, but a work in progress. The point, of course, is that sensitive information vulnerable to the predations of identity thieves may be located almost anywhere. Section 7 offers guidance on how consumers can make thoughtful decisions in limiting the proliferation of this information.

4 How Identity Thieves Operate

SECTION OVERVIEW

As suggested in the General Course Overview, identity theft is carried out on a battlefield where the two sides are in constant competition to overcome the latest weapons developed by the combatant. Identity thieves fall into several operational categories, starting with those who commit one-time crimes of opportunity. They generally access vulnerable information from individual consumers by various means. Organized crime purveyors of large-scale data utilize premeditated breaches. There are also terrorists bent on disrupting economic and societal activities, and even State-sponsored cyber-warfare.

It is appropriate for this purpose to review and analyze the modalities used by identity thieves according to where the sensitive information is kept, how they gain access to it, and what they do with it. For convenience, identity theft based on information taken from the consumer may be viewed as "retail" and identity theft based on information taken from holders of information of many consumers as "wholesale."

Typically, if the identity thief gets unauthorized access to information directly from the consumer, the identity thief uses it very quickly and directly. An example would be copying credit card information during the course of a legitimate transaction, such as payment for a restaurant meal. For a period of time, the credit card is out of the cardholder's sight, and the thief can simply copy the name, card number, expiration date, and 3-digit security code, usually located on the back of the card. Using this information, the identity thief can make purchases online or in other "card not present" transactions.

On the other hand, identity theft schemes against the individual consumer using remote or more complex means to collect a wider variety of PII. The identity thief then uses the illicit information to perpetrate theft of products or services, or by selling it to a third party who may use it for any number of purposes. These unauthorized uses are reflected in the major types of identity theft listed in Section 2 on Magnitude and Trends in Identity Theft.

In contrast, wholesale events of identity theft against holders of PII of many consumers tend to be deliberate, well planned and executed, and even designed to make it difficult for law enforcement to identify and locate the perpetrator. While wholesale identity theft may include crimes of opportunity, like finding a lost laptop computer and accessing the sensitive information it may contain, they are in a distinct minority. The preponderance of such incursions against holders of large volumes of consumer PII tend to be data breaches carried out by either physical or remote means.

The following discussion covers how identity thieves get access to sensitive PII, how they use it for financial gain or other purposes, and lays the foundation for what consumers and other holders of their PII can do to manage this risk.

"RETAIL" IDENTITY THEFT AGAINST CONSUMERS

Incidents in which the identity thief gets the consumer's PII directly from the victim are further categorized as low-tech or high-tech. The low-tech methods are well established, and tend to be repetitive in situations where the identity thief simply has access to and illicitly takes and uses the victim's information. There are few innovations in low-tech events – it has all been done before, and it happens repeatedly because it works.

Low-tech incidents tend to be situations in which the perpetrator physically steals or gets access to the PII and uses it right away. They may be crimes of opportunity, like finding a lost wallet or copying the information from a credit or debit card.

CASE IN POINT:

While dining at a restaurant, the consumer receives the bill and gives the server a credit card for payment. The server goes to another area in the restaurant and copies the name, credit card number, expiration date, and 3-digit security code from the back of the card into a notebook (on onto a napkin). After work, the server goes home and places an online order (or makes a catalog order by phone), pretending to be the victim, and using the victim's credit card information. In Section 5, there is detailed discussion about how credit card technology is developing to address this kind of fraud, but it is very challenging in "card not present" sales.

High-tech incidents tend to be planned in advance and carried out against more than one consumer, using the same method over and over, like getting a person's information from social networking web site and using it to perpetrate a fraud by pretending to be that person in a scam. Such activity tends to be part of a scheme pattern, which may be launched against one person at a time or spread to many potential victims at once. High-tech methods are constantly being developed and refined, reflecting developments and weaknesses in the technology they utilize. Such a scheme may be conducted from anywhere, even an internet café in a distant country, as long as the payment method is viable.

CASE IN POINT:

The "grandparent scam" falls into this category. Family and travel or vacation information about the grandchild is posted online to let friends know of the plans. The identity thief waits for the dates of travel, and contacts the grandparent via e-mail or call from an unknown phone number, claiming to be law enforcement from the country where the grandchild is vacationing. Usually there is a demand for money for bail or other payment made by Western Union or other domestic or international payment mechanism to an account of the perpetrator. Here there are two victims: the grandchild whose information has been stolen and the grandparent who makes the payoff. This scam may be run against multiple pairs of victims simultaneously, and repeated over and over. Picture the identity thief, sitting in an internet café sending thousands of e-mails a day; it only takes a few hits to make the day's "work" worthwhile.

Following is an illustrative list of "low tech" methods used by identity thieves. Note they may not appear to be very sophisticated or elegant, just practical ways in which they take advantage of unsuspecting consumers.

Shoulder surfing. The thief observes transactions at ATMs and writes down (or records with a cell phone camera) the PIN used to complete the deposit or withdrawal. This information may then be aggregated with other PII to access accounts illegally.

Changing The Victim's Mailing Address: Thieves divert billing statements to another location by completing a change of address form. They then request a replacement card, and use that to make bogus purchases.

Physical Stealing: Thieves take wallets and purses, or anything from the mail, such as bank and credit card statements, pre-approved credit offers, new checks, tax information, personnel records, and Social Security numbers. Laptop, tablet computers, and smartphones are also targets, as they usually carry a great deal of sensitive information.

Dumpster Diving: Thieves will go through trash containers looking for accounts information, credit card statements, and other PII. Once the trash barrel is put out in the street for pickup, it is considered abandoned, and becomes easy prey for identity thieves.

Skimming: This illicit gathering of credit card information can be done manually or by using a skimmer, a device that reads and stores the information from the card's magnetic strip. The skimmer may be handheld, attached to an ATM or even a pay-at-the-pump gas station facility, and large numbers of credit cards may be harvested this way. Currently, the magnetic strips on credit cards are migrating to a more secure technology, utilizing a computer chip embedded in the card to augment, and ultimately replace, the magnetic strip. The chip may be used in conjunction with a PIN, for additional security. However, it is predictable that identity thieves and hackers who assist them will be working on a way to crack this security device, too. Section 5 includes a more detailed discussion of developing credit card technology. Organized crime may be a factor in this scheme.

CASE IN POINT:

Authorities say they've caught the leader of a prolific credit card skimming operation at the Seattle-Tacoma airport, but not before he targeted thousands of people at parking lots near the airport. According to court documents, employees at two parking facilities were paid by a guy they knew as 'Big Homie' to skim more than 17,000 credit card numbers from people who parked in their lots between November of 2013 and April of 2014. [34]

Less subtle means: Identity thieves with criminal ties or backgrounds may also blackmail or bribe employees and others who have access to such sensitive information. Criminal organizations don't limit their use of PII to unauthorized purchases; they may also sell bulk information through syndicates for use in broader systematic abuses.

CASE IN POINT:

A fast-growing criminal enterprise referred to as "cracking" or "popping" credit cards, has been reported in the media and the subject of a warning from the banking industry and the Federal Bureau of investigation. The targeted individuals appear to be mainly young adults and military personnel with credit cards, who may actually be cooperating in the scheme, making the card physically available to the crooks.

According to reports, criminals are using Instagram, Twitter, and Facebook to solicit young adults for a so-called fast-cash scheme. The consumer hands over his or her debit card information and PIN number. The idea is that they will get something, maybe a cut of the money.

Once legitimate bank account information is in hand, the thief deposits counterfeit checks that were created by the con artist. These deposits may be made via smartphones or other mobile devices, using the card account information.

In the next phase, an associate with the account information, card, and PIN, withdraws the money from an ATM or possibly a point-of-sale terminal at a local retail store.
In some cases, the alleged "victim" later calls the bank to report a stolen debit card or compromised credentials. The consumer might never mention that he or she handed over the bank information from the start.

In-depth coverage from USAA (formerly United Services Automobile Association) indicates that the practice occurs when fraudsters pose as USAA officials on social media channels and offer money or deals in exchange for members' account information. Fraudulent funds are deposited into members' USAA accounts, and the posers take what they want as payment before the check bounces and the fraud is detected.

On Instagram, for example, the fraudsters hunt for users who create or like posts containing hashtags such as #ArmyStrong and #USAA, then make direct contact with those users. Results from USAA investigations show that nearly 87% of members lured by this scam are younger than 31 and 47% are active military personnel — 59% of which are Army.

Because members participate in the scam — regardless of whether they're aware it's a scam — they can be held responsible for the fraudulent funds. This could risk the financial well-being of the account holder and any co-signers.

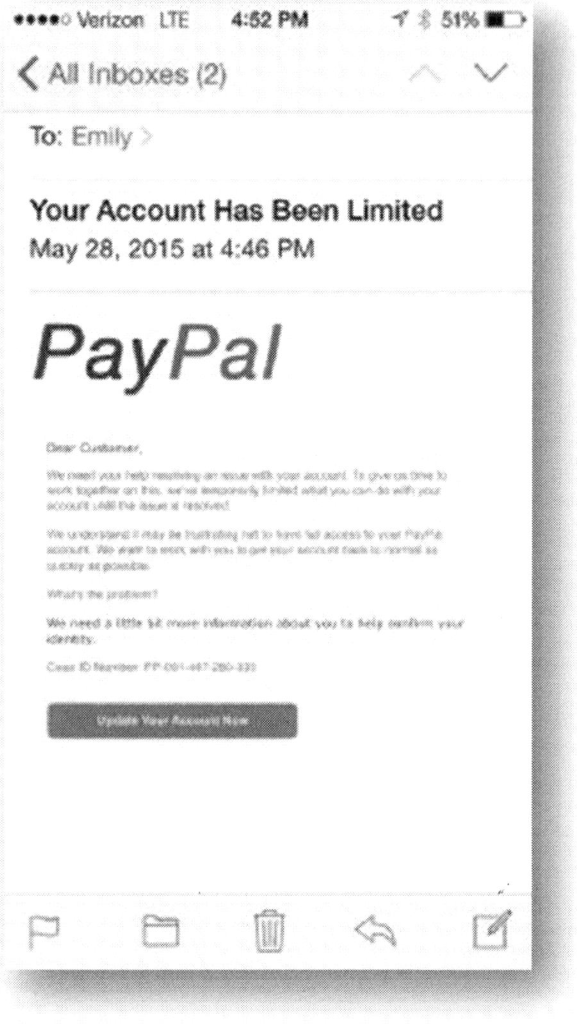

"It could affect their credit rating, their ability to get a car loan and mortgage," says True Brown, USAA's director of financial investigations. "It's a possibility that their wages will be garnished, and they could be at risk of losing their USAA membership. Even their military status could be affected if they are active duty or reserve. It depends on how culpable they are found to be in the activity." [35]

Hybrid Low/High Tech: Internet access, using search engines and other web site inspection, is used to collect many elements of PII; these are the building blocks of identity theft schemes when they are aggregated together to form a full picture of the victim's identity.

Following is an illustrative list of "high tech" methods and facilities used by identity thieves, generally avoiding face-to-face communications and using electronic means to collect and abuse sensitive consumer information. These methods are dynamic and change regularly with technological developments, both on the protection and criminal sides. Details of several technological aspects of identity theft vulnerability are in the Section 5 discussion of Specialized Areas of Concern.

Phishing: Thieves pretend to be financial institutions or companies that provide services or products to consumers and send phony e-mails, with hidden "execute" files or targeted pop-up messages to get the potential victim to 'click" on Reply or on a link that allows them to get access to personal information. Many of the e-mail utilities detect the underlying pattern and send such messages to the Spam folder – but they still carry the means of causing damage if the recipient does open the message anyway. There are several variants, which have been given derivative names, such as Spear Phishing, Vishing, and even SMiShing.

Spear-phishing: Similar to the email phishing scam, spear-fishing attacks businesses and other organizations, through emails to large groups of people with something in common. They may be employees, customers, students at an academic institution, members of a community group, or have something else in common that would be found in a single data base, which the attacker may already have hacked. The e-mails appear to be sent from organizations or individuals the potential victims would normally get e-mails from, even showing the organization's logo, making them even more deceptive. The email might require every recipient to reply with his user name and password for verification purposes. Alternatively, clicking on a link that appears to be from the real organization's web site – but takes them to the thief's bogus web site, where they are asked to log on with their user names and passwords or fill in additional sensitive information. Potentially, this gives the attacker access to both the employee's PII and the company's sensitive information.

CASE IN POINT:

Beware of tricky phishing scams like this recent one. These fraudsters would collect all kinds of information if the recipient clicked this link. Legitimate companies will NEVER solicit information from customers like the following:

It should be noted that commonly available computer programs make it very easy for identity thieves to create official-looking documents using scanned copies or facsimiles of authentic documents and manipulating them with such programs as Photoshop. Be aware that even high-quality color-printed graphics may have been created for use in identity theft schemes.

Vishing: A contraction of "voice fishing," this identity theft method utilizes the telephone to initiate contact with the consumer. The call may be live or recorded ("robocall"), and may even ask the consumer to call back. The caller pretends to be calling on behalf of a company with which the consumer already has a relationship, or selling a "one-time opportunity" for a special deal, and usually starts with a demonstration the caller already knows a variety of PII about the consumer. This "authentication" is usually based on information gleaned from other public sources or even from a data breach at a legitimate company. The object is to get the consumer to share additional PII, with which the thief then uses for illicit purposes.

Variants of vishing include institutionalized credit card scams. They have been around a long time, and show no sign of going away. It's not enough depend on "Do Not Call" list enforcement by the FTC, since the companies involved simply go out of business and set up in a new location with new phone numbers. Regulators have described their efforts as a "whack-a-mole" game. From the persistence of this type of scam, it must work or the perpetrators wouldn't keep doing it.

CASE IN POINT:

"Rachel from Card Services"

This scheme may sound familiar, since it has been so prevalent. It's not just an irritation, but a potentially costly scam. It starts out with a robo-call, and the greeting: "This is Rachel from Card Services." Then the voice claims to be calling from the card issuer of the consumer, with an offer of a reduction in the rate the consumer is paying on credit card accounts. Finally, at this stage, the consumer is invited to "Press 1" to be connected with an agent who can set up the rate reduction.

In fact, the call is not coming from the bank of other issuer of the consumer's credit card. It is from a boiler room operation seeking only to scam the consumer out of money. The "agent" claims to be associated with the real card issuer, and may even have the complete 16-digit card number and expiration date. That is why it seems so convincing, because this information has been illicitly obtained (either skimmed or purchased from identity thieves), and entices the consumer to share more information – usually by responding to the agent's questions to "confirm" information they do not have, such as the PIN associated with the card or the consumer's Social Security Number.

Finally, to complete the scam, the consumer is transferred to another person, the "supervisor," who advises that this rate-reduction service costs a substantial amount, but due to the consumer's good credit, has been reduced. The charge may be in excess of $1,000, and if the consumer balks, the scammers may charge the card anyway.

The only sure way to avoid this scam is to hang up as soon as "Rachel" starts to speak. With most cell phone providers, the calling number can be added to the "reject" list; however, the scammers call from many different numbers from many area codes. Even though it may be illegal for the scammers to continue to call, this identity theft scheme is not going away. [36]

SMiShing: A contraction of "SMS fishing," this method uses texting ("Short Message Service" or "SMS") to contact the consumer through the smartphone. The text appears to come from a bank or other financial service with which the consumer has a relationship, and usually includes an "urgent" request for immediate response, based on a fictional transaction that must be verified. Once engaging the consumer in communication, the thief asks for additional confirming information from the consumer – only in order to use it to gain unauthorized access to the victim's own financial accounts, or to prepare the consumer to authorize an upcoming bogus transaction, and reject an inquiry from the real bank.

CASE IN POINT:

While most Americans are worried about credit card and bank fraud, they should treat safety "alerts" with a degree of skepticism as well.

Many consumers have received a seemingly legitimate credit-card or debit-card alert that is actually part of a scam. In a recent poll, about 70 percent of respondents said they received a fraudulent fraud alert from a card company. [37]

Search Engine Phishing. Similar to phishing, the identity thief creates a website that advertises ridiculously low prices or terms for well-known products and services. The website is properly registered and shows up when the consumer searches for the product or service through popular search engines, but the offers are not real. They are only to get the consumer to go to the web site and enter purchasing and payment information, which the thief then uses to perpetrate his crime.

Pretexting or "social engineering": Thieves use false pretenses by phone or other forms of communication to obtain the consumer's personal information directly or from financial institutions, telephone, cable, and other service companies, and other businesses of which the consumer is a customer. They initiate the call either to "update your information" or issue a warning about an account problem, claiming to be from the business of which the consumer is a customer, and start by asking to confirm basic information they have already collected from another source. Once getting the consumer to believe they are legitimate, they ask for more and more sensitive information, until they get enough to perpetrate fraudulent schemes.

Remote thievery: Thieves can read contactless or smartcard credit cards remotely with a compact radio frequency device. More detail on Radio Frequency Identification Devices (RFIDs) is in Section 5.
Computer identity theft. With the use of computer viruses, hacking, and other malware attacks, thieves can get personal information from anyone's computer. It is common for new computers to come pre-loaded with anti-virus software, but only for a limited period of time. Then the provider asks the consumer to renew the program. The cost of renewal, to keep the protection in place, often seems more costly than a breach might be – however, it is not advisable to let it expire. Software upgrades and fixes may also give rise to computer-based attacks.

CASES IN POINT:

Reports of a fake tech-support operation have recently been made public. The caller, pretending to be from a software company, tells the consumer there is a virus on the computer and the consumer needs to pay $200 to fix it remotely. In most cases, there is little detail given, other than the scare tactic of telling the consumer if it's not fixed, the computer will crash. [38]

The "Windows Tech Support" scam has already affected thousands of unsuspecting consumers. Scammers pretend to be Microsoft employees to gain access to victim's computers to install malware and tracking devices.

The caller tries to get remote access to a victim's computer. They then either implant a virus to steal personal information or ask for money to remove a non-existent virus. [39]

Employment scams: These scams advertise a non-existent position in a real or fictional company and request detailed personal information and employment history from applicants. The depth and breadth of such information makes it easy for the identity thief to open new loan accounts, pretend to be the victim to get a real job, or otherwise abuse the victim's creditworthiness and good reputation.

Social networking: Thieves often visit several social networking sites to collect elements of personal information about the potential victim. The basic information, as well as personal matters often the subject of passwords or challenge questions, can be aggregated from various sources and use to commit fraud of all types.

Pharming: In this scheme, the identity thieves set up web sites with names and extensions very similar to legitimate companies. The spelling may be off by one letter, or a transposition, or a different extension. Sometimes, the thief sends an e-mail to targeted consumers, perhaps from a list of respondents to a survey, and masks the bogus web site with authentic-looking graphics and text. The object is to get the unwary consumer to sign on, using the correct user name and password. This information is captured by the thief and used to log on to the real account and drain the victim's funds or place orders for merchandise paid for by the victim.

A note about Aggregation, using the Building Blocks of Identity Theft

Many of the methods identity thieves use may be coordinated for the collection of numerous elements of PII, no single one of which would be sufficient to carry out the particular identity theft scheme. They may gain access to the victim's name and address in one place, the Social Security number in another, a user name and password from a secure web site, and other items of sensitive information in still others. By aggregating the individual pieces of the puzzle, the identity thief is able to construct a bogus profile, based on all true facts about the victim, but subject to manipulation and perpetration of an identity theft event in any of the multitude of reported categories.

Once access to a source is set up, even information that has been "anonymized" and integrated into a data base can still be used in the aggregation process. Any information that can be used to distinguish one person from another can then be used for de-anonymizing anonymous data can be considered PII. [40]

WHOLESALE IDENTITY THEFT AGAINST HOLDERS OF CONSUMER PII

In contrast to consumer identity theft, attacks against businesses and other organizations that have relationships with consumers are carried out with a wider range of goals both against the organization itself and against the consumers who information they hold. Consequently, these attacks tend to occur on a broader scale, potentially affecting much larger numbers of people.

The selection of the target company, the data to be accessed, and the methods used reflect the purpose of the attack. For instance, if the goal is to obtain PII on customers or members of the organization, data such as payment arrangements may be sought, in order to make unauthorized credit card charges or drain customer bank accounts. If the intent is to clone company's own identity in order to collect payment for sales made in the victim company's name, with no intention to deliver, human resource and accounting files may be hacked. In the case of an intrusion into a government data base, the purpose may be political or terrorism.

The target may also be selected based on knowledge of systemic weaknesses, such as software that has not been regularly updated for security flaws, weak security practices among employees and others with access to the company's computers, or vulnerability to bribes or extortion.

As in the analysis of magnitude and trends, the means and methods of perpetrating identity theft against organizations that hold consumer PII continue to develop, with identity thieves seeking to defeat security measures and security professionals trying to plug the gaps that seem to appear on a regular basis.

Using a systematic approach, identity thieves may start a well-planned attack on an organization by researching public information, much of which is available online through a variety of official and non-confidential web sites. With the publicly available information as a foundation, the next steps would include deliberate deceptions leading to accessing the internal files and other data bases held by the target organization. Ultimately, the abuse or unauthorized use of the information is the means by which the identity thieves achieve their goals of stealing money, disrupting the target organization, or committing other criminal acts.

Access to public information on corporate entities.

It should be noted that much of the information on which attacks on companies and other organizations in this arena is available in public records and open web sites. This kind of data is where many identity thieves start and use it as a foundation to facilitate their direct attacks on the target organization.

Government and Official Sources

EDGAR® Online

As discussed in Section 3, most corporations, limited liability companies, and other entities used for business or financial or even charitable purposes are chartered by the authority of one of the States. Usually, it is the State Secretary of State or Corporations Commission or other similar agency that issues such charters. Almost all corporate filings are accessible online, either free of charge or for a nominal fee. In the case of free access, the person seeking corporate information need not disclose his or her identity or purpose. For paid access, a credit card is normally required (although an identity thief seeking this kind of corporate information might well employ-unauthorized use of a credit card or an entirely bogus one). For public companies (traded on a stock exchange, with many shareholders), a wealth of information is filed with the federal Securities and Exchange Commission, and is available online through the "EDGAR" (Electronic Data Gathering, Analysis, and Retrieval) system. Even non-profit organizations are subject to public disclosure of much sensitive information.

CASES IN POINT AND INFORMATION SOURCES:

In order to determine the contact information, mailing address, names of officers and directors, and much more detailed corporate information, the identity thief only needs to go to the main web site of the State in which the company was set up, search for the company by name, and read this information immediately. The URL for each state is usually in the format www.[Name of State OR 2-letter state designation].gov
For publicly traded companies, the proxy statements and periodic reports are available through www.sec.gov and contain very detailed information, which can be used to further an identity theft scheme. Similar information is available on non-profit organizations, including copies of their annual "Form 990" reports to the IRS, disclosing personal and financial information, online at the web site of the GuideStar service at www.guidestar.org

Employment Web Sites

Public information on both job applicants and potential employers is easily accessed from classified advertisements and online employment job posting sites. Such information may be used as elements of PII to create new identities and sell them to people who are unable to gain employment in their own names. Examples of buyers would include convicted felons, people not in the country legally, and deadbeat parents whose earnings may be subject to attachment by child support agencies, even from other States. It may take a months or years for the victim to learn of another person using his Social Security Number and other identifying information. This type of identity theft is pervasive in the victim's records and is very difficult to resolve and restore the integrity of the victim's identity.
Information in employment listings are also subject to abuse against the posting company. Identity thieves posing as job applicants may telephone to learn detailed information about the company from unsuspecting individuals fielding the calls. As in the case of consumers, the company information may be misused to add to other available facts, laying the foundation for wider identity theft schemes.

CASE IN POINT:

Monster.com describes itself: "We connect people and job opportunities" on its web site. For over 20 years, Monster.com has provided services for both prospective employers and job applicants, and is a public company with a broad base of shareholders. As a publicly-held company, Monster files reports with the U. S. Securities and Exchange Commission; these reports are available to the public.
Although Monster.com requires setting up an account and signing in to access the posted jobs and resumes, and the Terms of Use are very specific and restrictive as to how this facility may be used. However, identity thieves rarely honor such limitations.

Note that there are also search engines provided by various media organizations with the capability of conducting a wide-area search for resumes, including Monster, many social networks, referral facilities, and even access to information about internal candidates from posting companies.

Community Bulletin Boards

Whether for economic, financial, commercial, religious, charitable, or other purposes, the current array of places to connect locally via the internet is vast. Personal preferences, names and addresses and other contact information, patterns of presence and absence, and a host of other sensitive information may appear in these web sites. Generally, they include the ability for someone to post and respond through e-mails that allow anonymity, until both parties are comfortable communicating directly – by telephone or their normal e-mail addresses.

CASE IN POINT:

Craigslist is intended to be a community bulletin board for local people and companies to post items for sale or wanted to buy, services, personal ads, and a wide variety of other legitimate purposes. Identity thieves who have stolen identifying information on a legitimate business pretend to offer products and services, with a link to a web site that appears to be the real company, but in fact is a pharmed web site. They take payment information from the unsuspecting consumer, and then use that to make unauthorized purchases for themselves; or, they may sell the consumer's payment information in the underground market, so others may use it as well.

Methods Identity Thieves Use to Steal Non-Public Confidential Information

Once armed with information from public or other available sources, identity thieves are prepared to fill in the gaps in the information they need to perpetrate their schemes. The most intrusive way to steal information for this purpose is also the one that potentially affects the largest number of individuals: the data breach. Other means are used to steal and abuse internal information about the company, such as vendor accounts and payment systems, in order to drain funds directly from the target company.

Data Breaches

Detailed discussion of the magnitude and trends in data breaches appears in Section 2. Here, the focus is on what identity thieves do with the breached data to further their objectives. Of course, at this point, the specific perpetrators are not known, and their purposes can only be the subject of conjecture. Nonetheless, based on what is known about the individual data breaches, the following discussion can be considered more than speculation.

For this purpose, the selected data breaches involve the records of millions of individuals, and have received a great deal of media attention and commentary. The four breaches for further study are Target, Anthem, the Internal Revenue Service (IRS), and the U.S. Office of Personnel Management (OPM).

Target Corporation

- Date made public: December 13, 2013
- Nature: Malware infected point-of-sale (POS) systems
- Number of Records: 70 million
- Information: Credit card purchase details
- Likely use:
    - Primary: Sale of credit card details, then unauthorized purchases
    - Secondary: Calls and e-mails used by scammers claiming to work for Target in resolving the breach, but actually obtaining additional sensitive information from affected individuals

Anthem Blue Cross (formerly WellPoint)

- Date made public: February 15, 2015 (discovered as early as April 2014)
- Nature: "Very sophisticated external cyber-attack"
- Number of Records: 80 million
- Information: Personal Data, including Social Security Numbers
- Likely use: Analysis points to Chinese hacker group "Deep Panda," but purpose of the attack is not known; speculation there may be resale of information to set up fraudulent medical insurance accounts.

Internal Revenue Service (IRS)

- Date made public: May 2015
- Nature: Hack by Russians into "Get Transcript" files of taxpayer forms, using PII already stolen by the hackers, including Social Security Numbers, names, addresses, and birthdays, as well as correct answers to challenge questions.
- Number of Records: 104,000 tax records exposed
- Information: Historical and pending tax filings
- Likely use:
    - Primary: Some 15,000 were reportedly used to file for and receive fraudulent tax refunds (from the accounts of real taxpayers)

  - Secondary: Use information to open bank accounts, credit lines, and file for tax refunds in the future

United States Office of Personnel Management (OPM)

- Date made public: June 2015
- Nature: Cyber-attack on official data base
- Number of Records: Originally 4 million, now 18-32 million
- Information: Detailed data from personnel files, including name, date and place of birth, Social Security Number; later found to include security-clearance-relate background information
- Likely use: Based on speculation that Chinese hackers were responsible, and they may have been acting with official support, the purpose may be disruption of personnel functions and penetration of intelligence assets.

As of the time of this writing, a continuing stream of reports have disclosed that there were two separate incidents, and admitted number of individual files exceeds 25 million; information includes intimate details. As characterized by FBI Director James B. Comey, Jr., in a Congressional hearing:

- "If you have my SF-86, you know every place I've lived since I was 18, contact people at those addresses, neighbors at those addresses, all of my family, every place I've traveled outside the United States since I was 18. If I had substantial contact with any non-United States person, it's on there, along with the contact information of that person. Just imagine you were a foreign intelligence service and you had that data, how it might be useful to you. So it's a big deal." [41 42]

As indicated in Section 2, although large-scale breaches such as these have garnered the broadest news coverage, and potentially affected the largest number of people, the vast majority of data breaches involve smaller organizations and smaller groups of individuals. Regardless of the size of the organization, or number of consumers potentially affected, the data breach threat is a daily challenge to the ongoing viability of the business or entity holding such vulnerable information.

Another aspect of the adverse results of a data breach is the identity theft threat to the consumers whose PII is compromised. All of the methods used by identity thieves directly against consumers can be leveraged with information accessed through data breaches. This information may be used for a variety of illicit purposes, such as making unauthorized purchases, opening new accounts, and even setting up bogus credit files.

Dun & Bradstreet and Other Credit Listings

As with consumer credit files, business credit reports provide information for would-be lenders, investors, and business associates to make decisions to enter into transactions. In reviewing the financial capability and credit-worthiness of business enterprises, they rely heavily on disclosures directly from the company as well as reports of the experiences of others who have done business with them.

Identity thieves use collected and stolen information to set up fake accounts in the name of the victim, companies to access funds through loans, investments, and other business relationships. In effect, they create an entity with a parallel existence however, based on the vital information of the victim. Note that the personal credit reports of the officers, directors, and other owners of record maybe used to bolster this scheme.

Note also that federal consumer protection laws and regulations do not necessarily protect businesses. For instance, there is no free annual credit report, no statutory right to include a written statement to be included with every credit report issued, and no procedure for businesses to enforce correction of erroneous information. Some States are starting to adopt similar protections for businesses, but so far, only those falling under the definition of "consumers" enjoy these rights.

Business listings and publications

Once the identity thieves have set up a "business" based on the good will and name of the victim company, they take measures to advertise for the sale of products and services, as well as to collect more PII from unsuspecting consumers who make contact thinking they are calling or e-mailing the victim company.

In extreme cases, the identity thieves may pay for listings in directories of telephone and internet services, set up web sites with similar names to the victims, and virtually "clone" the victim to siphon off legitimate business. Of course, they take payments, but never deliver the goods.

In the Anthem (formerly Wellpoint) case, the thieves set up a web site using the numeral "1" instead of the letter "l" in the URL address. With masked hyper-links sent in e-mails to the affected individuals, in order to entice them to click on the highlighted link and land on the bogus web page, where they were asked to enter their user name and password information. That created a secondary and very valuable body of information, and facilitated further exploitation of Anthem, the original victim of the data breach.

Unauthorized access to employee information

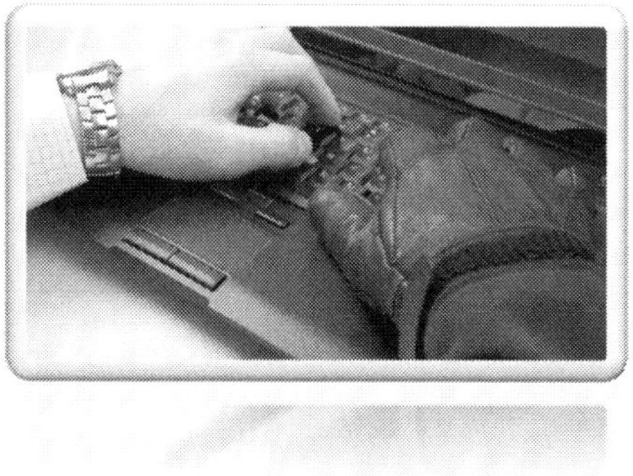

Businesses and other organizations with employees are often the targets of identity thieves who take advantage of information gained on the financial, health, and other benefits of employees. This may occur at several levels, such as access to the specific information, ability to modify it from a remote location, and even deny the target access to its own records.

At the lower-tech end, the identity thieves may just use the information to withdraw money from employee accounts, or re-direct payments to a fake account set up in the employee's name, or abuse health care benefits by making them available to others not affiliated with the target company.

Another means of extracting value from hacking would be to interfere with the company's access to its own database, and demand a ransom to restore that capability.

A high-tech intrusion with sufficient remote control over the digital books and records of the organization would make it possible for identity thieves to add phantom employees, perhaps with stolen Social Security Numbers, to the payroll, and siphon off money into controlled accounts.

Bogus invoices from "real" suppliers

Identity thieves may also use stolen information from the accounts of the target company or any of its suppliers to obtain money. In this case, the stolen information may come from the target company, an employee, the supplier, or a combination.

Typically, such documents as invoices, purchase order forms, and payment sources are generated and sent to the accounts payable office of the target. They appear to be from the supplier of products or services with which the target already has a relationship, even showing the correct Employer Identification Number (EIN), but the address and payment information has been changed to direct payment to the identity thieves.

In a variation of this method, the fraudulent entity may be set up as a customer of the target company. Payment is made to the target with a fake check, apparently drawn on the account of the real customer, and in an amount in excess of the amount indicated on the fraudulent invoice. The target company is asked to send back its own check for the excess amount. By the time the fake check bounces at the bank on which it is drawn, the identity thieves have cashed the excess payment from the target company and disappeared.

Intellectual Property (IP), including trademarks, copyrights, software and services

Any situation in which royalty payments are at stake may lend itself to identity theft. Whether in hard copy, digital format, or limited term license, the opportunity to claim to be the owner of the intellectual property, in order to seek new or recurring or upgrade payments from users, may be abused.

The means of perpetrating this scheme is usually by e-mail, in which the identity thief purports to be the owner of the intellectual property, and advises the consumer that a payment is due. The e-mail may carry the logo and other graphics from the real company or organization, and may have a link to a cloned web site, where payment can be made.

Any payment-related activity may be the subject of this scheme, including renewal of subscriptions, donations to charitable organizations, and even utilities and communications services.

Review and Perspective

The field of identity theft is rich with opportunity. Whether the target is the individual consumer, a group of individuals, a business, public or private organization, or even a government entity, the means of access to information and the ways to transform the information into money literally know no bounds.

As long as there are incentives for identity thieves to collect and manipulate sensitive information, and a market into which they can sell, or simply drain vulnerable accounts, this crime is not going away.

As long as there are practicing identity thieves, both official and private efforts will be made to deny them access to sensitive information and the means to use it for illicit purposes.

Only by understanding the methods used by identity thieves, and learning how to combat them, is it possible to contain its cost to our community, economy, and society.

5 Specialized Areas of Concern

SECTION OVERVIEW

In drafting this ISG, it became apparent certain current phenomena are worthy of specific mention and deeper study. Among them are both technological and demographic developments that suggest growing vulnerabilities to identity theft.

Included in these principal technological trends, as mentioned in the General Course Overview, are Credit Cards, Cloud Computing, Radio Frequency Identification Devices, Smartphones, Cyber Warfare and Social Networking, Search Engines, and so-called "Big Data." Special mention is also made of encryption, as it is a technological capability that crosses over concerns between privacy and security.

On the demographic and activity side, further detail is offered on vulnerabilities faced by medical patients, active and veteran military personnel, children, and seniors. Also of interest are the developments in consumer financial protection, including federal and State initiatives. In addition, recent reports indicate the Internal Revenue Service is a lucrative target, with billions of dollars' worth of tax refunds being claimed by identity thieves.

These examples are representative of the vast and swift developments in the field of identity theft prone technologies. There is no doubt that this trend will continue, and new technologies will offer future challenges to professionals working to help clients and consumers manage the risk of identity theft.

No discussion of developments in identity theft would be complete without mention of privacy issues. The history of identity theft is firmly rooted in privacy issues. It's notable that concerns about maintaining confidentiality and privacy of personal information were expressed by individuals and consumer groups well before the identity theft phenomenon became apparent.

Historically, privacy concerns came from the desire to exercise the *right to privacy*, with the intention of preventing known and unknown parties' access to personal information. Initially, privacy constituted an end in itself. For many years, there has been a major movement devoted to maintaining the individual's own control over access to and use of personal information.

As the misuse of such information has grown over the intervening years, the need to control and protect such personal information has expanded from the desire to exercise the right to privacy, to the need to control and protect against identity thieves who use such information for a broad variety of illicit uses. Uses that wreak financial and personal damage to the person whose identifying information has been stolen. Today, the right to privacy and management of the risk of identity theft are inextricably intertwined.

In response to the destructive nature of identity theft, a major industry has grown up, to educate professionals and consumers, undertake preventive measures, and perform restoration and remediation services for victims of identity theft. Holders of protected personally identifiable information (PII) are also subject to a growing body of laws and regulations, as well as receiving support services from trained and equipped professionals who assist in compliance and preventive actions to forestall data breaches. Breaches that can result in financial liability and loss of customers who are wary of the reputation of companies that fail to protect their PII.

In the past, the pattern of government action was based on a centralized organizational focus, mainly placing responsibility in the hands of the Department of Health and Human Services (HHS) for Protected Health Information (PHI) and the Federal Trade Commission (FTC) for most other types of PII. The Consumer

Financial Protection Bureau (CFPB) has begun to take an interest in regulating aspects of identity theft vulnerabilities that may fall outside the purview of HHS and FTC.

Nearly every State has adopted some form of notification requirement for events that could result in identity theft since the original CITRMS® course was published, and there is currently consideration of a federal law to impose uniformity on this requirement. Adoption of a federal standard, if it does occur, will likely take into consideration the experience of the States in their administration of notification requirements that tend to respond to particular needs of their own populations and business climates.

It is important to note the proliferation of the means of identity theft, and the resulting response involving several more specialized State and federal actions to assure compliance with law and regulation. It is a certainty this trend will continue to keep pace with both technological and demographic developments.

Subsection I – Technological Areas

These six technological areas of concern have been selected for discussion, though it should be noted immediately they are illustrative, not exhaustive.

- Credit cards
- Cloud Computing
- Radio Frequency Identification Devices (RFIDs)
- Smartphones
- Computer "warfare"
- Social Networking, Search Engines, and "Big Data"

Credit cards

Nearly everyone either has one or more credit cards or is at least aware of credit cards as a payment device. Credit card use is pervasive in our economy, and the nearly universal ease of completing transactions has naturally attracted the interest of identity thieves. The use of credit cards in fraudulent transactions was discussed in Section 4. Here the focus is on developing credit card technology, and the implications for Identity Theft Risk Management.

In the early days of credit cards as the "plastic" payment device, the typical card had a number, expiration date, and a place for the signature of the card holder. It was not unusual for the merchant accepting the card to ask for a picture identification, unless the cardholder was already familiar. Transactions with both the card and cardholder present were fairly simple and not very vulnerable to unauthorized use.

As telephone sales from catalogs and advertising grew, "card not present" transactions became more prevalent. Another security element was added: the "3-digit security code," usually found on the back of the card, printed in the signature block. That device at least helped assure the card was in the hands of the person placing the order, although it was (and still is) subject to being copied by hand and used for unauthorized purchases of goods and services.

Additional data capabilities were added to credit cards, mainly on the magnetic strip on the back, carrying much more identifying information about the card, cardholder, account, and issuer. On one hand, this provided the ability to hold and communicate more complete information; on the other hand, it made more detailed information to criminals who were able to apply technical means, such as skimmers to read and abuse this authentication protocol.

Meanwhile, more attention was paid to the issue of liability for unauthorized transactions. Initially, if credit card information was stolen, and a purchase made, the issuer (usually a bank) could hold the cardholder responsible for the entire amount, and usually did so unless the consumer could prove the charge was unauthorized and without any benefit.

In 1974, the Fair Credit Billing Act (FCBA) was adopted as an amendment to the Consumer Credit Protection Act (popularly known as "Truth in Lending" or "TILA"). Among other provisions, FCBA limited cardholder liability for unauthorized transactions to $50, with several specific conditions. In practice, as long as there is no indication the cardholder was complicit in a scheme to defraud the card issuer, since that time most card issuers do not hold the cardholder liable for the $50 amount. The issuers' decision to write off such charges appears to be based on two considerations: the cost of enforcing the $50 collection (and probably losing the customer), and competitive reasons (maintaining good will and customer service).

The internet and its vast capabilities to support commerce added huge volume to the challenge of authenticating every transaction. "Card not present" transactions have grown exponentially, and the authentication challenges have similarly grown, along with the temptation for identity thieves to profit from this huge opportunity. Accordingly, to combat the abuse of credit cards, currently a transformation is taking place in the industry. It is important to note that the immediate solution is applicable to "card present" transactions, and not yet to online or telephone orders, though additional protections are being developed for this purpose.

The most fundamental and visible technological change is the advent of the metal "chip" embedded in most newly issued credit cards. This device is sometimes referred to as the EMV chip. The acronym EMV stands for Europay MasterCard Visa, as these are the three organizations involved in its development and application. The chip stores information on all transactions, assigning each one a unique number, but does not transmit the card number to the point-of-sale terminal. This prevents identity thieves from gaining access to sufficient information to allow them to make unauthorized charges.

At this point, the magnetic strip on the back is still used in parallel with the chip. As discussed in Section 4, the magnetic strip is vulnerable to access using a skimmer, so it is contemplated the migration process will soon entail the removal of the magnetic strip. With the chip as the sole readable device, it will be much more difficult for identity thieves to create fake credit cards by transferring magnetic information from a real card to a bogus one. Note also the chip may be used in conjunction with a PIN, for additional security, in point-of-sale transactions where the card is present; this authentication routine is similar to the PIN used in debit card transactions.

As of October 2015, new rules for credit cards are in effect to change how liability for unauthorized transactions is assessed between card issuers and merchants. Compliance with EMV capability won't be mandatory as such, but the liability for fraud will fall on the merchant rather than the card issuer if the merchant's system has not been enabled to read the chip.

It is reported that both the Visa and MasterCard organizations are developing technologies to authenticate online and other card not present transactions. It is not expected that these programs will be in general use for some time, but it is worth noting there is current information available online from the card service companies. MasterCard: Chip Authenticated Program (CAP) [43]

- Which system promotes conducting regular back-ups and conforms most closely to the user's needs for remote access?

CASE IN POINT

News media have reported that Amazon.com's cloud computing service has become a popular conduit for fraudsters looking to create automated [sometimes called "bot"] traffic and disseminate it over the Web, according to new research from advertising fraud detection firm Fraudlogix.
The hackers use computer generated bots to mimic the actions of real consumers and trick marketers into paying for ads displayed on Web pages. A number of techniques are used to generate artificial traffic, such as infecting consumers' personal computers with software that loads Web pages without their knowledge, or installing similar software on cloud computing services such as Amazon's to simulate real users.

It is only a short step from this type of hack to placing purchase orders on Amazon using the victim consumer's payment information already on file. [45]

Privacy

Privacy issues arise in cloud applications in several ways. They range from data use by the operator of the cloud server to access by law enforcement and homeland security officials. In general, cloud services require acceptance of "Terms of Use" and "Privacy Policy" conditions prior to the consumer using the service. It is fair to say that these conditions are principally for the benefit of the cloud service operator, not the consumer. Careful reading usually discloses there are many opportunities for the cloud operator to use or sell information about the consumer – although that does not typically extend to the content of the user's data.

The Terms of Use and Privacy Policies of cloud services generally run parallel to those for search engines and e-mail services. The provider may have access to the meta-data (such data as time and date, terms in a search or message, URLs accessed from a search or included in a message, e-mail recipients or addresses to which URL addresses are sent, and patterns of use), and in some cases the content of the material itself.

"Agreed-upon" uses may include sending unsolicited messages based on preferences or products or services mentioned in communications or stored content, sale of such information to third parties for marketing purposes, and other unspecified legitimate purposes.

"Cloud searches," for employment, for example, now include access to content that may not appear in internet searches, and subject to additional permissions for posting to cloud services. So far, it appears a positive action must be taken by the consumer to include personal information in such search results, but the combination of Terms of Use and Privacy Policies should be carefully considered prior to making such information accessible to any and all users of such search services.

In addition to private uses of cloud information, there is a growing trend toward law enforcement and homeland security expressed needs to get access to content stored in the cloud. Current coverage indicates there are several areas of conflicting forces at work.

- Access: Under the Foreign Intelligence Surveillance Act (FISA), and amendments, access to electronic communications has been utilized by national security and law enforcement agencies, both with and without warrants. In some circumstances, no notice is given to the person whose communications or remotely stored data is accessed. Privacy professionals and other interested parties have frequently disputed the constitutionality of such searches, and have advocated legislative restrictions on such activities. At this time, the discussion continues.

- Encryption: In many cases, government agencies get access to information held in consumer accounts on cloud servers, but such information is encrypted and not open to plain reading. In response, initiatives have been undertaken to require the operators of the cloud storage servers to restrict encryption of consumer data or otherwise hinder the use of encryption by consumers. This, too, is an ongoing tug-of-war.

- It appears that there is no unanimity among government agencies in determining what the standard should be for protection of consumer information and getting access for homeland security and law enforcement functions. A particularly trenchant discussion of this situation was posted by the International Association of Privacy Professionals (IAPP), and is included in the following excerpts:

> "On one side, we saw the Office of Personnel Management (OPM) announce that 21.5 million individuals had some of the most sensitive personal information imaginable hacked. This data, which includes in some cases financial and mental history, Social Security numbers and the like, is tremendously valuable for adversaries—particularly if they're a nation-state looking to exploit government workers, informants, military personnel, and so on.
>
> We also learned in the last few weeks that much of the OPM's stored data was not encrypted and access to much of it did not require even something as simple as two-factor authentication (something most users of Gmail should already employ)…."

In contrast, the post goes on to ask: "So why, then, are [FBI] Director Comey and others in law enforcement asking for backdoors into encrypted communication technology?"
The seemingly insoluble task is then described: "find a solution to the encryption problem by creating encryption that can both prevent access by adversaries but also allow access by law enforcement authorities." [46]

For the CITRMS® XV professional, the takeaway is to consider all these considerations in helping the consumer to make an informed choice. In this case, it is clear that one size does NOT fit all.

Radio Frequency Identification Devices (RFIDs)

"RFIDs" as they are usually referred to, are tiny chips embedded in various types of hardware to facilitate communication with other devices, such as security access cards, tracking capabilities, and embedded devices that capture information to support financial transactions. The proliferation of RFIDs is due to their relatively inexpensive cost, multiplicity of uses in exchanging and holding sensitive information, and (to date) low level of concern for the vulnerability they can create.

The internet is replete with "How To" articles on RFID hacking. While this is not the place to provide direct links, the techniques are relatively simple, and demonstrate the vulnerability of all sorts of RFID access devices. The information they carry is easily captured, transmitted, corrupted, and replaced for nefarious purposes.

RFIDs are embedded in many credit cards to effect non-contact transactions, and are vulnerable to being read by unauthorized scanners. Examples include credit cards that enable transactions without touching a swipe or skimming device, store security tags, and even medical devices for tracking purposes.

For credit cards, the convenience of not swiping the card to complete a purchase may be outweighed by the potential vulnerability to unauthorized RFID readers that can capture the card number, expiration date, and 3-digit security code – without even touching the card. It's the equivalent of picking the consumer's pocket without making physical contact. Fortunately, there are countermeasures available, principally in the form of RFID-proof credit card sleeves.

ICFE is pleased to advise such protective sleeves are available for purchase through ICFE's web site. See www.icfe.org for more information. [47]

Smartphones

Smartphones contain a broad variety of personal data, such as extensive PII, e-mail files, photos, financial information and payment applications, phone logs, and even passwords or automatic sign-on routines. The hardware alone may sell for hundreds of dollars, so there is also a secondary market for stolen phones and parts.

These mobile phones use a variety of advanced operating systems that enable the devices to provide a growing array of computer functions. No longer are they devices for voice communications through cell or Wi-Fi connections; now full e-mail and internet connectivity is the norm. However, unlike conventional computers, smart phones tend to be more vulnerable to malware attacks than full-function computers with anti-virus software installed. Due to rapidly developing technology, the following discussion should be considered as illustrative, and subject to continuing review.

Whether the operating system is Android, Microsoft, or Apple, there has been a huge increase in the number and types of applications. Many of these are prone to exploitation by identity thieves. The most commonly targeted functions are in financial transactions, either based on online access to deposit and credit card accounts or mobile "wallet" uses that replace physical credit or debit cards.

Removable media constitutes a very accessible means for identity thieves if they get possession of a smartphone. Most smartphones have two removable storage devices, for very different purposes: a SIM card and an SD card.

The subscriber identity module or subscriber identification module (SIM) is an integrated circuit that is intended to store the international mobile subscriber identity (IMSI) and the related key used to identify and authenticate subscribers on mobile telephony devices (such as mobile phones and tablet computers). The smartphone will not operate or connect to the cell phone system or via wi-fi to the internet without a SIM card. While the SIM card is intended to be secure, it is still subject to hacking by professional criminals.

The secure digital (SD) card is a memory card used extensively in portable devices, such as mobile phones, cameras, and tablet or notebook computers. In contrast to the SIM card, even if the phone cannot be operated, the SD card can be removed and the data accessed using any other compatible device like a computer card reader or another similar phone. Typically, the SD card holds potentially damaging information, such as downloaded attachments to e-mails, personal photographs, and intentionally or unintentionally stored information related to applications. Precautions for SD cards may include read-only restrictions, Digital Rights Management (DRM) copy protection, and password protection; but these are subject to hackers as well. [48]

Note the default settings on many smartphones include automatic backup routines, in which data stored on the device is sent to cloud servers operated by the phone service company or the provider of the operating system. Typically, the transmission and storage are not encrypted, and subject to unauthorized access, as discussed above. Moreover, even if the consumer changes the initial settings, it may not cause this backup routine to stop.

CASE IN POINT:

Users of the Google Photos application who later decide to cease using it, must make sure they also turn photo backup off in the Android phone's Google Settings menu, or else the program will continue uploading new pictures to the service. This is reported to occur even when the consumer deletes the pictures and uninstalls the application itself from the phone, because Google Photos uses Android's centralized Google settings menu to launch the backup routine. As a result, if the consumer has selected automatic uploads of new pictures to the cloud when installing the Google Photos application, that setting will continue to upload photos even after the application is removed from the phone. [49]

Another function on smartphones is the dual Global Positioning System (GPS) and mapping program for using real-time directions to find and go to a specific location. In most cases, this function requires a permission to track the user's movements, either as an option on the phone or as part of the Terms and Conditions of Use requirements to utilize the application.

While the GPS and mapping capabilities are very convenient, they may also give rise to identity thieves gaining access to information such as when the user is absent from home or office. Such information may be obtained through introduction of malware on the phone device, or by hacking into the supporting system for the program. In either case, identity thieves and their associates may take advantage of the consumer's absence to perpetrate crimes involving physical access to the target premises.

Other developing technologies, such as near field communication (NFC) encompass a set of standards for smartphones and similar devices to establish radio communication with each other by touching them together or bringing them into close proximity, usually no more than a few centimeters.

It has also been reported that "lab-on-a-chip" capabilities are being developed to support medical analysis using the smartphone device to monitor, capture, and transmit information such as the qualities of blood, urine, sweat, saliva, or breath. These fiber optic sensors may even be used to detect and monitor conditions such as pregnancy, sexually transmitted diseases (STDs), or diabetes. [50]

The question remains as to how to maintain the security and privacy of this information, which is stored on the smartphone itself, and also on any number of remote servers.

Smartphone software can also be the source of vulnerability. In particular, programs and applications that are integral to the operating system may cause weaknesses that are the most difficult to protect.

CASE IN POINT

A report on some 600,000 Samsung Galaxy devices discloses such a weakness, though the solution to the apparent problem is not clear.

According to researchers at NowSecure, a cybersecurity firm, the vulnerability comes from the keyboard software, and potentially allows hackers to spy on anyone using a Samsung Galaxy phone. This software can't be deleted, as it is integral to the operating system.

Information on the phone can be exposed by using public or insecure Wi-Fi. But some researchers think users are exposed even on cell phone networks.

NowSecure CEO Andrew Hoog said that, on a well-established system that ranks cybersecurity problems from 1 to 10, this vulnerability stood at 8.3. [51]

Some vulnerable situations may occur due to temporary use of convenient facilities, especially when it's not apparent that information is being shared with a device that later comes under the control of a third party. There are potentially many of these situations, such as connection to a passworded wi-fi router, where the phone may connect again without knowledge of the user. Bluetooth connections may present a point of vulnerability for two reasons: once recognized, another Bluetooth device may be inadvertently connected again without further action by the user; information accessed by another Bluetooth device may be stored there and accessed by a subsequent user.

CASE IN POINT

Many rental cars have the latest infotainment systems, which let the renter connect, or "pair," his smartphone via Bluetooth with the car. This supports making calls over the car's audio system, dialing from the center console, getting directions or streaming music, for example.

Once connected to the car with Bluetooth, the car's onboard computer stores the user's phone number to make it easier to connect later. It also stores the call logs, including any contacts dialed. All that information is saved inside the system and may be accessed by the car rental staff or the next renter. [52]

Computer "warfare" or CyberWar

"War is the continuation of politics by other means."

– *Carl von Clausewitz*

For our purposes, these terms are intended to be viewed broadly, rather than just the immediate definition of institutionalized hacking for political and warfare objectives. In point of fact, consumers may well be vulnerable to collateral damage from the compromise of confidential data held by a broad variety of official and unofficial data bases.

Intrusive and disruptive attacks on personal and organizational computer systems and data banks have become an everyday occurrence, and threaten the integrity of all kinds of identity theft related information. The example that has most actively captured the attention of news media is the breach at the federal Office of Personnel Management (OPM), covered in more detail in Section 2. Official commentary is posted at the following web site:

OPM -- http://www.opm.gov/news/latest-news/announcements/frequently-asked-questions/

At the time of this writing, it seems undisputed that the hackers were from China, and most likely sponsored by the government of that country. While the final chapter of this story may not be written for some time, perhaps the best contemporary analysis of the situation and commentary on balancing priorities is from former NSA and CIA chief Michael Hayden is the following (excerpts):

"The current story is this was done by the Ministry of State Security—very roughly the [Chinese] equivalent of the CIA. Those records are a legitimate foreign intelligence target. If I, as director of the CIA or NSA, would have had the opportunity to grab the equivalent in the Chinese system, I would not have thought twice, I would not have asked permission. So this is not shame on China. This is shame on us for not protecting that kind of information. This is a tremendously big deal. …
"American military doctrine says this cyber thing is a domain. There are no rivers or hills up here. It's all flat. All advantage goes to the attacker. That's one reality. …

"… [A]ll of us just fell in love with the ease, convenience, and scale, so we decided to take things we used to keep if not in a safe, at least in our desk drawer, and put it up here, where it's by definition more vulnerable. …

"What's the impact for you? The impact is the next sound you hear will not be a digital bugle signaling the arrival of the digital cavalry to come save the day. The government ain't coming. You're not quite on your own, but you are more on your own up here [in cyberspace] than you in your lifetime have ever experienced being on your own down here. …

"We [the United States intelligence organizations] only steal stuff to keep you free and to keep you safe. We do not steal stuff to make you rich. I know of four other countries that can say those last two sentences. Everyone else steals for commercial advantage. …" [53]

Social Networking, Search Engines, and Big Data

These related areas represent companies and organizations that collect and use sensitive information provided by the consumer, usually under "Terms of Use" and "Privacy Rules." These conditions are subject to change solely at the initiative of the social network, search engine, or collector of the information. The following discussion concentrates on what they do with this information, how it may put the consumer at risk, and the trends in use and control of the potentially vulnerable data.

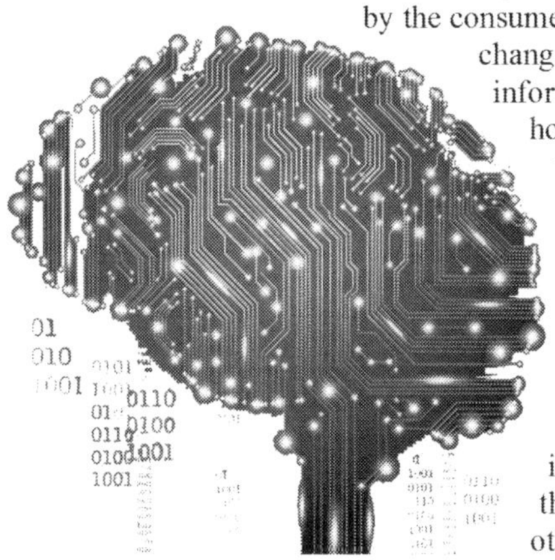

The choice of organizations for this discussion is based on their preeminence and representative practices in their respective fields: for social and business networking Facebook and LinkedIn; and for search engines and related services Google. "Big Data" is in a class by itself and is discussed with a broader perspective.
While it is difficult, if not impossible, for consumers to prevent breaches, or unauthorized intrusions, into data bases that contain their personally identifiable information, risk management against this phenomenon can be improved by limiting the submission and distribution of such information by diligent opting-out and otherwise restricting its use.

Information consumers don't post on networking and other public web sites, for example, can't be hacked and used by identity thieves. That may seem elementary, but it also emphasizes the role of the CITRMS® XV in constantly bringing to the attention of consumers the vulnerabliities that are, in fact, within their control.

CASE IN POINT

Most e-mail programs include a directory of the user's contacts. This list may include notes and other user comments, as well as basic information such as the contact's name, address, e-mail address and phone numbers. It's a given that the online support of this type of program generally allows the service provider access to the content of this directory. These directories are often shared or "sync'd" between the user's computer and smartphone.

Beyond that, however, many business and social networking web sites offer the convenience of adding all of the user's contacts from the e-mail program and smartphone. Utilizing this "convenience" can compromise a great deal of sensitive information. Moreover, it works both ways – what if someone who has you in his e-mail contact list (with notes about your business and personal info) uses this "convenient" facility?

Social and Business Networking

The "poster child" for social networking is, of course, Facebook, currently reporting nearly 1.5 billion monthly active users worldwide. The depth and breadth of user information is unprecedented. Facebook collects not only detailed personal information, but also likes and dislikes, friends and other connections, items of interest shared with others, and virtually any other actions or behaviors that help the organization determine the user's needs and preferences.

According to public reports and commentary, Facebook is always monitoring user behavior. That information is used to help determine the content that shows up in the user's News Feed. The company takes into account more subtle cues, such as turning on sound, making a video full screen, or enabling high definition. From these actions, Facebook will infer that the user found the video interesting, and populate your News Feed with similar content in the future. [54]

The potential for sharing this kind of information, intentionally or otherwise, can form a stepping-stone for identity thieves to learn how to approach consumers to inveigle them into falling victim to a variety of scams.

On the business networking side, the current leader in the field is LinkedIn, with a reported 364 million members. Extensive information on participants is listedfor anyone with a LinkedIn account to see. In most cases, this includes name, photo, location, education, employment history, skills, areas of expertise, and anything else of a professional nature. Once an individual is connected with another individual, each has access to information on all of the connections of the other. For free accounts, there may be limitations on access to those paid participants who wish to restrict access to their information. Paid accounts also offer anonymous browsing of other LinkedIn participants, and enhanced ability to communicate with them. LinkedIn does offer a facility for the user to share a complete list of contacts (e-mail or otherwise) for the purpose of sending each of them an invitation to connect. As mentioned above, this "convenience" should be used with care and forethought in order to avoid unexpected repercussions.

Trends indicate online networking is only going to grow in size and participation in the future. For the consumer concerned with Identity Theft Risk Management, it is important to understand the nature of information shared on these web sites, the uses to which it may put, and the vulnerability to access of sensitive information by potential identity thieves.

Search Engines

Companies operating internet search engines are a huge factor in the collection and use of consumer information. It is no coincidence that after searching for a particular product or service, consumers find pop-ups or other links to providers of the product or service in the search appearing on other pages from other web sites. One of the value propositions for the search engine companies is to sell information on searches to providers or to program in the pop-ups and links for a fee.

The Terms of Service and Privacy Policy documents posted online by leading search engine companies, such as Google, are extensive. They provide for display of advertising content along with the search results. While they may be subject to some user preferences, generally they allow use of information, such as metadata (terms used in the search) gleaned from user searched for commercial purposes. The privacy policy allows the company to send data on the user's search queries to websites or advertisers to help them determine the words that led to the search results. [55]

It should be noted there are also private browsing options available on some browser applications. If this option is activated, it may help maintain anonymity or even prevent capture of the history of searches and web sites visited by the user. However, private browsing facilities are only as effective as the application's terms of use and the terms of use of the browser or other program the consumer is using. For working purposes, it is fair to say that private browsing may or may not be completely private.

Big Data

Who or what is "Big Data" ?

"Big Data" is not so much a specific term of art or single concept as it is a general description of the huge array of places where exceedingly large quantities of information about individuals and organizations is collected, transmitted, stored, analyzed, and disseminated. Big Data encompasses every entity that engages in these activities, whether for public or commercial use, and whether the information and the analytical products are used internally or sold or rented to other parties.

The Wikipedia definition appears to have been submitted by a Big Data advocate:

"Big data is a broad term for data sets so large or complex that traditional data processing applications are inadequate. Challenges include analysis, capture, data curation, search, sharing, storage, transfer, visualization, and information privacy. The term often refers simply to the use of predictive analytics or other certain advanced methods to extract value from data, and seldom to a particular size of data set. Accuracy in big data may lead to more confident decision making. And better decisions can mean greater operational efficiency, cost reductions and reduced risk." [56]

Big Data participants include private companies, government entities, and hybrids. They carry or have access to vast amounts of PII, and are used for analytical, tracking or marketing or other decision-making purposes. And they are subject to hackers' attempts to break into their data bases. For the consumer/user, there are weaknesses built into the systems. In addition to the Terms of Service and Privacy Policies, to which the user must agree in order to access their web sites and/or services, there are usually limitation of liability provisions, and all subject to change without notice to or agreement by the consumer.

It is not the purpose of this course to study in depth the nature and ramifications of Big Data, but the phenomenon is important to recognize as a factor in the extent to which PII is subjected to such collection and analysis activities beyond the control of the consumer.

It is worth noting that organizations concerned with consumer interests, and privacy in particular, have initiated a variety of legal and regulatory actions to modify the balance in favor of the users. As in the case of the EMV chip security device for credit cards, the European Union has led the trend toward giving consumers more control over the collection and sale of personal information.

CASE IN POINT

The "Right to be Forgotten" by Search Engines

On May 13, 2014, the Court of Justice of the European Union (CJEU) granted people the right to request removal of search results for queries including their names if the results are inadequate or irrelevant, on the grounds that the information might be outdated or otherwise unfairly cast them in a negative light. Google has continued to protest that decision, but in the meantime, hundreds of thousands of EU citizens have made requests for the purge of such search results. Two observations are of particular interest: the vast majority of the requests have come from individuals with no public notoriety, such as politicians and celebrities; Google has, for one reason or another, rejected the majority of such requests. [57]

Government Surveillance

Whether for law enforcement or national security reasons, there appears to be a growing trend toward collection of PII and behavioral traits by government agencies, principally at the federal level. Such surveillance over online communications and other activity is most often carried out without notice to the target. As a result, statistics on this phenomenon are not available to the individual consumer, but do appear in the aggregate twice a year.

Due to actions by public interest groups, certain internet companies now publish so-called "Transparency Reports," which disclose how often a company receives requests for customer data, such as a subpoena or search warrant, from government bodies, as well as how often that company complies with such requests.

Recently, Amazon for the first time released a report on the number of government data requests it receives, offering the public more information on how often it hands over its customers' data to judges and law enforcement agencies. Amazon runs the largest public cloud-infrastructure business in the world, so it is an appropriate measure of these government requests.

Among the details mentioned in the report, Amazon said it received 813 subpoenas from January 1 to May 31 of 2015, and fully responded to 542 of them. It received 25 search warrants and fully responded to 13 of them. In comparison, Facebook disclosed in March that it received a total of 35,051 requests for user data from international governments during the second half of 2014.
Twitter released its own government transparency report, revealing that requests on Twitter user information was up 40 percent in the second half of 2014. A total of 2,871 individual requests were received during the period.

Reddit, another popular social networking site, reported receiving only 55 requests for user information for all of 2014. Details of the nature of the information sought are not revealed, so no reliable estimate or breakdown can be made on the underlying purpose or intent of these government requests. [58]

A Special Note on Encryption

Encryption of data, both local (on the user's computer or smartphone) and remote (on the internet or in the cloud), has developed into a two-edged sword. On one edge, the government agencies (mainly law enforcement and national security) want to be able to use encryption to protect the security and integrity of official data against breaches by criminals and foreign intelligence organizations. On the other edge, these same government agencies want to be able to defeat encryption protections utilized by nearly everyone else.

On the flip side, privacy and civil rights advocates want to be able to protect private information from government (or any third party) surveillance by using encryption techniques. They also tend to want to get public access to government practices, as discussed above.

Recent reports bring focus to this clash between privacy and security, and place the internet and software companies in the buffer position between consumers and the government. In the first instance, the government agencies want clear and immediate access to all data, either by denying the user the ability to encrypt information or by getting access to a master "key" to override the encryption program.

Some of the companies thrust into this situation, Apple for example, have responded by furnishing the consumer with an encryption key that can't be used by anyone else, not even Apple. Ceding control to the user removes the company from the buffer role. A similar facility has been developed by Google for application in devices with Android operating systems.

The continuing challenge will be to guarantee government access to a locked device without introducing security flaws others could also find.

So far, quoted technology experts do not accept that such a solution is within the realm of possibility. [59]

It should not go without comment that the standard sought by leading government agencies does not appear to be accepted for application to encryption of information stored in official data bases.

As reported in a national publication, a spokesperson for the federal Office of Personnel Management (OPM), which experienced a pair of major breaches, told *Fortune* the agency sometimes uses encryption to protect data, though he did not reveal when or how. "OPM does utilize encryption in some instances and is currently increasing the types of methods utilized to encrypt data," he wrote in an email. "These methods include not only data at rest, but data in transit, and data displayed through masking or redaction."
He added: "Though data encryption is a valuable protection method, today's adversaries are sophisticated enough that encryption alone does not guarantee protection." [60]

This set of developments is far from being resolved in any meaningful way. It is the intention of ICFE and the author to continue research and reporting on these and other relevant news items through the ICFE web site and e-News sent periodically.

SUBSECTION II - Demographic and Activity Areas

Special demographic or activity areas of concern include the following, though again they are illustrative, not exhaustive.

- Medical and Health Records
- Children
- Seniors
- Military personnel, active and veterans
- Consumer financial protection
- Tax return fraud

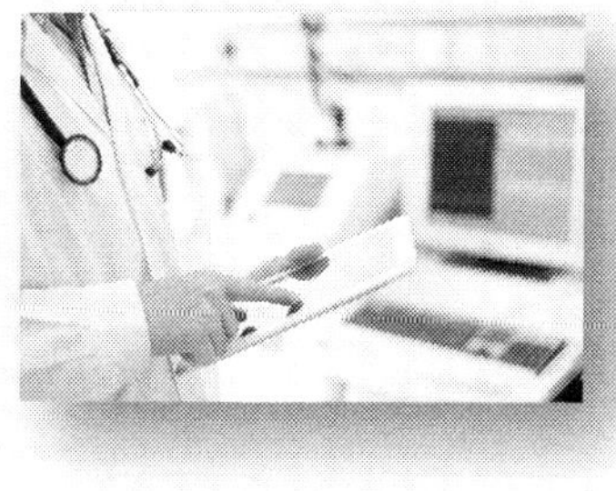

Medical and Health Records

Much has been written and discussed about Medical Identity Theft and in-depth analysis of this risk and regulations to meet the threat are included elsewhere in this independent study guide. With developing changes in health care and insurance law and practice, and the impact of these changes based on age, health, and economic status, it is appropriate to include medical patients as a demographic group with increasing vulnerability to identity theft.

Both the trend toward increased reports of incidents of medical identity theft and the value of individual medical files and data suggest a confluence resulting in a major shift of the activities of identity thieves into this potentially lucrative sector. Estimates of the "street value" of a complete medical profile, including name, date of birth, Social Security Number, insurance policy, diagnosis codes, billing details, and other particulars about the patient are some 10 times the value of corresponding credit card information. [61]

AN UNUSUAL DEVELOPMENT – Application of the Law of Unintended Consequences

Recently, the federal Consumer Financial Protection Bureau (CFPB) and the New York State Attorney General took action at behest of consumer groups to overcome a perceived credit-reporting problem involving delinquent medical debt.

Due to delays in payment of insurance claims and final resolution of the amounts actually due from the patient/consumer, it has been alleged the consumer is inappropriately penalized. As a result, based on the urging State and federal authorities, the principal credit reporting agencies (TransUnion, Experian, and Equifax) have acted in concert to postpone the reporting of delinquent medical debt for 180 days. The delay in order to allow time for insurance payments to catch up with the invoices submitted to the insured consumer by the medical service provider.

In practice, this will mean credit report monitoring, a principal means of early detection of identity theft, will no longer be able to notify consumers promptly in the event a fraudulent bill has been submitted for a medical service or insurance claim. In effect, the identity thief will be given a six-month head start on abusing medical information from a breach without being discovered.
None of these measures is or should be considered to exclude consumers from active participation in education and vigilance over both credit report and identity theft issues. There is no doubt that consumer engagement is key to responding to this set of growing challenges.

CITRMS® XV practitioners are encouraged to inquire about and discuss any medical records issues for consumers they counsel, and to raise awareness of this developing area of concern.

Children

Both statistics and anecdotal evidence indicate children are at risk of identity theft for numerous reasons. These center on the creation and use of PII of children combined with any financial activity by or on behalf of the child. Once a Social Security number is created for any legitimate purpose, such as setting up a savings account at a financial institution, the child becomes vulnerable to identity theft.

Credit reports, including Social Security numbers and other PII, are often maintained on children as well as adults; the difference is children don't usually apply for credit or have any reason to monitor such records. The result is that normally, children under the age of 18 don't have credit records at all.

However, that doesn't prevent identity thieves from creating a parallel identity and applying for credit in the name of the child. Identity thieves can use Social Security numbers, addresses, and supporting information to apply for credit and use it for weeks or months before being discovered. Indications identity thieves are involved include the receipt of pre-approved offers to apply for credit being mailed directly to the victim, or to attend financial seminars, or open other types of accounts.

Parents are well advised to check with the principal credit reporting agencies on whether they have credit files on their children. Unless it has been initiated by the parent for some reason, there should be no such files. However, if a credit file has been set up without parental action, it would suggest there has been unauthorized activity, and steps can be taken to close it out. Care should be taken to avoid setting up a credit file by making such an inquiry, and the purpose of the parental inquiry should be made clear.

Some situations involve innocent actions on the part of the victim. Children (especially teenagers) participate extensively in social networking online in order to keep up with their families and friends. The nature and extent of information they share may be accessed, aggregated, and ultimately used by identity thieves. The vulnerability arises from the likelihood children are not as discerning and protective about information they share as adults with more experience. Not only may peers use information on social networks for unauthorized purposes, but identity thieves are able to target children based on their posting of information about their activities, whereabouts, and other personal matters.

Full discussion of laws and regulations in place to protect children against identity theft and related crimes is included in Section 6.

Seniors

The changing lifestyles of older people reveal various issues that make them especially prone to identity theft. Both statistics and institutional trends point out several areas where criminals target seniors in identity theft schemes.

According to the FTC, seniors are particularly vulnerable to identity theft because they tend to have more assets and readily available cash than others. Identity thieves may also view seniors as attractive targets based on their belief they may be more trusting or easier to exploit, and may even suffer from dementia or Alzheimer's Disease. The "grandparent scheme," discussed in Section 4 spells out one example of this vulnerability in detail.

While medical identity theft and tax return fraud are discussed in detail elsewhere in this ISG-XV, it is also an area of concentration of such abuse against seniors.

They also may be impacted by tax and government benefits-related identity theft, especially as they may not be prepared to safeguard their PII in light of the movement of government benefits away from paper into internet-based or other automated facilities. They often do not learn of the identity theft for months, if at all, due to their unfamiliarity with online facilities.

Older consumers are also susceptible to identity theft in nursing home settings and assisted living situations, both by family members and professionals who hold powers of attorney and other means of implementing decisions that may not be in the best interests of the seniors.

CASE IN POINT:

Former Certified Nursing Assistant and Co-Conspirators Sentenced for Identity Theft Tax Scheme
On April 17, 2014, in Albany, Ga., Kimberly Banks, Donalene Mosley and Arneshia Austin were sentenced to serve 192 months, 37 months and 21 months in prison, respectively, for crimes relating to filing fraudulent income tax returns using stolen identities. After a weeklong jury trial, Banks was convicted on Jan. 14, 2014, of conspiring to file false federal income tax returns in the names of stolen identities, wire fraud, aggravated identity theft and theft of government money. Mosely and Austin each pleaded guilty to conspiracy. In addition to their terms of imprisonment, the court ordered Banks, Mosley and Austin to pay $275,134 in restitution and to serve three years supervised release. According to court documents and evidence introduced at trial, Banks, who is a former certified nursing assistant, obtained the names and Social Security numbers of nursing home patients from her employer and conspired with Mosely, Austin and others to use the stolen identifying information to filing fraudulent tax returns. The tax returns were filed from internet protocol addresses assigned to Banks, and the fraudulent tax refunds were deposited onto prepaid debit cards that were mailed to addresses belonging to Banks, Mosely, Austin and others. During the course of the conspiracy, Banks and her co-conspirators prepared 187 fraudulent tax returns that claimed over $600,000 in false refunds. [62]

Elder abuse is manifested in many forms and situations. Identity theft may be only one aspect of this shameful phenomenon, but an important one nonetheless. CITRMS® XV professionals are encouraged to explore with the consumers they counsel how seniors in particular can be adversely affected by these schemes, and how to help them maintain awareness and protection against such criminal activities.

Military personnel, active and veterans

Military service personnel and their families constitute a group for special concern because of the proliferation of data bases where their sensitive information may be stored, and consequently subject to breach of confidentiality. This concern has been increased with the overlap of security clearances for military and homeland security personnel, since detailed background information on all military personnel with security clearances is also maintained in civilian records data bases.

Due to the transient nature of military life, including frequent Permanent Change of Station (PCS) or Temporary Duty (TDY of up to 6 months), and the likelihood that the service member may have a separate address and contact information from his or her family, the many records and changes in records give rise to increased vulnerability to intrusion by identity thieves.

Additional concerns may arise during the process of separation/discharge from the military, as new needs for financial, insurance, and other benefit arrangements also occur during such periods. Increased attention should be paid to maintaining confidentiality with the proliferation of applications and updating financial and other personal files.

The Veterans Administration (VA) is a huge and complicated organization serving a broad variety of needs of some 22 million military veterans, including educational and health benefits, among others. Like the Social Security Administration and Internal Revenue Service, the VA will never contact the veteran by telephone to ask for personal information. Such communications are made by letter or through a secure messaging system operated by the VA.

Even having implemented various levels of precautions, the VA has reportedly been the target of several data breach incidents, some as far back as 2006, involving a stolen laptop computer with information on an alleged 26.5 million individuals (which may have included military family members and civilian VA employees). A settlement was reached in that case, and the VA has continued to institute protective measures in managing sensitive information.

However, it appears recent developments, including the breach of federal Office of Personnel Management (OPM) records of over 20 million current and past government employees, may also have an impact on active military and veterans. Public source reports indicate the compromised OPM files include information on background checks underlying the security clearances of many of these individuals and their families and friends. See Section 2 for more detailed information on this data breach.

In recent years, more attention has been given to keeping track of military benefits that may be subject to misuse or outright abuse. In addition to participating law enforcement organizations, in 2014, for the first time, the U.S. Departments of Defense, Education and Veterans Affairs began collecting educational institution and student lending complaints from military members and their dependents. It is likely the upward trend in medical identity theft will result in a similar initiative being undertaken for military health benefit complaints.

Consumer financial protection

Developments in consumer financial protection have occurred in both structural and conceptual ways. The structure of agency activities has been changes with the addition of the Consumer Financial Protection Bureau (CFPB) at the federal level and increased interest demonstrated by several State Attorneys General on identity theft issues. The conceptual evolution has concentrated on liability issues, especially regarding the nature of damages and responsibility in the aftermath of a data breach.

As discussed further in Section 6, the CFPB has undertaken initiatives in parallel to the existing reporting, investigation, and enforcement activities of the Federal Trade Commission. The Attorneys General of several States have joined the CFPB directly or in several companion legal actions. There are bureaucratic territorial issues at stake, as well as the potential of sharing in funds that may come from financial settlements with the companies being investigated. So far, consumers appear to have benefited from this increased level of activity by the various government entities. Identity theft services sold by financial institutions have been a focal point for CFPB.

CASES IN POINT:

Add-on products, such as identity theft protection services, offered by financial institutions, caught the attention of CFPB early in its regulatory endeavors. In 2012, CFPB published a compliance bulletin for credit card issuers on the marketing of add-on products. The bulletin pointed out several "deceptive practices" in this line of marketing, and promulgated standards under cited statutory authority.

Within months, CFPB had instituted three enforcement actions against major banking firms: Capital One ($210 million), Discover ($214 million), and American Express ($112.5 million). Major portions of these settlement figures were to be paid in restitution to the customers who had been adversely affected by the marketing practices. Since that time, CFPB has continued to levy fines and reimbursements for similar activities, with settled cases approximating 50 at this time.

One case of particular interest came to a head in 2013, where CFPB required JPM Chase to refund $309 million to more than 2.1 million credit card customers. The reason cited was "unfair billing practices for certain credit card "add-on products" by charging consumers for credit monitoring services they did not receive."

Since that time, Chase, as well as several other financial institutions, have ceased offering identity theft protection services as an add-on product. Looking at the marketplace overall, it is worth noting this kind of influence by the CFPB will likely have a substantial impact on the way identity theft monitoring and restoration services are sold and delivered. [63]

Tax return fraud

The number of reports of tax return fraud, generally involving bogus claims for refunds in the name of the identity theft victim, has exploded in recent years. There is anecdotal evidence that seniors may be more vulnerable to tax return fraud than other age groups, due to their reliance on third parties (usually not professionals) preparing their returns, but the practice apparently goes far beyond those who may require others to file their tax returns for them.

There are several ways this fraud can be perpetrated. It may be based on a direct personal relationship with the victim, as in the case of a criminal family member or care giver. In some cases, it appears to be the result of identity thieves obtaining enough information about the taxpayer to submit a tax return with real income information, but directing the refund check to be sent to an address controlled by the criminal.

In terms of magnitude, however, the concentration of reported tax return fraud appears to have been initiated through a hack into the computer facilities of the Internal Revenue Service itself. While several reports in news media indicate there may not be a direct relationship between the IRS hack and suspicious tax return filings, it is likely there may be a delay between the unauthorized access to the information and the filing of fraudulent refund applications.

In any case, the IRS, in cooperation with State authorities and private sector firms, has instituted a series of preventive measures to authenticate the identity of persons filing tax returns, especially where refunds are claimed. As indicated below, even the authentication process is subject to a somewhat complicated set of steps.

CASE IN POINT:

Hackers gained access to personal information of 104,000 taxpayers in the spring of 2015, downloading an online service the Internal Revenue Service uses to give Americans access to their past tax returns, the agency said Tuesday.

[IRS Commissioner] Koskinen said the incident was probably not related to a spike in suspicious tax filings this year, which raised red flags for the IRS state tax authorities, which saw fraud jump by as much as 3700 percent. [64]

Faced with a surge of identity theft tax-refund fraud, the IRS and private tax-preparation firms Thursday united in a new public-private effort to protect U.S. taxpayers.
The agreement comes weeks after an embarrassing breach in which cyber-thieves stole as much as $39 million by filing fraudulent tax refunds based on taxpayer information hacked from an IRS website.
Starting with the 2016 tax-filing season, the IRS, state tax agencies and private tax firms will join in taking new steps to authenticate taxpayers' returns at the time of filing. The participants will also identify and share information about suspected tax fraud schemes as they develop.
http://www.usatoday.com/story/money/2015/06/11/irs-identity-theft-protection/71058624/

The Internal Revenue Service may determine a tax return is suspicious, with the real taxpayer's name and Social Security Number, but with other indications of identity theft. In these cases, the IRS sends a letter to the person whose identity has been used to file the return. This letter is referred to as "Letter 5071C," and requests that the taxpayer verify the authenticity of the identity. Letter 5071C is mailed through the U.S. Postal Service to the address on the return.

As is the practice for other government agencies, the IRS does not make such requests by e-mail or telephone. The IRS will not call a taxpayer directly to ask for this information without sending a letter 5071C first. The letter will carry a unique identification number, enabling the taxpayer to confirm that any follow-up communications are actually from the IRS.

Taxpayers who have received the IRS Identity Verification Letter 5071C should respond promptly, if possible using the Identity Verification Service website, ID Verify. See https://idverify.irs.gov/IE/e-authenticate/welcome.do. For taxpayers without access to the internet, a toll-free number is included in the letter. However, due to the high-volume on the toll-free numbers, the IRS Verify ID website is the preferable option for taxpayers.

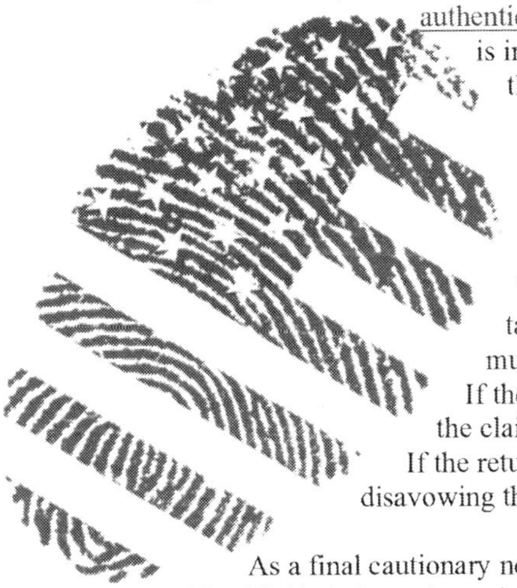

In responding to the verification inquiry, taxpayers should have available the subject year tax return and current year tax return, if it has been filed, including supporting documents, such as Forms W-2 and 1099 and any attached schedules. [65]

The website authentication starts with a series of questions that only the real taxpayer should be able to answer. Upon completing the verification, taxpayers must confirm whether or not they filed the subject return.

If the return is legitimate, it takes about six weeks for the IRS to process it and issue the claimed refund.

If the return is bogus, the IRS will take steps at that time to assist the taxpayer in disavowing the fake claim and re-filing a correct return.

As a final cautionary note, taxpayers should always be wary of tax scams, efforts to solicit personally identifiable information using IRS impersonations. The CITRMS® XV professional can be helpful in preventing and responding to this increasingly common trend in identity theft. [66]

6 Legal and Regulatory Responses to the Identity Theft Challenge

IMPORTANT NOTICE

The ICFE and the author intend for this discussion of Laws and Regulations to enable CITRMS® XV credential holders to discuss intelligently the legal framework in which identity theft is being addressed. Unless the CITRMS® XV holder is a qualified attorney, licensed to practice in the relevant jurisdiction, it is not recommended that any attempt be made to undertake rendering legal opinions on compliance issues. In contrast, the ICFE and the author believe that familiarity with these concepts and their application can make the CITRMS® XV a valuable part of a legal team, facilitating and increasing efficiency for the client to achieve compliance.

SECTION OVERVIEW

While the initial section on definitions and concepts included relevant specifics that are based on legal language, this section provides a broader and more in-depth presentation of the provisions of federal and selected State laws and regulations. It is worth noting the very nature of statute and regulation makes it difficult, if not impossible, to be pro-active rather than re-active – government actions can rarely be taken in advance of the new and creative actions of criminals. Nonetheless, through legal requirements for holders of vulnerable information to undertake protective and preventive measures, the growth of identity theft can be slowed, if not brought to a halt.

This section should be studied in coordination with the definitions set out in Section 1. Further specifics on the application of these laws are detailed in Section 8, on Risk Management for Businesses.

The following discussion of laws and regulations is structured to start with the most general applications, from federal to State levels, follow legislative and regulatory responses to trends in identity theft, and finally address provisions adopted to combat particular situations. Among the most noteworthy are the following:

- Federal laws defining identity theft, setting penalties for violations, and empowering agencies to regulate and enforce the laws
- Regulatory structure and responsibility for regulation and enforcement
- State laws requiring notification to consumers of identity theft incidents, such as data breaches, and filling in other gaps in federal requirements
- Sector and demographic-specific provisions, such as:
    - Requiring banks and other creditors to shield their customers from actions of identity thieves
    - Protecting sensitive medical/health information
    - Addressing children's issues
    - Providing protections for military personnel

A NOTE ON THE DISTINCTION BETWEEN LAWS (STATUTES) AND REGULATIONS

It is a common error to fail to understand the difference between a law and a regulation. For the CITRMS® XV professional to speak with authority and maximize the value of advice, this distinction is essential. Accordingly, a brief exposition is offered here.

Laws (also referred to as statutes) are adopted by the legislative branch of government, whether State or federal, and then signed into law by the chief executive of the government. In general, federal laws are superior to State laws, where there is a conflict between them. The legislative process tends to be lengthy and subject to the influence of partisan positions. Amendments to laws must be passed by the legislative branch and approved by the chief executive; in the federal government, that is the Congress and the President, respectively.

Regulatory bodies promulgate regulations. The regulatory bodies are generally created by laws, and given authority to carry out specific functions. Regulatory entities are considered to be part of the Executive branch, though they may be constituted as independent agencies, answerable directly to the legislative branch. The regulatory process may be formal or informal, and (for good or ill) may result in legal disputes by those subject to the particular regulation.

Formal regulatory action usually requires posting of a draft regulation in the appropriate publication (the Federal Register, for federal agencies), a comment period for the affected parties to be heard, receipt of written comments and hearings (usually in a public setting), modifications of the draft regulations, and further consideration before final regulations are adopted and enforced.

Informal regulatory action may be taken to adopt and enforce regulations where there is an emergency or other overwhelming public need. Without opportunities for the affected parties to comment and influence the terms and conditions of the regulation, there is a greater chance the enforcement of the regulation may be called into question and challenged in court.

Remedies against onerous or inappropriate regulatory provisions include legislative action to modify or limit the power of the agency to adopt or enforce such regulations. Law suits in court may also be undertaken, if the agency has exceeded its lawful authority in the process of promulgating or enforcing the regulation.

For our purposes, it's also important to note neither the statutory nor regulatory landscape of identity theft issues is static. There is a continual process of evaluating the application and effectiveness of both laws and regulations in responding to the developing threats of identity thieves.

Federal Identity Theft Laws

FEDERAL TRADE COMMISSION
IdentityTheft.gov

The following perspective on the range and scope of federal identity theft laws relies extensively on the presentation provided by the United States Department of Justice Office for Victims of Crime (OVC) at: http://www.ovc.gov/pubs/ID_theft/idtheftlaws.html [67]

Legislative efforts to create federal identity theft laws must balance the competing needs of victims, government agencies, and businesses, yet stay flexible enough to anticipate future identity crime issues.

Prior to 1998, crimes that would now be considered identity theft were charged under "false personation" statutes, which go back to the late 19th century. False personation can be defined as "the crime of falsely assuming the identity of another to gain a benefit or avoid an expense."

When Congress passed the Identity Theft and Assumption Deterrence Act of 1998 identity theft was officially designated as a federal crime. Specifically, it amended 18 U.S.C. § 1028 ("Fraud and related activity in connection with identification documents") to make it a federal crime to —
…knowingly transfer or use, without lawful authority, a means of identification of another person with the intent to commit, or to aid or abet, any unlawful activity that constitutes a violation of Federal law, or that constitutes a felony under any applicable State or local law.
(See: http://www.gpo.gov/fdsys/pkg/PLAW-105publ318/pdf/PLAW-105publ318.pdf)

The Identity Theft and Assumption Deterrence Act accomplished four things:
It made identity theft a separate crime against the individual whose identity was stolen and credit adversely impacted. Previously, victims had been defined solely by financial loss and often the emphasis was on banks and other financial institutions, rather than on individuals.

It established the Federal Trade Commission (FTC) as the Federal Government's one central point of contact for reporting instances of identity theft by creating the Identity Theft Data Clearinghouse.
It increased criminal penalties for identity theft and fraud. Specifically, the crime now carries a maximum penalty of 15 years imprisonment and substantial fines.
It closed legal loopholes, which previously had made it a crime to produce or possess false identity documents, but had *not* criminalized stealing another person's personal identifying information. Closing loopholes also included a provision making it a federal crime to engage in an act that constitutes a felony under any applicable State or local law.

Additional federal laws have been enacted to address the growing complexities surrounding identity theft and fraud. Some address the practices of holders of PII. Others are oriented toward protecting the security and privacy of consumers in general. Still others focus on specific population groups, as mentioned in Section 5.

The most important, for our purposes, include the following:

Fair Debt Collection Practices Act (FDCPA)
The Fair Debt Collection Practices Act (15 U.S.C. §§ 1692-1692p, as amended by Pub. L. 109-351, §§ 801-02, 120 Stat. 1966) prohibits debt collectors from using unfair or deceptive practices to collect overdue bills that a creditor has forwarded for collection.

Fair Credit Reporting Act (FCRA) and the Fair and Accurate Credit Transactions Act (FACTA) of 2003
FCRA is the law governing the accuracy and privacy of credit reports. FACTA amended the Fair Credit Reporting Act in 2003 to strengthen and add to the protections for victims of identity theft.

These laws require consumer reporting agencies (CRAs) and creditors to help victims recover from identity theft, and allow consumers to place alerts on their credit files if they are or believe they may become victims of identity theft (fraud alerts). Consumers have the right to dispute inaccurate information, and CRAs and creditors must investigate the claim and correct information if it is inaccurate.

These laws also entitle consumers to a free credit report once per year from each of the three credit reporting agencies.

As part of their responsibilities under FACTA, the Federal Trade Commission and the federal financial agencies established "Red Flag Rules" requiring creditors and financial institutions to establish programs designed to prevent identity theft. A detailed discussion of the Red Flag Rules follows in this Section.

Identity Theft Penalty Enhancement Act of 2004
This act (Pub. L. 108–275 § 1028A) establishes penalties for "aggravated" identity theft, which is using the identity of another person to commit felony crimes, including immigration violations, theft of another's Social Security benefits, and acts of domestic terrorism.

Identity Theft Enforcement and Restitution Act of 2008
This act amends 18 U.S.C. § 3663(b) to make it clear that restitution orders for identity theft cases may include an amount equal to the value of the victim's time spent remediating the actual or intended harm of the identity theft or aggravated identity theft. The new law also allows federal courts to prosecute when the criminal and the victim live in the same state. Under previous law, federal courts only had jurisdiction if the thief uses interstate communication to access the victim's PII.

Gramm-Leach-Bliley Act of 1999

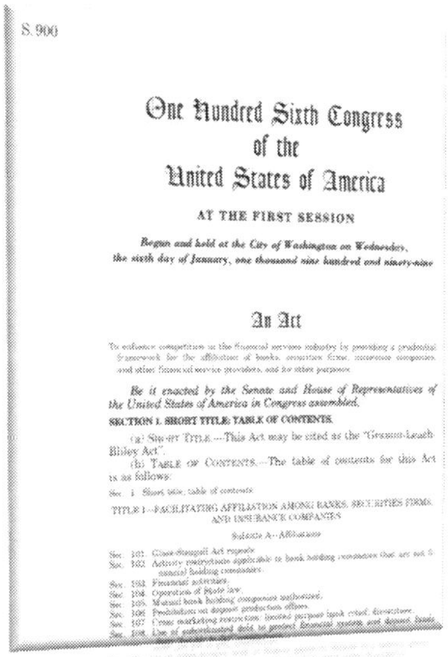
S.900

One Hundred Sixth Congress of the United States of America

AT THE FIRST SESSION

Begun and held at the City of Washington on Wednesday, the sixth day of January, one thousand nine hundred and ninety-nine

An Act

Be it enacted by the Senate and House of Representatives of the United States of America in Congress assembled,

SECTION 1. SHORT TITLE; TABLE OF CONTENTS.

The Gramm-Leach-Bliley Act (Pub. L. 106-102, 113 Stat. 1338) includes a Financial Privacy Rule, which requires financial institutions to provide consumers with a privacy notice when the consumer relationship is established and annually thereafter. The privacy notice must explain what information the institution collects about the consumer, where that information is shared, how it is used, and how that information is protected. The notice must also explain the consumer's right to opt out of the information being shared with unaffiliated parties and notify him or her if the privacy policy changes.

In practice, compliance with this "opt-out" provision has been achieved by periodically mailing a "Privacy Notification" or similar document to the customer. Typically, this notification is sent to the account holder by mail. It covers the required information in detail, along with instructions for the consumer on how to limit the extent of sharing personal information.

It is notable not all sharing of the consumer's information can be limited. Examples of this sharing include normal business purposes, such as processing transactions, maintaining accounts, responding to legal inquiries, and reporting to credit bureaus. Internal and joint marketing activities are also exempt from consumer limitations.

The consumer can limit sharing of creditworthiness information by financial institution affiliates, as well as for marketing purposes by affiliates and non-affiliates. "Affiliates" are considered to be those companies under common ownership or control. "Non-affiliates" may still include companies participating in joint marketing agreements with the financial institution making the notification.

A few States have enacted laws that further restrict the sharing of information. They either provide for an automatic opt-out of sharing information (such as California and Vermont) or give the consumer a means of limiting marketing calls from the financial institution and its affiliates (Nevada). These State actions are illustrative, and may change from time to time.

Red Flags Rules

The Federal Trade Commission (FTC), in coordination with the federal financial agencies established "Red Flag Rules" requiring financial institutions and other specified creditors to establish programs designed to address identity theft threats. This set of required actions was developed and implemented after an extensive regulatory process. The final deadline for compliance was November 1, 2008 for all financial institutions except state chartered credit unions. Enforcement for organizations subject to oversight by the Federal Trade Commission was extended several times and the final compliance deadline to avoid penalties was June 1st, 2010.

The authority for promulgation of the Red Flags Rules is rooted in the Fair and Accurate Credit Transactions Act (FACTA) of 2003. Specifically, Sections 114 and 315 include the concept of "red flags." Section 114 requires all organizations subject to the legislation to develop and implement a written "Identity Theft Prevention Program" to detect, prevent, and mitigate identity theft in connection with the opening of certain new and certain existing accounts. Section 315 further requires actions to be taken to verify and reconcile the addresses of account holders.

The following six financial regulatory agencies were given responsibility for the adoption and enforcement of the Red Flags Rules:

- Department of Treasury - Office of the Comptroller of the Currency under 12 Code
- of Federal Regulations (CFR) Part 41 (National Banks)
- Federal Reserve System under 12 CFR Part 222 (State-chartered banks members of the Federal Reserve System)
- Federal Deposit Insurance Corporation under 12 CFR Parts 334 and 364 (State-chartered banks not members of the Federal Reserve System but insured by the FDIC)
- Department of the Treasury – Office of Thrift Supervision under 12 CFR Part 717 (Federally Chartered Savings Banks)
- National Credit Union Administration under 12 CFR Part 717 (Federal and State-chartered Credit Unions insured by the NCUA)
- Federal Trade Commission under 16 CFR Part 681. (All other "Creditors" as defined)

During the regulatory process under which the Red Flags Rules were adopted, numerous groups of professional service firms and other businesses objected to being considered as covered organizations. On one hand, they fit the description of a creditor extending payment terms to customers. On the other hand, various aspects of their services and customer relationships provided a basis to exempt them from such requirements. Examples are attorneys and providers of health care, as they are already subject to other governmental requirements that serve similar purposes.

Due to voluminous commentary from these and other interested parties, Congress again took action in passing the Red Flag Program Clarification Act of 2010, which was signed into law on December 18, 2010. This amended the Fair Credit Reporting Act regarding the applicability of identity theft guidelines to creditors. The effect is to limit the scope of the FTC's Red Flags Rule to creditors that regularly and in the ordinary course of business:

1) obtain or use consumer reports, directly or indirectly, in connection with a credit transaction;
2) furnish information to consumer reporting agencies in connection with a credit transaction; or
3) advance funds to or on behalf of a person, based on a person's obligation to repay the funds or on repayment from specific property pledged by or on the person's behalf.

The revised definition of "creditor" excludes creditors "that advance funds on behalf of a person for expenses incidental to a service provided by the creditor to that person." This exclusion responds to the comment that the original FCRA definition improperly extended the Red Flags Rule's scope to cover organizations not typically thought of as creditors, including such services as law firms and health care providers.

Additional coverage and exemption issues

As noted above, the statutory and regulatory processes have resulted in a broad net being cast over the organizations and relationships subject to the Red Flags Rules. In applying the definitions of "creditor" and "covered account" for this purpose, certain specific applications and exemptions have come into play.

FTC Red Flag Rules: [68]

There is a two part analysis to determine whether an organization is subject to the Red Flags Rules: According to the Federal Trade Commission, as of the date of this writing:

The Red Flags Rule [*sic*] requires "financial institutions" and some "creditors" to conduct a periodic risk assessment to determine if they have "covered accounts." The determination isn't based on the industry or sector, but rather on whether a business' activities fall within the relevant definitions. A business must implement a written program only if it has covered accounts.

DEFINITION OF "CREDITOR"

The Red Flags Rule defines "creditor" based on conduct.[5]
To determine if your business is a creditor under the Red Flags Rule, ask these questions:
Does my business or organization regularly:

- Defer payment for goods and services or bill customers?
- Grant or arrange credit?
- Participate in the decision to extend, renew, or set the terms of credit?
- If you answer:
- No to all, the Rule does not apply.
- Yes to one or more, ask:
- Does my business or organization regularly and in the ordinary course of business:
- Get or use consumer reports in connection with a credit transaction?
- Give information to credit reporting companies in connection with a credit transaction?
- Advance funds to — or for — someone who must repay them, either with funds or pledged property (excluding incidental expenses in connection with the services you provide to them)?
- If you answer:
- No to all, the Rule does not apply.
- Yes to one or more, you are a creditor covered by the Rule.

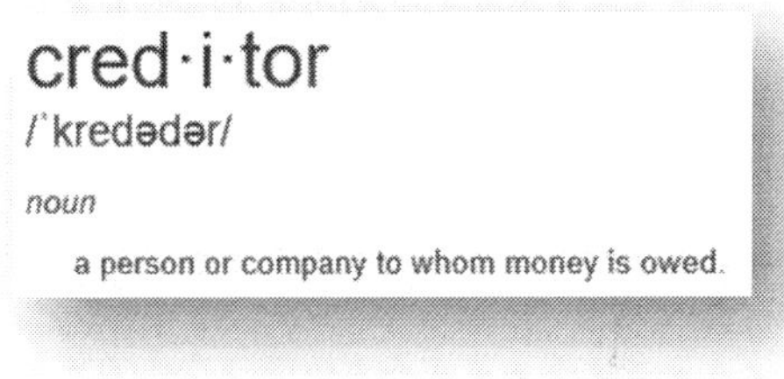

Covered Accounts

If you conclude your business or organization is a financial institution or a creditor covered by the Rule, you must determine if you have any "covered accounts," as the Red Flags Rule defines that term. You'll need to look at existing accounts and new ones. Two categories of accounts are covered:

1. A consumer account for your customers for personal, family, or household purposes that involves or allows multiple payments or transactions.[7] Examples are credit card accounts, mortgage loans, automobile loans, checking accounts, and savings accounts.
2. "Any other account that a financial institution or creditor offers or maintains for which there is a reasonably foreseeable risk to customers or to the safety and soundness of the financial institution or creditor from identity theft, including financial, operational, compliance, reputation, or litigation risks."[8] Examples include small business accounts, sole proprietorship accounts, or single transaction consumer accounts that may be vulnerable to identity theft. Unlike consumer accounts designed to allow multiple payments or transactions — always considered "covered accounts" under the Rule — other types of accounts are "covered" only if the risk of identity theft is reasonably foreseeable.

In determining if accounts are covered under the second category, consider how they're opened and accessed. For example, there may be a reasonably foreseeable risk of identity theft in connection with business accounts that can be accessed remotely — say, through the Internet or the telephone. Your risk analysis must consider any actual incidents of identity theft involving accounts like these.

If you don't have any covered accounts, you don't need a written program. But business models and services change. You may acquire covered accounts through changes to your business structure, process, or organization. So it's good policy and practice to conduct a periodic risk assessment. [69]

CAVEAT: Due to changes in business processes and relationships, an individual organization may become subject to (or cease to be subject to) the Red Flags Rules, in the event of setting up covered accounts and establishing a "creditor" relationship with customers. For this reason, even organizations not currently subject to the requirements of the Red Flags Rules would be prudent to stay vigilant regarding any such operational changes that could cause them to have to comply with these Rules.
Conceptually, these actions are designed and enforced to assist covered lenders in tracking and identifying patterns in customer behavior and data in order to avoid unauthorized uses of customer information by potential identity thieves. In practice, these are steps are generally accepted as being prudent and appropriate for this purpose. The requirements are applied in a manner that recognizes one size does not fit all. It is not unreasonable to consider a form of Red Flags Rules would be appropriate for any organization to adopt and implement, regardless of whether it falls into a covered category.

Developing the plan must be appropriate for the specific organization, based on a review of its business methods and operations, and its previous experience with identity theft. The program must provide for policies and procedures that will: identify patterns, practices or activities to alert the firm to the possible occurrence of identity theft, and achieve compliance with the Red Flags Rules.

The FTC describes compliance as a "Four-Step Process:"

- Identify Relevant Red Flags
- Detect Red Flags
- Prevent & Mitigate Identity Theft
- Update the Program

The following is a summary of the steps listed by the FTC to be taken in the implementation phase of the program. [70]

- ***Identify Relevant Red Flags***

  - Potential patterns, practices, or specific activities indicating the possibility of identity theft

  - Risk Factors in the industry or activity specific to the organization (FTC suggests "think about the types of accounts you offer or maintain; the ways you open covered accounts; how you provide access to those accounts; and what you know about identity theft in your business.")

  - Sources might include the experiences of other competing businesses or of organizations with related activities; keeping abreast of technological changes is important in identifying these Red Flags

  - Categories of Common Red Flags (Examples of Suspicious Items)

    - Credit Reporting Agency notifications

    - Financial or other documents with inaccurate information

- Personal ID documents (or other PII) with errors or inconsistencies in photo or other information
- Account activity in conflict with experience or raising fraudulent issues such as unaccustomed patterns of use
- Notices from other sources, such as law enforcement, benefits statements, employer, landlord or tenant activity
- *This list is illustrative, not exhaustive*

Detect Red Flags

- Adopt Verification and Authentication Procedures to Detect Red Flags
- New Accounts
  - Verify identity using official documents
  - Compare with other sources of information
  - Utilize challenge questions (known only to the customer)

  - Existing Accounts
    - Authenticate with updated information
    - Monitor activity of account
    - Online procedures: use multi-factor authentication such as passwords, PINs, smart cards, biometrics, and tokens
    - *Caveat:* Easily accessible confirming information, such as mother's maiden name, Social Security number, or mailing address is not reliable for this purpose.

Prevent & Mitigate Identity Theft

- How to Respond to a Red Flag Detection
  - Contact customer
  - Monitor account
  - Confirm or modify challenge questions
  - Close/Reopen account with new account number
  - Notify Law Enforcement
  - *NOTE:* "No Response" may be appropriate in cases where it can be determined the lapse is an error not attributable to identity thieves
    - Other legal obligations, e.g., maintain the confidentiality of privileged information as in attorney/client or doctor/patient relationships

- Update the Program (Periodically) to Take into Account
    - New Red Flags, from regulators
    - Technology changes in the systems used by the business
    - New detection methods from software vendors
    - Specific experience of the enterprise
    - Business changes in the organization

Guidance on Administering the Program

- Conduct continuing review and approval of the program by Board of Directors (or Senior Management)
- Assignment specific responsibilities to a senior employee
- Periodically evaluate staff training and assignments
- Coordinate with and monitor the activities of partners, affiliates and outside service providers

Once the Red Flags Rules program is in place, in addition to continuing updates and administration, the covered organization must be prepared to be audited for compliance from time to time. Such an audit may be initiated as a result of any one of several occurrences. A consumer complaint may be filed with the responsible agency, or a data breach may occur (requiring reporting and notification), or at the initiative of the regulatory agency, for instance.

Failure to maintain compliance with the Rules may result in enforcement actions, such as agreements (formal or informal) to take the actions necessary to achieve compliance, monetary sanctions, or other appropriate actions. Fines and penalties may be compensatory in nature, result in payments to the individuals affected by the compliance failure or punitive, and result in payments directly to the regulatory agency. State agencies, such as Attorneys General who may participate in the enforcement actions, may also share in the funds from the penalties.

The Advent of the Consumer Financial Protection Bureau

One of the most notable changes, in terms of governmental regulation, is the establishment in 2010 of the Consumer Financial Protection Bureau (CPFB) which was given broad oversight authority of the credit, credit reporting, identity theft safeguards and debt collection industry, among many other groups. The CFPB was established pursuant to Title X of the Dodd-Frank Wall Street Reform and Consumer Protection Act. Despite various legal and legislative challenges to the Board's constitutionality and alleged overreach beyond statutory authority, as of this date, the CFPB is in full operation, with executives and staff carrying out its statutory duties. Nonetheless, even with certain activities overlapping with the FTC and other federal agencies, the full extent of the CFPB's authority in promulgating and enforcing identity theft standards is still developing. While the political back story may be interesting in its own right, for purposes of this ISG-XV, focus remains on CFPB's activities regarding identity theft.

The agency's online resources include educational materials, opportunities to participate in the process of regulation, and a place to submit and check on the status of a consumer complaint. The consumer complaint data base lists the complaints by product, sub-product, and issue, as well as a place for narrative and even a response from the company against whom the complaint was filed. Unfortunately, at least for our purposes, there is no "product" or "sub-product" listed as "identity theft." The complaints involving identity theft issues tend to be about sales practices or add-on products associated with credit card accounts. In this context, a view of CFPB's regulation activities is better focused on published enforcement actions. [71]

The following examples are representative of the CFPB's identity theft-related investigative and enforcement actions. They have concentrated on remedies for consumers who were charged for add-ons to their credit card accounts, such as credit report monitoring and identity theft protection services they were charged for but did not receive, or were sold by making unsupported claims about the nature and value of the service. Note that at least one of the actions was imposed jointly with the Federal Deposit Insurance Corporation (FDIC). This list is not exhaustive, and will no doubt such actions will no doubt continue in the future.

- July 2015: CFPB took action against two credit card add-on product vendors – Affinion Group Holdings, Inc., Affinion's affiliated companies, and Intersections Inc. – for unfairly charging consumers for credit card add-on benefits they did not receive. Under the proposed consent orders, Affinion would pay approximately $6.8 million in monetary relief for eligible consumers who have not yet received refunds and $1.9 million in civil money penalties, while Intersections would pay approximately $55,000 in monetary relief to eligible consumers who have not yet received refunds and $1.2 million in civil money penalties. [72]

- April 2014: The Consumer Financial Protection Bureau (CFPB) has ordered Bank of America, N.A. and FIA Card Services, N.A. to provide an estimated $727 million in relief to consumers harmed by practices related to credit card add-on products. Roughly 1.4 million consumers were affected by Bank of America's deceptive marketing of their add-on products. Bank of America also illegally charged approximately 1.9 million consumer accounts for credit monitoring and credit reporting services that they were not receiving. Bank of America will pay a $20 million civil money penalty to the CFPB. [73]

- December 2013: The Consumer Financial Protection Bureau (CFPB) today ordered American Express to refund an estimated $59.5 million to more than 335,000 consumers for illegal credit card practices. These practices included unfair billing tactics and deceptive marketing with respect to credit card "add-on products" such as payment protection and credit monitoring. American Express will pay an additional $9.6 million in civil penalties to the CFPB. [74]

- September 2013: The Consumer Financial Protection Bureau (CFPB) ordered Chase Bank USA, N.A. and JPMorgan Chase Bank, N.A. to refund an estimated $309 million to more than 2.1 million customers for illegal credit card practices. This enforcement action is the result of work started by the Office of the Comptroller of the Currency (OCC), which the CFPB joined last year. The agencies found that Chase engaged in unfair billing practices for certain credit card "add-on products" by charging consumers for credit monitoring services that they did not receive. [75]

- September 2012: Today, the Federal Deposit Insurance Corporation (FDIC) and the Consumer Financial Protection Bureau (CFPB) announced a joint public enforcement action with an order requiring Discover Bank to refund approximately $200 million to more than 3.5 million consumers and pay a $14 million civil money penalty. This action results from an investigation started by the FDIC which the CFPB joined last year. The joint investigation concerned deceptive telemarketing and sales tactics used by Discover to mislead consumers into paying for various credit card "add-on products" – payment protection, credit score tracking, identity theft protection, and wallet protection. [76]

As discussed further in Section 9, investigations and enforcement actions like these have had an effect on the way Identity Theft Risk Management products and services are marketed and provided. Little doubt remains this trend will continue to develop in the future.

Health Information Portability and Accountability Act of 1996 (HIPAA)

Comprehensive rules promulgated by the U. S. Department of Health and Human Services (HHS) under HIPAA and its statutory amendments regulate the treatment of patient information. They set national standards for protecting the confidentiality, integrity, and availability of hard copy and electronic Protected Health Information (PHI).

As with the survey of identity theft laws from the U. S. Department of Justice, and the Red Flags Rules from the FTC, the most authoritative exposition of the HIPAA Privacy, Security, and Enforcement Rules comes directly from the Department of Health and Human Services. The specificity with which HHS has reduced this analysis to writing makes it a preferred source for the interpretation of the provisions.

The following citations are for the convenience and further study of these provisions.

Privacy Rule – http://www.hhs.gov/ocr/privacy/hipaa/understanding/summary/index.html including a 25-page Summary in .pdf format

Security Rule – http://www.hhs.gov/ocr/privacy/hipaa/understanding/srsummary.html

Enforcement Rule -- http://www.hhs.gov/ocr/privacy/hipaa/administrative/enforcementrule/index.html

Health Information Technology for Economic and Clinical Health Act (HITECH) –
Implementation of regulations under this Act modify HIPAA and the Privacy, Security, and Enforcement Rules http://www.hhs.gov/news/press/2013pres/01/20130117b.html (Press Release)
Deeper analysis of these rules are found at these same URLs, and CITRMS® XV certificants are encouraged to review this information from time to time.

The following discussion of HIPAA, with special attention to the Privacy, Security, and Enforcement rules, should be understood as an introduction only. Each of these rules and its application has been discussed, analyzed, written about, and even litigated by full-time professionals who practice in this area.
Privacy Rule

The formal name for the HIPAA Privacy Rule is "Standards for Privacy of Individually Identifiable Health Information." The Privacy Rule standards address the use and disclosure of individuals' health information — called "protected health information" by organizations subject to the Privacy Rule — called "covered entities," as well as standards for individuals' privacy rights to understand and control how their health information is used. Within HHS, the Office for Civil Rights ("OCR") has responsibility for implementing and enforcing the Privacy Rule with respect to voluntary compliance activities and civil money penalties.

A major goal of the Privacy Rule is to assure that individuals' health information is properly protected while allowing the flow of health information needed to provide and promote high quality health care and to protect the public's health and well-being. The Rule strikes a balance that permits important uses of information, while protecting the privacy of people who seek care and healing. Given that the health care marketplace is diverse, the Rule is designed to be flexible and comprehensive to cover the variety of uses and disclosures that need to be addressed.

The Privacy Rule applies to health plans, health care clearinghouses, and to any health care provider who transmits health information in electronic form in connection with transactions for which the Secretary of HHS has adopted standards under HIPAA (the "covered entities"). It also extends to "Business Associates," which must operate under contracts with covered entities including obligations to comply with the same Rule.

Privacy Rule Definitions:

- Health Plans -- Individual and group plans that provide or pay the cost of medical care are covered entities.
- Health Care Providers -- Every health care provider, regardless of size, who electronically transmits health information in connection with certain transactions, is a covered entity.
- Health Care Clearinghouses -- Health care clearinghouses are entities that process nonstandard information they receive from another entity into a standard (i.e., standard format or data content), or vice versa, are covered entities.
- Business Associate -- In general, a business associate is a person or organization, other than a member of a covered entity's workforce, that performs certain functions or activities on behalf of, or provides certain services to, a covered entity that involve the use or disclosure of individually identifiable health information.
- Business Associate Contract -- When a covered entity uses a contractor or other non-workforce member to perform "business associate" services or activities, the Rule requires that the covered entity include certain protections for the information in a business associate agreement (in certain circumstances governmental entities may use alternative means to achieve the same protections).

- Individually identifiable health information is information, including demographic data, that relates to:
    - the individual's past, present or future physical or mental health or condition,
    - the provision of health care to the individual, or
    - the past, present, or future payment for the provision of health care to the individual, and
    - that identifies the individual or for which there is a reasonable basis to believe can be used to identify the individual.

[NOTE: The Privacy Rule excludes from protected health information employment records that a covered entity maintains in its capacity as an employer and education and certain other records subject to, or defined in, the Family Educational Rights and Privacy Act (FERPA, which is discussed later in this Section).]

- De-Identified Health Information -- There are no restrictions on the use or disclosure of de-identified health information. De-identified health information neither identifies nor provides a reasonable basis to identify an individual. There are two ways to de-identify information; either: 1) a formal determination by a qualified statistician; or 2) the removal of specified identifiers of the individual and of the individual's relatives, household members, and employers is required, and is adequate only if the covered entity has no actual knowledge that the remaining information could be used to identify the individual.

- Privacy Rule Principles and Disclosures:
    - Basic Principle -- A major purpose of the Privacy Rule is to define and limit the circumstances in which an individual's protected heath information may be used or disclosed by covered entities. A covered entity may not use or disclose protected health information, except either: (1) as the Privacy Rule permits or requires; or (2) as the individual who is the subject of the information or the individual's personal representative) authorizes in writing.

    - Required Disclosures -- A covered entity must disclose protected health information in only two situations: (a) to individuals (or their personal representatives) specifically when they request access to, or an accounting of disclosures of, their protected health information; and (b) to HHS when it is undertaking a compliance investigation or review or enforcement action.

    - Permitted Uses and Disclosures - A covered entity is permitted, but not required, to use and disclose protected health information, without an individual's authorization, for the following purposes or situations:
        1. To the Individual (unless required for access or accounting of disclosures);
        2. Treatment, Payment, and Health Care Operations;
        3. Opportunity to Agree or Object;
        4. Incident to an otherwise permitted use and disclosure;
        5. Public Interest and Benefit Activities; and
        6. Limited Data Set for the purposes of research, public health or health care operations.

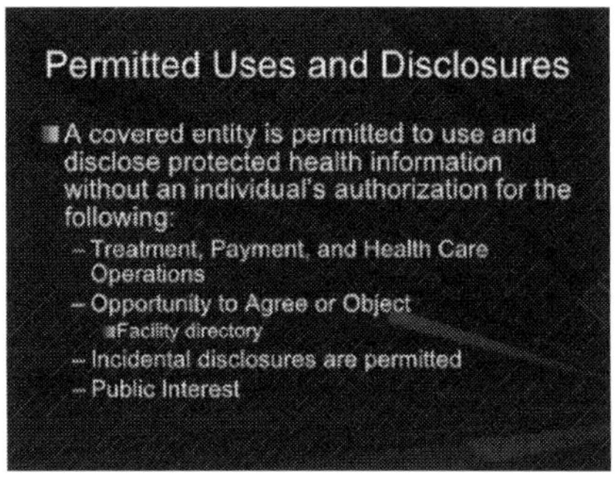

- Covered entities may rely on professional ethics and best judgments in deciding which of these permissive uses and disclosures to make.

    i. To the Individual -- A covered entity may disclose protected health information to the individual who is the subject of the information.

ii. Treatment, Payment, Health Care Operations -- A covered entity may use and disclose protected health information for its own treatment, payment, and health care operations activities.

These protections are under periodic review, in light of the technological and business practice developments that continue to take place in the health care industry. As indicated in the discussion in Section 2 on trends and magnitudes in identity theft, it is clear the value of PHI is growing apace with the cost of delivering and paying for health care services. [77]

CITRMS® XV professionals should note detailed knowledge of the administrative procedures, including access and appeals, remedies, compliance exercises, penalties, and other aspects of the Privacy Rule and its applications is beyond the scope of this course. ICFE offers no legal opinions on the effectiveness of any specific actions on compliance with this Rule.

Security Rule

The *Security Standards for the Protection of Electronic Protected Health Information* (the Security Rule) establish a national set of security standards for protecting certain health information held or transferred in electronic form. The Security Rule operationalizes the protections contained in the Privacy Rule by addressing the technical and non-technical safeguards that organizations called "covered entities" must put in place to secure individuals' "electronic protected health information" (e-PHI). Within HHS, the Office for Civil Rights (OCR) has responsibility for enforcing the Privacy and Security Rules with voluntary compliance activities and civil money penalties. The following is the description of the "General Rules" from HHS.

- Sets the security standards for the protection of electronic protected health information.
- Requires the implementation of administrative, technical and physical security safeguards to ensure the secure passage, maintenance and reception of PHI.

The Security Rule requires covered entities to maintain reasonable and appropriate administrative, technical, and physical safeguards for protecting e-PHI.

Specifically, covered entities must:

1. Ensure the confidentiality, integrity, and availability of all e-PHI they create, receive, maintain or transmit;
2. Identify and protect against reasonably anticipated threats to the security or integrity of the information;
3. Protect against reasonably anticipated, impermissible uses or disclosures; and
4. Ensure compliance by their workforce.

The Security Rule defines "confidentiality" to mean that e-PHI is not available or disclosed to unauthorized persons. The Security Rule's confidentiality requirements support the Privacy Rule's prohibitions against improper uses and disclosures of PHI. The Security rule also promotes the two additional goals of maintaining the integrity and availability of e-PHI. Under the Security Rule, "integrity" means that e-PHI is not altered or destroyed in an unauthorized manner. "Availability" means that e-PHI is accessible and usable on demand by an authorized person.
HHS recognizes that covered entities range from the smallest provider to the largest, multi-state health plan. Therefore the Security Rule is flexible and scalable to allow covered entities to analyze their own needs and implement solutions appropriate for their specific environments. What is appropriate for a particular covered entity will depend on the nature of the covered entity's business, as well as the covered entity's size and resources.

Therefore, when a covered entity is deciding which security measures to use, the Rule does not dictate those measures but requires the covered entity to consider:

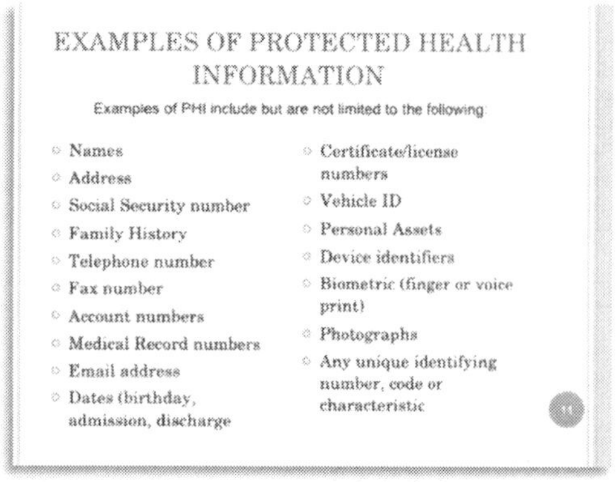

- Its size, complexity, and capabilities,
- Its technical, hardware, and software infrastructure,
- The costs of security measures, and
- The likelihood and possible impact of potential risks to e-PHI.

Covered entities must review and modify their security measures to continue protecting e-PHI in a changing environment. [78]

Enforcement Rule

The HIPAA Enforcement Rule contains provisions relating to compliance and investigations, the imposition of civil money penalties for violations of the HIPAA Administrative Simplification Rules, and procedures for hearings. Within HHS, the Office for Civil Rights (OCR) is responsible for discharging this responsibility.
OCR enforces the Privacy and Security Rules in several ways:

- Investigating complaints filed with it
- Conducting compliance reviews to determine if covered entities are in compliance
- Performing education and outreach to foster compliance with the Rules' requirements.
- OCR also works in conjunction with the Department of Justice (DOJ) to refer possible criminal violations of HIPAA.SOURCE [79]

Resolution Agreements and Civil Money Penalties -A resolution agreement is a contract signed by HHS and a covered entity in which the covered entity agrees to perform certain obligations (e.g., staff training) and make reports to HHS, generally for a period of three years. During the period, HHS monitors the covered entity's compliance with its obligations. A resolution agreement likely would include the payment of a resolution amount. These agreements are reserved to settle investigations with more serious outcomes. When HHS has not been able to reach a satisfactory resolution through the covered entity has demonstrated compliance or corrective action through other informal means, civil money penalties (CMPs) may be imposed for noncompliance against a covered entity. As of June 30, 2015, HHS has entered into 21 resolution agreements and issued CMPs to one covered entity.

The following are representative examples of corrective actions with identity theft implications, in which identity thieves could have breached the confidentiality of PHI.

- HMO Revises Process to Obtain Valid Authorizations
  Covered Entity: Health Plans / HMOs
  Issue: Impermissible Uses and Disclosures; Authorizations

A complaint alleged an HMO impermissibly disclosed a member's PHI, when it sent her entire medical record to a disability insurance company without her authorization. An OCR investigation indicated the form the HMO relied on to make the disclosure was not a valid authorization under the Privacy Rule. Among other corrective actions to resolve the specific issues in the case, the HMO created a new HIPAA-compliant authorization form and implemented a new policy that directs staff to obtain patient signatures on these forms before responding to any disclosure requests, even if patients bring in their own "authorization" form. The new authorization specifies what records and/or portions of the files will be disclosed and the respective authorization will be kept in the patient's record, together with the disclosed information.

- Private Practice Implements Safeguards for Waiting Rooms
  Covered Entity: Private Practice
  Issue: Safeguards; Impermissible Uses and Disclosures
  A staff member of a medical practice discussed HIV testing procedures with a patient in the waiting room, thereby disclosing PHI to several other individuals. Also, computer screens displaying patient information were easily visible to patients. Among other corrective actions to resolve the specific issues in the case, OCR required the provider to develop and implement policies and procedures regarding appropriate administrative and physical safeguards related to the communication of PHI. The practice trained all staff on the newly developed policies and procedures. In addition, OCR required the practice to reposition its computer monitors to prevent patients from viewing information on the screens, and the practice installed computer monitor privacy screens to prevent impermissible disclosures.

HIPAA Privacy & Security Rule Complaint Process

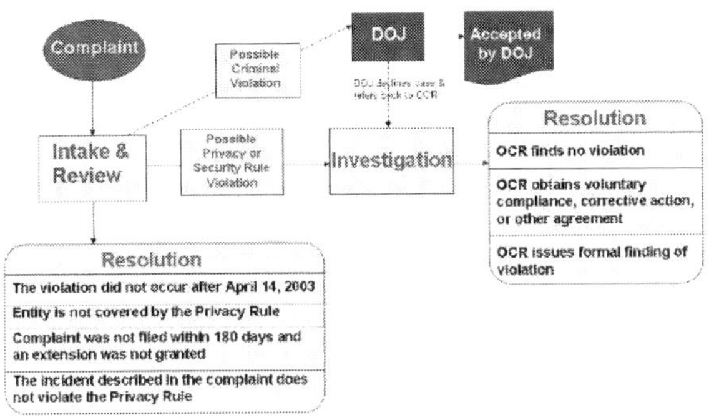

- Pharmacy Chain Institutes New Safeguards for PHI in Pseudoephedrine Log Books
  Covered Entity: Pharmacies
  Issue: Safeguards
  A grocery store based pharmacy chain maintained pseudoephedrine log books containing protected health information in a manner so that individual protected health information was visible to the public at the pharmacy counter. Initially, the pharmacy chain refused to acknowledge the log books contained protected health information. OCR issued a written analysis and a demand for compliance. Among other corrective actions to resolve the specific issues in the case, OCR required the pharmacy chain implement national policies and procedures to safeguard the log books. Moreover, the entity was required to train of all staff on the revised policy. The chain acknowledged log books contained protected health information and implemented the required changes.

SOURCE [80]

Health Information Technology for Economic and Clinical Health Act (HITECH)

The Health Information Technology for Economic and Clinical Health (HITECH) Act, enacted as part of the American Recovery and Reinvestment Act of 2009, was signed into law on February 17, 2009, to promote the adoption and meaningful use of health information technology. Subtitle D of the HITECH Act addresses the privacy and security concerns associated with the electronic transmission of health information, in part, through several provisions that strengthen the civil and criminal enforcement of the rules.

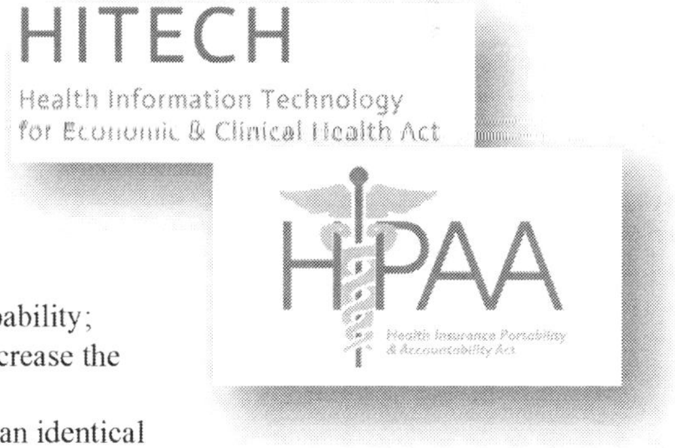

Relevant provisions of HITECH establish:

- Four categories of violations that reflect increasing levels of culpability;
- Four corresponding tiers of penalty amounts that significantly increase the minimum penalty amount for each violation; and
- A maximum penalty amount of $1.5 million for all violations of an identical provision.
- It also amended section 1176(b) of the Act by:
- Striking the previous bar on the imposition of penalties if the covered entity did not know and with the exercise of reasonable diligence would not have known of the violation (such violations are now punishable under the lowest tier of penalties); and

- Providing a prohibition on the imposition of penalties for any violation that is corrected within a 30-day time period, as long as the violation was not due to willful neglect.
- SOURCE [81]

In all, the HIPAA and HIPAA-related body of law and regulation continues to develop to meet the challenges of changing technology and vulnerabilities in the health care and medical information system. The coming years will no doubt bring more attempts by identity thieves to penetrate the places where PHI is held, and more responses by the legislators and regulators to frustrate the efforts of these criminals.

Family Educational Rights and Privacy Act of 1974 (FERPA)

The Family Education Rights and Privacy Act of 1974 (FERPA) is the principal federal law here. FERPA limits the disclosure of educational records maintained by agencies and institutions that receive federal funding. It protects "records, files, documents, and other materials" that "contain information directly related to a student" when held by a federally-funded educational institution or by someone who works for one. In practice, this covers almost every educational institution, as nearly all have federally funded programs. The Family Policy Compliance Office in the federal Department of Education administers FERPA. [82]

As the Family Policy Compliance Office (FPCO) is the primary and original authority for this information, the following discussion is sourced at the web site of FPCO.
FERPA gives parents certain rights with respect to their children's education records. These rights transfer to the student when he or she reaches the age of 18 or attends a school beyond the high school level. Students to whom the rights have transferred are "eligible students."

- Parents or eligible students have the right to inspect and review the student's education records maintained by the school. Schools are not required to provide copies of records unless, for reasons such as great distance, it is impossible for parents or eligible students to review the records. Schools may charge a fee for copies.
- Parents or eligible students have the right to request that a school correct records which they believe to be inaccurate or misleading. If the school decides not to amend the record, the parent or eligible student then has the right to a formal hearing. After the hearing, if the school still decides not to amend the record, the parent or eligible student has the right to place a statement with the record setting forth his or her view about the contested information.
- Generally, schools must have written permission from the parent or eligible student in order to release any information from a student's education record. However, FERPA allows schools to disclose those records, without consent, to the following parties or under the following conditions (34 CFR § 99.31):
- School officials with legitimate educational interest;
- Other schools to which a student is transferring;
- Specified officials for audit or evaluation purposes;
- Appropriate parties in connection with financial aid to a student;
- Organizations conducting certain studies for or on behalf of the school;
- Accrediting organizations;
- To comply with a judicial order or lawfully issued subpoena;
- Appropriate officials in cases of health and safety emergencies; and
- State and local authorities, within a juvenile justice system, pursuant to specific State law.

Schools may disclose, without consent, "directory" information such as a student's name, address, telephone number, date and place of birth, honors and awards, and dates of attendance. However, schools must tell parents and eligible students about directory information and allow parents and eligible students a reasonable amount of time to request that the school not disclose directory information about them. Schools must notify parents and eligible students annually of their rights under FERPA. The actual means of notification (special letter, inclusion in a PTA bulletin, student handbook, or newspaper article) is left to the discretion of each school.

These provisions are prone to being extended to areas where they may or may not have been intended to reach. A recent advisory from a covered educational institution to alumni admissions interviewers makes mention of regulations under FERPA: they "entitle enrolled students and alumni to review their admissions files, including interview reports. While information about the interviewer is redacted, and interviews of admitted students will presumably be complimentary, we should be aware of this right in connection with future interviews."

On one hand, such access may, in some measure protect the interviewee's privacy and personal rights to know what is in his or her admissions files. On the other hand, it could provide another opportunity for identity thieves to pretend to be the student, in order to receive PII as part of an identity theft scheme.

Ultimately, as the parties involved gain greater experience with such access and protection, a balance will likely be reached. In the meantime, consciousness-raising about these issues will be the best means of avoiding adverse actions by the FPCO.

Children's Online Privacy Protection Act of 1998 (COPPA)

The Children's Online Privacy Protection Act of 1998 (COPPA), authorized the Federal Trade Commission (FTC) to regulate use of the internet by children under the age of 13. Under this Act, the FTC requires internet services "directed to children under 13" and collect personal information from internet users to institute broad protections against the abuse or unauthorized collection and use of the PII of these children.

The operative language of the COPPA Rule is set out in §312.3 -- Regulation of unfair or deceptive acts or practices in connection with the collection, use, and/or disclosure of personal information from and about children on the Internet. *General requirements.* It shall be unlawful for any operator of a Web site or online service directed to children, or any operator that has actual knowledge that it is collecting or maintaining personal information from a child, to collect personal information from a child in a manner that violates the regulations prescribed under this part. Generally, under this part, an operator must:
(a) Provide notice on the Web site or online service of what information it collects from children, how it uses such information, and its disclosure practices for such information (§312.4(b));
(b) Obtain verifiable parental consent prior to any collection, use, and/or disclosure of personal information from children (§312.5);
(c) Provide a reasonable means for a parent to review the personal information collected from a child and to refuse to permit its further use or maintenance (§312.6);
(d) Not condition a child's participation in a game, the offering of a prize, or another activity on the child disclosing more personal information than is reasonably necessary to participate in such activity (§312.7); and
(e) Establish and maintain reasonable procedures to protect the confidentiality, security, and integrity of personal information collected from children (§312.8).
These requirements are subject to relief under the "Safe Harbor" clause, which permits internet service providers to submit for approval by the FTC self-defined guidelines to achieve compliance with the protections

of the COPPA Rule. To date, few of these submissions have been approved. At the time of this writing, the oversight and application of COPPA continue to develop. [83]

Active Duty Military Freeze & Fraud Alert Provisions

Service members who deploy can place an active duty alert on their credit reports to help minimize their risk of identity theft. An active duty alert on a credit report means businesses have to take extra steps before granting credit in the service member's name. Active duty alerts last for one year, and can be renewed to match the period of deployment.

As for civilians, to place a fraud alert on the individual's credit reports, it's required to contact one of the nationwide credit reporting companies. A fraud alert is free. The individual must provide proof of his/her identity. The credit reporting agency so advised must tell the other credit reporting companies, which in turn must place an alert on their versions of the credit report.

Additional information on freezes and alerts is covered in Section 7 on steps consumers can take to minimize the risk of identity theft. [84]

Driver's Privacy Protection Act of 1994 (DPPA)

The Driver's Privacy Protection Act imposes limits on disclosures of personal information in records maintained by state departments of motor vehicles. DPPA prohibits, with certain exceptions, the disclosure of personal information without the express consent of the person to whom such information applies.
It is worth noting that the exceptions, called "permissible uses," are extensive; at the time of this writing, the published permissible uses are:

1. For any government agency to carry out its functions
2. For use in connection with "matters of motor vehicle or driver safety and theft"…
3. For use in the normal course of business by a legitimate business or its agents, employees, or contractors, but only to:
    A) verify the accuracy of personal information
    B) correct information
4. For use in connection with any matter before a court or arbitration proceeding.
5. For producing statistical reports and other research, provided that personal information is not published.
6. For use by insurance companies.
7. For providing notice to owners of towed vehicles.
8. For use by licensed private investigation agencies, for a permitted DPPA use.
9. For use by employers.
10. For use by private toll transportation facilities.
11. For response to requests from motor vehicle departments.
12. For the bulk distribution or surveys, marketing materials, or solicitations (opt-in only).
13. When written consent of the individual is provided.
14. For other users specifically authorized by state laws.

SOURCE [85]

Regarding use #13, it should be noted that "express consent" may be obtained in seemingly innocuous ways. For example, is some States, online or in-person renewal of vehicle registrations and driver licenses include a "one-time" authorization to share any and all information with nearly anyone who requests access. [86]

Two additional identity theft-related provisions are included in the Act:

- DPPA makes it illegal to obtain drivers' information for unlawful purposes or to make false representations to obtain such information.

- DPPA establishes criminal fines for noncompliance, and establishes a civil cause of action for drivers against those who unlawfully obtain their information.

State Actions

Over time, state legislative bodies also started to pass laws that helped victims, and many of these laws have in turn become the basis for national laws. As most crimes are prosecuted on the state level, these laws tend to provide disincentives for identity thieves, as well as significant protective effects for potential victims.

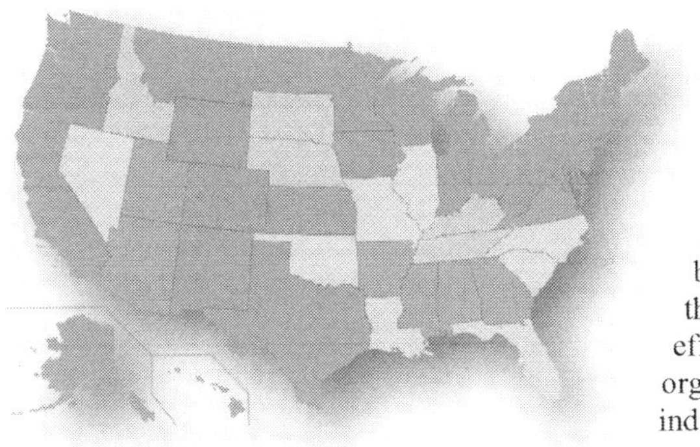

One area where States have taken the lead is enacting a notification requirement regarding data breaches. These laws make it mandatory for organizations that have suffered a data breach to notify the individuals whose PII was compromised of the event and certain additional information relating to the adverse effects they may experience. In most cases, the breached organization also offers a period of credit report monitoring to these individuals. [87]

For over 10 years, California has had on its books a law requiring organizations that experience a data breach to notify the affected parties of certain facts involved. The original California law required notification when unencrypted personal information was, or is reasonably believed to have been, acquired by an unauthorized person. The California model is the basis for most of the other State laws levying this requirement.

In general terms, the following are the elements forming the basis for these State laws.

- Delineating who must comply with the law
- Defining the terms "personal information" and "breach of security"
- Establishing the elements of harm that must occur, if any, for notice to be triggered
- Adopting requirements for notice
- Creating exemptions and safe harbors
- Clarifying preemption and relationships to other federal laws
- Creating penalties, enforcement authorities, and remedies

Following are the principal provisions in the California law describing the actions the breached organization must take:

1. The security breach notification shall be written in plain language.
2. The security breach notification shall include, at a minimum, the following information:
    a. The name and contact information of the reporting agency subject to this section.
    b. A list of the types of personal information that were or are reasonably believed to have been the subject of a breach.
    c. If the information is possible to determine at the time the notice is provided, then any of the following: (i) the date of the breach, (ii) the estimated date of the breach, or (iii) the date range within which the breach occurred. The notification shall also include the date of the notice.
    d. Whether the notification was delayed as a result of a law enforcement investigation, if that information is possible to determine at the time the notice is provided.
    e. A general description of the breach incident, if that information is possible to determine at the time the notice is provided.
    f. The toll-free telephone numbers and addresses of the major credit reporting agencies, if the breach exposed a social security number or a driver's license or California identification card number.
3. At the discretion of the agency, the security breach notification may also include any of the following:
    a. Information about what the agency has done to protect individuals whose information has been breached.
    b. Advice on steps the person whose information has been breached may take to protect himself or herself. [88]

Currently, nearly every State has adopted some form of breach notification requirement. Such laws generally apply to organizations with offices in or doing business in the particular State, and may even apply to breaches involving customers or clients in other States, even though the breached organization may have no presence there.

Specific information on individual States can be obtained by referring to the web site of each State, or by searching "State data breach notification law" in your internet browser. [89]

There are, of course, certain unintended consequences to the effect of numerous notifications to consumers of data breaches. If anything, the now-routine letters from holders of sensitive information to consumers may have had the effect of dulling the concerns consumers would otherwise have about the theft of this information. Further, the assumption of consumers they will be protected from financial or other loss by the senders of such notifications also may lull consumers into a false sense of security about non-financial losses.

In a developing area, there may also be civil litigation rights against the organization whose data was breached for victims who can demonstrate financial or economic loss as a result of the breach. In some pending cases it is alleged financial harm is not a required element for money damages to be awarded. However, it should also be noted there also appears to be a duty on the part of the consumer to mitigate damage and participate actively in preventing financial or economic harm. It appears this line of inquiry will continue to be debated and litigated for years to come.

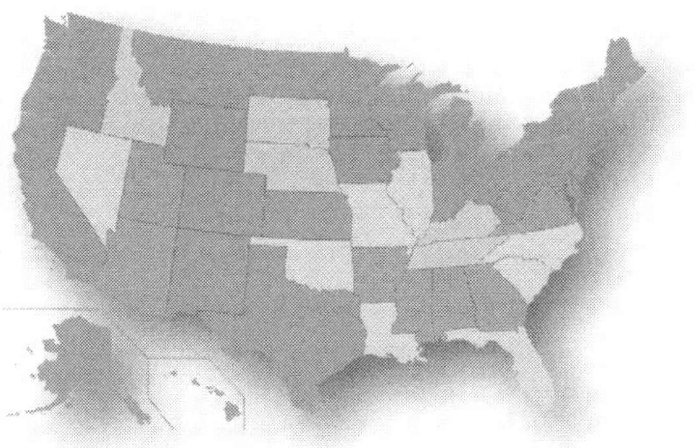

Cooperation or Preemption on the Federal Level

For some time, there has been consideration of enactment of an omnibus federal breach notification law. While there are several industry-specific notification requirements at the federal level, such as financial institutions and health care records, there has not been any consensus on the enactment of an umbrella requirement.

Arguments both for and against such action at the national level have been advanced by interested parties. It is beyond the scope of this course material to delve deeply into the debate, but it is safe to observe the discussion of a companion or preemptive federal law will not soon be abandoned.

Before leaving the subject, there is one area of overlap that appears to be working well in cooperation between national and State agencies.

The HIPAA Breach Notification Rule requires covered entities and their business associates to notify the Secretary, individuals, and in some cases, the media, regarding breaches of unsecured (unencrypted) protected health information (PHI). Compliance with the standards was required as of September 23, 2009.

The Health Information Technology for Clinical and Economic Health (HITECH) Act, part of the American Recovery and Reinvestment Act of 2009, gave State Attorneys General the authority to bring civil actions on behalf of state residents for violations of the HIPAA Privacy and Security Rules. The HITECH Act permits State Attorneys General to obtain damages on behalf of state residents or to enjoin further violations of the HIPAA Privacy and Security Rules. [90]

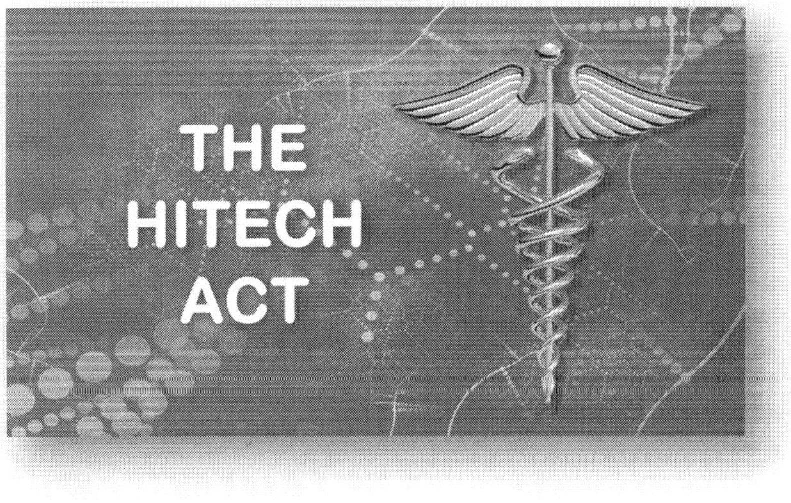

7 Preventive and Remedial Steps for Consumers

SECTION OVERVIEW

The personally identifiable information (PII) most subject to misuse is generally in the possession of either consumers or third parties with responsibilities to prevent it falling into the hands of identity thieves. This section draws on a broad variety of sources to present actions consumers can take to reduce the risk of becoming victims of identity theft. The first sub-section includes steps to avoid compromise of documentary and digital information within the control of the consumer, as well as ways to reduce the proliferation and sharing of information held by others. The second sub-section provides a detailed step-by-step guide for the consumer who has become a victim of identity theft.

The Risk Management Mindset

Creating awareness of the threat of identity theft is a basic technique in responding to the challenge of this growing phenomenon. Although it is by no means recommended we become a nation of fearful people, the ability to recognize and take appropriate steps to deal with a known threat is only prudent. It often happens that a longstanding habit may just need a minor adjustment in order to frustrate identity thieves.

CASE IN POINT

What's in the family car? If a criminal were to get into a car parked in an unprotected location, and search inside, several items of interest would be found. First, the registration and insurance papers, listing the name and address of the owner, are usually readily available. In many cars, there is also a garage door opener. The combination of those items tell the thief where to go and provide access to the inside of the garage. It is a common practice to leave the door between the garage and the inside of the home (usually a utility room) unlocked – after all, the garage is locked. Now the thief has full access to the home and its contents, including financial records and other sensitive personal information.

The vulnerability of any one of these elements can be protected with a minimum of effort. A copy of the registration papers can be made with the address obscured (though it would be wise for the driver to carry a full copy). The remote control for the garage can be removed from the car when it's parked away from home or outside the garage. The connecting door between the garage and the main house can be locked when everyone is away.

The point here is not necessarily to take these specific actions, but mostly to make consumers aware of these kinds of vulnerabilities, and to help them make mindful decisions on security in the context of Identity Theft Risk Management.

The Security-Convenience Spectrum

Consumers manage their sensitive personal information within a pattern that reflects the value they place on security and convenience. This spectrum has been observed and commented on as a means of drawing attention to the importance of making informed choices about how best to manage sensitive information.

At one end of the spectrum is security; a system that is 100% secure would employ numerous verification techniques to make it very difficult for an unauthorized person to gain access to the information. Examples would be authentication using various devices, such as facial recognition, fingerprints, and tokens. But multiple layers of authentications to reach 100% invulnerability would be so inconvenient as to make the system virtually unusable.

At the other end of the spectrum is convenience; in contrast, a system that is 100% convenient would be so insecure as to make it impractical to use. An example would be use of a single simple password for all accounts, one that never changes – easy to remember, but very vulnerable to identity thieves.

Typically, consumers are busy with other priorities and fail to educate themselves sufficiently to make informed decisions. Only popular knowledge of the growing trend in reported identity theft incidents can encourage them to choose where they want to place themselves along this spectrum – and then to live with the consequences.

As the old nostrum goes "To not decide is to decide." By the time a consumer has learned of a disruptive identity theft incident, it will likely be too late to take preventive steps. Still, the study and discussion of remedial actions can help prepare them for this eventuality.

An important objective of this course is to prepare the CITRMS® XV professional to assist consumers in making conscious choices in evaluating where they choose to be along this spectrum.

The following discussion of recommended preventive actions should be considered as a jumping-off point, illustrating the basic steps consumers can take to avoid becoming victims of identity theft. Acknowledged risk management techniques will always be subject to innovative attempts by identity thieves to overcome them and get access to sensitive personal information. Some of them may seem "old hat," but they still serve at least two functions:

- Directly confront known identity theft techniques
- Help consumers keep vigilant and maintain good identity theft prevention practices

Physical Documents in Consumer's Possession

Physical documents subject to identity theft misuse include any means of identification or financial access carried or stored by the consumer. Common examples carried by the consumer would be the driver license, insurance cards, Social Security card, and credit cards. In general, the fewer cards the consumer carries, the lesser the chance of information compromise resulting in an identity theft incident.

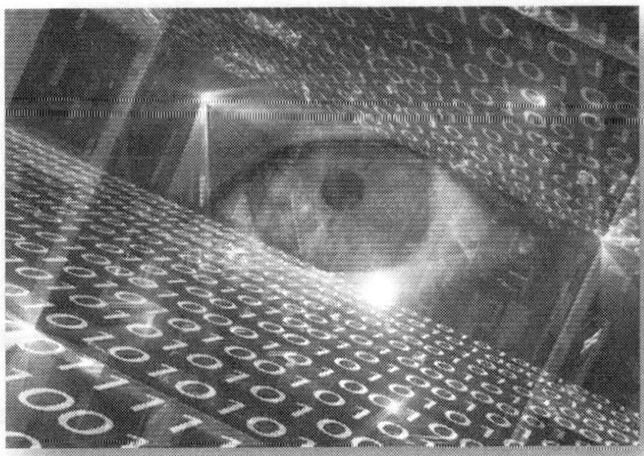

Some means of identification need not be carried at all, unless there is a specific use intended requiring physical demonstration of the particular means of identification. License and registration as well as proof of insurance are common items required in interactions with law enforcement. Many merchants ask to see picture identification in order to complete a credit or debit transaction. But the FTC recommends keeping the Social Security card in a secure place, not on the person of the consumer, as it is seldom required to be produced, and various versions of the card even carry the legends "Not for Identification," "Keep card in a safe place to prevent loss or theft," and "Do Not Carry It With You." [91]

It's been said with a fair degree of accuracy "Old habits die hard." It often seems easier to keep financial records, like paid bills, bank and insurance statements, credit card receipts, and other documents with sensitive information long past the time they need to be kept for tax or other purposes. That's why many people find themselves with boxes and boxes of such records, and no plan to dispose of them safely. Although it's not the job of CITRMS® XV professionals to give advice on how long to keep these documents, raising the consumer's consciousness about their vulnerability and appropriate disposal is an important aspect of effective counseling.

Even before considering ways to keep or dispose of physical records, attention should be paid to alternatives minimizing their creation and receipt. Paperless statements are an important way to reduce the chances of becoming a victim of identity theft. However, it should also be noted this option necessitates heightened awareness of vulnerabilities based on internet security issues and other means of direct contact.

Physical records with sensitive information should be kept in a secure place, not accessible to casual visitors or people who come to provide services at the consumer's home or place of business. Documents with no expected value for confirming payments or other financial or tax purposes should be disposed of promptly and safely, using a cross-cut shredder or other device making it difficult if not impossible for the papers to be re-assembled.

Periodically, outdated records should be disposed of in bulk. This task may be require more capability than a home-based shredder can provide. In some areas, burning in a safely-designed "burn barrel" may be a suitable means of secure destruction, though a burn permit may be required in many jurisdictions. That leaves commercial services as the next alternative.

Over the past several years, "shred-a-thons" have become commonplace. These events are usually sponsored by a local financial institution as a community service, with the participation of a mobile shredding service. They are usually well-advertised in local media, and publish the terms of service, including the maximum number of standard boxes per person, and any charges for additional boxes to be destroyed. Professionals who represent Identity Theft Risk Management services often attend these events for marketing purposes.

Document shredding companies serve most communities. These services often have central locations where consumers may deliver their documents to be shredded. Many have mobile shredding facilities, with large-capacity shredders installed on trucks. In either case, the pricing is competitive and the consumer is provided with a receipt describing the destroyed documents.

CITRMS® XV professionals may also take the initiative to set up a "shred-a-thon" for a neighborhood or community, either through a local sponsor or directly with the shredding company. Such an event may also serve as an educational opportunity to brief consumers on this and other ways to manage the risk of identity theft.

Keeping Up to Date on Consumer Records

The Federal Trade Commission advises the consumer to stay on top of financial statements as a good way to verify any charges as well as catch potential identity theft at the earliest possible moment. If something appears that shouldn't be there, contact the financial institution right away. It is important to determine promptly whether the problem is an identity theft incident or simply an error. In either case, there can be a substantial impact on the consumer's credit history and credit score.

The Consumer Financial Protection Bureau mentions several common indications of potential identity theft, including the following illustrations:

- Bills that do not arrive as expected
- Unexpected credit cards or account statements
- Denials of credit for no apparent reason (e.g., for credit you did not apply for)

- Calls or letters about purchases you did not make
- Charges on your financial statements that you don't recognize
- Incorrect information on your credit reports - accounts or addresses you don't recognize or information that is inaccurate

SOURCE [92]

Credit or Security Freezes and Fraud Alerts

These actions can be taken by consumers to protect against identity thieves getting access to or misusing the information in their credit reports. The two are quite different in application and effect. The choice of placing a security freeze or fraud alert should be made with a full understanding of the cost, potential inconvenience, and effectiveness of each step in advance. Note also there is a special provision for active duty military personnel using the credit freeze.

Credit or Security Freeze

The credit freeze or security freeze is a service of the credit reporting agencies. The main reason to impose a security freeze is to restrict access to the individual's credit report. Only companies with which the consumer already has relationships will have access to the individuals' credit report. This exception is to provide for certain types of account review, collection, fraud control or similar activities.

In effect, with the freeze in place, no one can receive the credit report, so no new application for credit can be evaluated using the credit report. The result is no new account or financial services will be opened in the name of the consumer who has instituted this freeze until the freeze is removed or "lifted." It may also interfere with applications for employment or housing rentals, or other situations in which the party receiving the application relies upon a credit report.

The cost to impose a freeze is set by each of the three main credit reporting agencies, or by State law in many cases. There is usually a separate charge to remove the freeze. In either case, this service is often provided at no cost for individuals over the age of 65 or who have been victims of identity theft, depending on the State in which they live. At the time of this writing, the cost to impose or lift a credit freeze may range from a low of about $3.00 to a high of about $20.00.

The consumer can impose the security freeze almost immediately upon request. The credit reporting agencies advise removing the freeze a few days before the consumer expects to apply for new credit or other action where the party involved would require a credit report, as the time to remove the freeze may not be immediate. The removal of a security freeze may be arranged to allow only a specified company or individual to gain access to the credit report for a limited period, or to have it removed entirely.
Upon requesting the freeze, the consumer is given a unique personal identification or password to assure secure authentication for future actions, such as temporarily suspending or removing the freeze in the future. In order to authorize such a temporary or permanent removal of the freeze, the consumer must be able to provide sufficient identification for verification purposes, the PIN or password, and a statement of the specific action requested.

If the individual is in a position to not rely on credit report being available for making applications for credit, housing, employment, and other common purposes, a credit freeze is often a good method of forestalling identity thieves in their attempts to gain access to sensitive information. This generally applies most closely to older people, who benefit more from this protection than any possible inconvenience involved in making these kinds of applications.

Fraud Alert and Extended Fraud Alert

The fraud alert is used when the consumer suspects his identification information has been or could be used fraudulently. The initial fraud alert is kept on the credit report for 90 days, after which it can be renewed for additional 90-day periods.

The fraud alert notifies potential creditors they must take steps to verify the consumer's identity prior to extending credit in his name, to prevent someone else from using the consumer's information without specific consent.

The fraud alert is free to the consumer. The consumer must provide proof of his identity to institute the fraud alert. Then the credit-reporting agency where the fraud alert is filed must notify the other two credit reporting agencies.

Should the consumer wish to remove the fraud alert during a 90-day effective period, it must be done by writing to each of the credit reporting agencies, including appropriate information to authenticate the consumer's identity.

Another benefit is the consumer filing the fraud alert is getting an additional credit report from each of the three credit reporting agencies.

If the consumer is a victim of identity theft and has submitted a copy of a valid identity theft report already filed with a Federal, State or local law enforcement agency, the consumer may request an Extended Fraud Victim Alert, which lasts for 7 years.

Active Duty Military Alert

For those in the military who want to protect their credit while deployed, this fraud alert lasts for one year. This provision was adopted in response to the vulnerability of active duty military personnel due to frequent travel and changes of assigned station. The background is discussed in Section 5.

Provisions for Veterans

Although there is no corresponding fraud alert provision for veterans, it's notable that for every person on active duty there are approximately 15 veterans. In consequence, the Veterans Administration (VA) has implemented the "More Than a Number" program for the benefit of veterans facing credit report and other identity theft issues.

In addition to the online resources posted at www.va.gov/identitytheft/ , the VA provides a toll-free phone Identity Theft Resource Line for veterans at 855-578-5492.

Access to Credit Reports and Other Consumer Reports

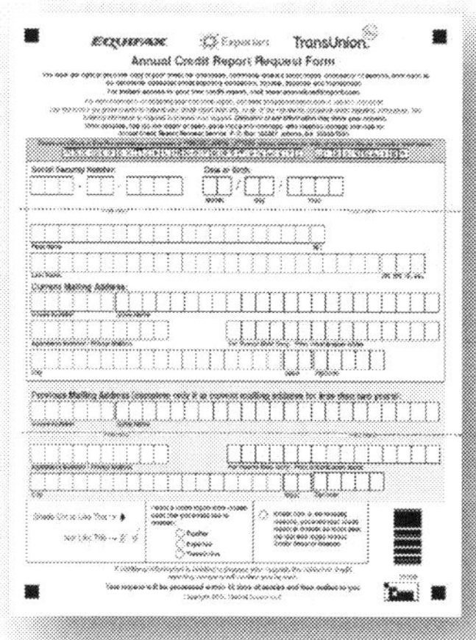

Under the Fair Credit Reporting Act (FCRA), every consumer is entitled to one free credit report per year from each of the three major credit reporting agencies. An appropriate way to keep track of credit report developments is to establish a rolling date to access each of them, getting one report every four months, and checking each for accuracy. The online facility is at the URL: www.annualcreditreport.com [93]

For those without internet access, application for the free credit report can be initiated by phone or mail.

The central toll-free phone number is 1-877-322-8228.
By mail, complete the Annual Credit Report Request Form and mail it to:

Annual Credit Report Request Service,
P.O. Box 105281, Atlanta, GA 30348-5281

A copy of the Annual Credit Report Request Form is included in the ISG Appendix. Note that the form requires substantial information to verify the identity of the applicant, including full name, Social Security number, date of birth, current and past (if at current address for less than two years) mailing addresses.
Do not contact the three nationwide credit-reporting companies individually. They provide free annual credit reports only through this central service.

In a technical sense, there is a difference between the terms "credit report" and "credit file." A credit report is the document provided by the credit-reporting agency to the company that requested it, based on the need to evaluate the consumer's application for credit or other relationship. A credit file is the contents of the credit-reporting agency's collection of information, or file, maintained on the consumer. The two terms are often merged together as "credit report" in regulations, commentary, and other official uses. However, according to the terms of the FCRA, the access rights of the consumer are to the contents of the file held by the credit-reporting agency, not any specific report issued to a requesting party.

In addition to annual access to credit reports, the Fair and Accurate Credit Transaction Act of 2003 (FACTA) specifies other situations in which consumers have the right to get copies of their current credit reports. These rights generally come into play when the consumer receives notice of an adverse action based on a credit report, and include the following:

- Denial of credit
- Denial of employment
- Denial of rental housing or mortgage loan
- Denial of insurance

The consumer has 60 days to request a free credit report from the time of receipt of notice of the adverse action by the company that has denied the application. This notice provides the name, address, and phone number of the credit reporting agency that issued the report. This requirement only applies to the credit reporting agency that issued the report, and the request should be directed to that specific credit reporting agency.
Consumers who are unemployed (and plan to seek employment within 60 days), on welfare, or whose credit reports have errors due to fraud or identity theft are also able to receive a free annual credit report.
Several States had enacted laws providing rights to free credit reports prior to FACTA. Residents of these jurisdictions can receive additional free annual reports: Colorado, Georgia (two each year), Maine, Maryland, Massachusetts, New Jersey, and Vermont. [94]

Credit Scores

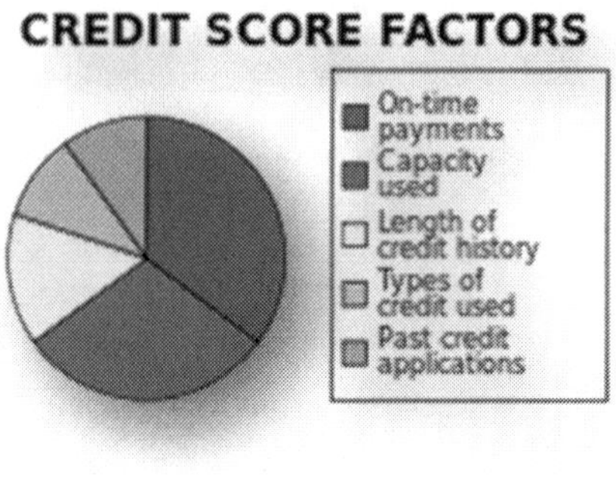

The consumer's credit report and credit score are not the same thing. The credit report includes all the information a credit reporting company has gathered about the consumer's borrowing relationships and payment patterns. Credit reporting companies calculate the credit score by using the information in the credit report to calculate a single number based on their licensed or proprietary credit score formula.
Federal law gives the consumer the right to receive a copy of the credit report from each nationwide credit reporting company every year for free. However, the law does not require the credit reporting companies to provide the credit score for free. Consumers can purchase their credit scores from the credit reporting agencies, usually for a nominal fee. Many financial institutions, such as credit card issuers offer no-fee access to credit scores along with other account benefits.

The credit score is based on the consumer's credit history, such as how much money is currently owed, how long it's been owed, how recently new accounts have been opened, how often the consumer misses or is late with payments, and what type of credit accounts the consumer has. Changes in any of those factors will cause the score to go up or down.

A credit score is a measure of risk. It is calculated using a mathematical formula based on the information in the consumer's credit file, such as timeliness of paying bills in the past, to estimate how reliable bill payment will be in the future.
Credit scores from different credit reporting agencies may not be the same. There are a number of reasons for this:

- Each credit reporting agency uses its own formulas for calculating credit scores. The differences in the formulas may lead to differences in credit scores.

- Credit reporting agencies may produce credit scores that give results on different numerical scales. The low end and high may each differ by 50 points or more.

- Creditors or lender reports don't always report to every credit reporting company. This means that information the credit reporting agencies use for their formulas may differ from credit reporting agency to credit reporting agency.

Most people's different credit scores are very close, despite the different credit reporting agencies calculate their scores using different formulas, and sometimes from different information. If one of the three credit scores is very different from the others, it may be useful to research why.

The credit score estimates how likely the consumer is to pay back loans or services that a lender may extend during the next few years. People with higher credit scores may be more likely to pay back their debts. People with lower credit scores may be less likely to pay their debts. Lenders take bigger risks when they lend money or provide services to people with low credit scores.

Credit reporting agencies can show the consumer's credit report and/or credit score to other companies who have a lawful reason to ask for it. These may include potential lenders. Lenders use credit scores to help decide how risky it will be to lend money or provide a service. Potential employers and landlords may use credit scores to help evaluate the consumer's dependability. [95]

Certified Credit Report Reviewer® - CCRR®
and Certified Credit Scoring Specialist™ - CCSS™
from the Institute of Consumer Financial Education (ICFE)

The ICFE's CCRR® program is the nation's only comprehensive training and certification specifically developed for credit industry professionals who are dedicated to educating and assisting consumers, clients, customers, businesses, and the general public in credit reporting, credit scoring plus how to maintain a good report and high score. With the formation of the Consumer Financial Protection Bureau (CFPB) in 2010, this agency took over the enforcement of the FCRA/FACTA laws from the FTC. This development, among others, led to the course and exam questions being completely updated in 2015.

The ICFE's CCSS™ program is the nation's only comprehensive training and certification specifically developed for credit industry professionals who are dedicated to educating and assisting consumers, clients, customers, businesses, and the general public in credit reporting, credit scoring and how to maintain a high score. With the birth, in 2010, of the Consumer Financial Protection Bureau (CFPB) which took over the enforcement of the FCRA/FACTA laws from the FTC. The CFPB is monitoring credit scoring and examining differences in credit scores purchased by consumers and those purchased by creditors, for example. This CCSS™ program is designed to enlighten participants to the side of credit scoring not often seen by the public. [96]

Specialty Reports

As noted in Section 3, in addition to the credit reports kept by the credit reporting agencies, databases of several other types of consumer information are maintained by other organizations. Consumers may request a free report annually from any of the specialty agencies. As in the case of credit reporting agencies, consumers may also request a free copy of these reports in the event of adverse action taken by a company based on the content of the specialty report. NSCRAs are also subject to the same requirements as credit reporting agencies regarding the restriction of issuance of reports to purposes allowed by the FCRA, and the rights of consumers to dispute any inaccurate information in the files of the agency.

It should be noted the Federal Trade Commission (FTC), responsible for administration of this law, does not publish a list of the companies meeting this definition. However, in 2012 the Consumer Financial Protection Bureau (CFPB) issued a bulletin to nationwide specialty consumer reporting companies clarifying the requirement for them to give consumers an easy way to get a free copy of their specialty reports. This action, under Regulation V, is pursuant to provisions of the Fair Credit Reporting Act (FCRA), as amended.

The bulletin is entitled: "The FCRA's 'streamlined process' requirement for consumers to obtain free annual reports from Nationwide Specialty Consumer Reporting Agencies (NSCRA)." The principal provisions include the following:

- NSCRAs are defined as consumer reporting agencies that compile and maintain files on consumers on a nationwide basis relating to
  (1) Medical records or payments;
  (2) Residential or tenant history;
  (3) Check writing history;
  (4) Employment history; or
  (5) Insurance claims.

- Compliance "expectations" are set out specifically as follows:

  (1) Enable consumers to request annual file disclosures by a toll-free telephone number, which is published and posted on the NSCRA's web site

  (2) Ensure that its streamlined process for obtaining an annual file disclosure has adequate capacity to accept requests from a reasonably anticipated volume of consumers

  (1) (3) Collect only as much personal information from a consumer requesting a disclosure as is reasonably necessary to identify the consumer properly

  (3) Provide clear and easily understandable information and instructions to consumers, including but not limited to: providing information on the status of a request, providing a "help" or "frequently asked questions" page for web-based requests, and providing a statement when the identity of the consumer requesting an annual file disclosure cannot properly be verified and directions on how to complete the request

  (4) Use or disclose personally identifiable information collected from a consumer because of the consumer's request for an annual or other disclosure required by the FCRA from the entity that the consumer made through the streamlined process only in ways permitted by Regulation V, and

  (5) Accept consumer requests for annual file disclosures from consumers who use methods other than the streamlined process or instruct such consumers on how to use the streamlined process.

SOURCE [97]

Accessing Consumer Information from NSCRAs

Following is specific information on how to obtain consumer files from individual NSCRAs. This information should be read in conjunction with the discussion in Section 3, on where sensitive consumer information is held.

(1) Medical records or payments

- MIB Group, Inc. (MIB), formerly the Medical Information Bureau, is a member-owned information exchange. MIB collects and distributes information on medical records, health services, and payments provided to or on behalf of patients by its member organizations.
- MIB has a robust online and telephonic system for consumers to receive copies of their MIB Consumer File. According to the MIB web site:
- Upon verification of your identity, MIB will process your request in a timely fashion and send you your MIB Consumer File by mail. If you do not have an MIB Consumer File, MIB will provide a "no record" letter explaining that a record does not exist. An MIB Consumer File will only exist if the consumer has applied for individually underwritten life or health insurance in the last seven years.
- Consumers may request the MIB Consumer File online through the MIB web site at http://www.mib.com/request_your_record.html or by toll-free telephone at 1-866-692-3901. There is no mail-in form to make this request.

- Records on the use of prescription drugs by consumers are also maintained by two additional NSCRAs, Milliman Intelliscript and Optum 360 (formerly OptumInsight MedPoint), which provide this information to insurance underwriters for evaluation of health care insurance applications. According to the information posted on their respective web sites, they both make reports available to consumers, but in quite different ways.

- Milliman Intelliscript uses the URL www.rxhistories.com for this purpose, as specifically http://www.rxhistories.com/RequestAReport/ for consumers to request their medication history reports. The following is posted on that web page:

- Milliman is not an insurance company and does not have any information about the insurance company's decision. If you are looking for information about your insurance application or the decision made about your insurability, please contact your insurance company or agent.

- Please know that Milliman IntelliScript will have prescription information about you only if you authorized the release of your medical records to an insurance company and that company requested that we gather a report on you. In such case, we will have a copy of that report in our files. Otherwise, we will have no information about you. If you would like a copy of your report please contact us.

- Your privacy is important to us, so please have each individual 18 years of age and older contact us separately to receive his/her report.
  Report request phone number: 877-211-4816
  Milliman IntelliScript email: intelliscriptsupport@milliman.com

- Please be prepared to provide the following information:
  - Full Name (please spell your name if you're leaving a message)
  - Mailing Address (and e-mail address if you'd like to receive your report via e-mail)
  - Phone number (we may call you if we have questions)
  - Date of birth
  - Last four digits of SSN
  - Insurance company to which you applied for insurance

- Optum 360 (formerly OptumInsight MedPoint) delivers its reports to consumers through a separate online facility operated by Ingenix, Inc., a wholly-owned subsidiary of United Health Group, Inc. The following information is posted at the consumer request web site: https://www.annualmedicalreport.com/order-your-medical-report-file-from-medpoint-by-ingenix-inc/

To obtain a copy of your medical report file from Ingenix, Inc., you must call 1-866-692-6901 and begin the request process. However, Ingenix, Inc. does not offer an online source to request, review, or dispute your medical report file contained within the MedPoint prescription profiling database.
THE TWO OPTIONS for obtaining a free annual copy of your medical report file from Ingenix, Inc. are:

1. CALL – To obtain a free copy of your consumer medical report file, U.S. residents may call the Ingenix, Inc. "MedPoint Compliance Line" by telephone at 1-888-206-0335. Please be prepared to provide the following six pieces of information:
   (1) Full Name (First and Last Name),
   (2) Date of Birth,
   (3) Complete Social Security Number (to identify your prescription information),
   (4) Physical Mailing Address (No P.O. Boxes),
   (5) The Name of the Insurance Company to which you applied for insurance,
   (6) Current Telephone Number where you can be reached.

2. MAIL – U.S. residents can request a copy by writing to Ingenix, Inc. at the following address: "MedPoint Compliance, Ingenix, Inc., 2525 Lake Park Blvd, West Valley City Utah 84120."

(2) Residential or tenant history

Unlike the field of medical records, in which the MIB operates as an industry-wide cooperative exchange, the array of services for searching residential and tenant history is very broad and even fragmented. Overlaps with other types of searches, such as background checks, criminal records, and employment history, have resulted in a variety of different approaches to finding and maintaining this consumer information.

The three principal credit reporting agencies, Equifax, Experian, and TransUnion offer tenant screening services. A simple internet search for will return links to many companies offering tenant screening services, though it may not disclose whether they are repositories for the information or only conducting record searches, either through online data bases or physical examination of records. It may also be effective to inquire with the tenant screening services listed in Section 3.

Many of these companies bundle together search and report services for the prospective landlord, employer, lender, or other legitimate users of this information. The pricing reflects the depth and extent of the search and detail of the report. Bulk pricing and purchase of services is usually available for commercial enterprises.

It is advisable for all consumers periodically to request their landlord or lender to furnish them with a copy of their tenant screening reports, regardless of whether they rent or own. In the event someone has stolen the consumer's identity to rent a home or other property, this will show up in the tenant history, and thus alert the consumer to identity theft. It is also likely the identity thief may default on the rent or lease payments; that information would eventually appear in the consumer's credit report. However, the early warning from the tenant screening would give the consumer an advantage in correcting the identity theft incident in a timelier manner.

(3) Check writing history

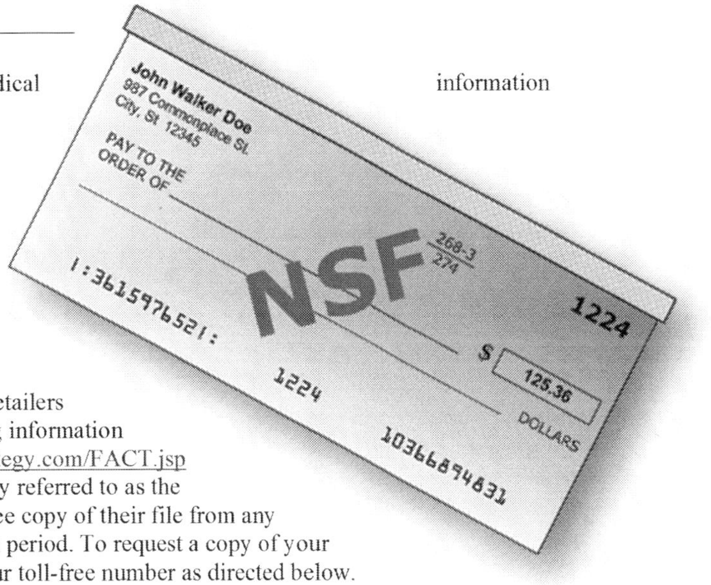

information

In between the patterns of the highly concentrated medical agencies and the diffuse tenant screening services, the principal providers of banking and check writing reports on consumers can be counted on the fingers of one hand. These five companies account for the preponderance of services in this area. While these companies are listed in Section 3, the procedures for obtaining copies of their consumer files appear below.

Certegy Check Services keeps a data base of check writing histories and provides screening services for retailers who accept checks at the point of sale. The following information is posted at the Certegy web site: https://www.askcertegy.com/FACT.jsp
The Fair and Accurate Credit Transactions Act, usually referred to as the FACT Act, gives consumers the ability to request a free copy of their file from any consumer reporting agency once during any 12-month period. To request a copy of your file from Certegy, you can mail your request or call our toll-free number as directed below.
To Request by Phone: 1-866-543-6315

To Request in Writing:
If you prefer, you may mail your request to us rather than using the automated telephone system. If you write to request, you will need to include your name, address, driver's license number, bank routing and account number and Social Security Number. Send the request for your file disclosure to:

Certegy Check Services, Inc.
P.O. Box 30296
Tampa, FL 33630-3296

Shared Check Authorization Network (SCAN) collects a database of returned checks and instances of fraud, to provide check authorization and verification services to member retailers. Although SCAN has become an affiliate of Certegy, its information is still posted at the following web site:
http://www.nobouncedchecks.com/SCAN-check.html

If you are a customer who wrote a check and it was declined by the merchant please visit the website www.askcertegy.com for complete instructions on what to do. If you want to receive a free copy of what is in your Certegy file please call 1-866-740-3276. Please do not call 800-717-1245 or 215-489-7878 as we do not have access to these records. Thank you.

ChexSystems collects and maintains information from member financial institutions. If a bank closes the consumer's checking account because of issuance of checks with insufficient funds, for example, the bank makes a report to ChexSystems; then other banks can check before opening new accounts for the consumer. The following information is posted at the ChexSystems web site

www.consumerdebit.com/consumerinfo/us/en/chexsystems/report/index.htm
You can order a report to learn what information, if any, is listed in your consumer file at ChexSystems. If you have been denied an account from a bank or credit union, and ChexSystems was used in the decision process, this information will help you understand what may have contributed to that decision.

To request your report, please read the following terms and conditions. If you would like to proceed, Click

AGREE below. By clicking AGREE, you confirm that you have read the terms and conditions, that you understand them and that you are in compliance with them.
Terms and Conditions

1. You may order only your own personal ChexSystems report. By clicking AGREE, you certify that you are the person whose report is being requested.
2. You understand that obtaining another person's consumer report is a violation of federal law punishable by fines and imprisonment.
3. YOU AGREE TO PROVIDE YOUR ACCURATE IDENTIFYING INFORMATION AND UNDERSTAND THAT CHEXSYSTEMS MAY ACCESS, STORE, AND USE THIS INFORMATION TO THE EXTENT PERMITTED BY LAW.

If you would like to proceed, please click AGREE. Your consumer report will be sent to you via U.S. mail within five business days. If you do not want to order your ChexSystems report at this time, you may CANCEL now.

Early Warning Services provides real-time verification of high-risk accounts and identifies checks offered to the retailer with a high likelihood of returning unpaid. There does not appear to be a facility for consumers to request report copies online, but the following information is posted at the Early Warning Services web site: http://www.earlywarning.com/consumer-information.html

If you wish to obtain Consumer Report Information, please contact Consumer Services at 1-800-325-7775. *Early Warning's Consumer Services provides interpretation services for over 160 languages.*

TeleCheck, an operating subsidiary of First Data Systems, maintains a database of returned checks and instances of fraud. Telecheck provides check authorization and verification services to member retailers. At the http://www.firstdata.com/telecheck/telecheck-consumer-contacts.html web site, the following instructions appear, as there is no direct online application procedure.
Free annual file disclosure pursuant to the Fair Credit Reporting Act
1-800-366-2425

(4) Employment history

Background screening for employment purposes is generally carried out by companies with individual professionals using a combination of network search facilities and physical record inspections. Although there is no complete listing of such providers, the trade association for these companies and individuals is the National Association of Professional Background Screeners (NAPBS). A current search of the Association's web site – www.napbs.com – and its member directory at https://portal.napbs.com/i4a/member_directory/feResultsListing.cfm?directory_id=9&viewAll=1 shows some 780 entries.

The identity theft application for the consumer in this area is complicated. First, there is no background screening report on an individual unless and until a prospective employer or other similarly qualified party requests one. Prior to requesting a background screening report, the requesting party must give notice to the person being screened, and receive written permission to conduct the background screening. This is important, because it is the first and sometimes the only opportunity the consumer has to learn the name of the firm conducting the screening. Without this knowledge, the consumer has little chance of ever obtaining a copy of the report.

Similar to the requirements for credit reporting agencies, there are consumer rights to receive free copies of reports in the first instance, and additional rights in the event the application for the position is denied. The employer's responsibility to provide a copy of the report only applies if the applicant is not hired or advanced within the company. Otherwise, the free report copy must come from the background screening company, and even then, only if there is a copy on file after the screening is complete. As a result, the consumer is well advised to learn the name of the background screening company at the outset, and request the copy as soon as possible.

In addition to the activities of professional background screeners, there are private databases maintained for reference in specific industries, such as retail. Among the principal providers in this field are the following, with their procedures for consumers to contact them :

National Retail Mutual Association (NRMA) is identified on its web site as a product of General Information Services, Inc. At http://theftdatabase.com/ the following legend appears:

Created in 2004, the National Retail Mutual Association (NRMA) Retail Theft Database is the product of GIS ingenuity and retailer experience, designed to help member retailers combat internal theft in new ways. NRMA states these points:

- Is only open to retailers who contribute to the database as well as use information from it
- Includes retail theft information only – No theft of time, no breaking of company policy
- Has a fully-automated inquiry process
- Offers an exclusive ongoing monitoring program
- Is backed by program management including case management and standard monthly management reports
- It's FCRA compliant, so you can legally use it in a hiring decision.

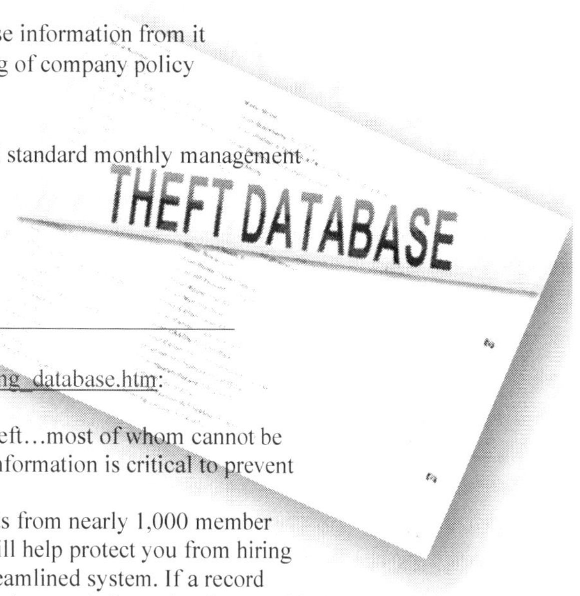

National Theft Database – reports at its web site

http://www.employmentscreeningservices.net/products/retail_theft_shoplifting_database.htm:

The retail theft database contains nearly 45,000 applicants with records of theft…most of whom cannot be found in standard public records because they were never prosecuted. This information is critical to prevent hiring thieves who would otherwise go undetected.
The National Theft Database records shoplifting and employee theft incidents from nearly 1,000 member companies. Checking your applicants against the National Theft Database will help protect you from hiring known thieves. The National Theft Database operates on an efficient and streamlined system. If a record indicates that an applicant has admitted to stealing from a member company, the case information is re-verified before being disseminated.
Most employee theft incidents are never prosecuted, meaning that the information in the National Theft Database is not available anywhere else. It contains exclusive information shared only between members. It is constantly updated with new incidents. Information in the National Theft Database is fully compliant with the FCRA.

First Advantage maintains a retail-oriented data base, which appears to include cases in which employees were accused, but not necessarily prosecuted or convicted, of retail crime, such as shoplifting or employee dishonesty. First Advantage also has a criminal history data base, described at https://my.fadv.com/myadvantage/prodinfo.do as containing over 200 million criminal records.

The First Advantage web sites offer self-check products for consumers, at http://www.fadv.com/Products/Solutions/Consumer-Solutions.aspx . There is also an extensive document posted for consumers to request a copy of a "Consumer Report" pursuant to FCRA at http://www.fadv.com/uploadedFiles/Screening_And_Assessment/I9_EVerify_Solutions/FreeReport_requestforcopyofconsumerreportpacket.pdf

HireRight is described as having developed the industry's first Internet-based background screening solution. This company maintains the proprietary National Theft Database, collecting information on incidents of retail theft and shoplifting. At the HireRight web site for consumers, http://www.hireright.com/applicants , consumers may request a report by following these instructions:

> You may request at any time a free copy of your background reports (if any) previously prepared by HireRight, and/or your active database files (if any) maintained on you by HireRight, by completing and submitting the form below.

NOTE: There is a hyperlink to the form at https://ows01.hireright.com

If you are unable to access or complete the form, if you would prefer to submit your request by telephone, fax or regular mail, or if you require additional assistance, please contact HireRight Customer Service at:

HireRight Customer Service
Telephone: (800) 381-0645 (Monday-Friday, 7am to 7pm Central Time)
Fax: (918) 664-5520
Address:

HireRight
Attn: Consumers Department
14002 E. 21st Street, Suite 1200
Tulsa, OK 74134

NOTE: If the consumer is able to determine at the time of making application to a prospective employer which background screening service is used, it will be easier to contact the specific service to obtain information.

(5) Insurance claims

There are two main companies specializing in reporting on claims the consumer has made on homeowner's or automobile insurance policies. LexisNexis and Verisk Insurance Services.

- Reed Elsevier (now RELX Group)/Lexis-Nexis subsidiary, the former independent company ChoicePoint Request forms and instructions for the consumer's "Full File Disclosure" are posted online at https://personalreports.lexisnexis.com/access_your_full_file_disclosure.jsp . Toll-free telephone requests can also be submitted at 1-888-312-8076 or 1-888-497-0111.

- Verisk Analytics

The free annual "A-Plus" loss history report is available to consumers through the Consumer Report Request Line at 800-627-3487 or online at http://www.verisk.com/underwriting/a-plus-underwriting-verisk-insurance-solutions.html.

Verisk also advises the following:
To dispute information on a claim record or to obtain a copy of an A-PLUS report resulting from an adverse action notice by an insurance company, consumers can call the Consumer Inquiry Center at 1-800-709-8842, option 2. We will send a Request for Disclosure Form for you to complete and return.

Electronic Data and Devices

Section 5 discussed several technological developments in detail; in that context, this section provides information on specific steps consumers can take to manage the risk of electronic devices they use being compromised by identity thieves. The principal points covered are personal computers, internet connections, and smartphones. Since many of the protective steps involved apply to more than one of these points, discussion proceeds from the general to the particular.

In general, any electronic data is subject to interference by identity thieves during any of four main processes: collection, transmission, storage, and distribution. The devices used for these processes have grown more sophisticated and serve many more functions as technology has developed. With a literal explosion in the availability and installation (wittingly or otherwise) of all sorts of applications, the consumer has become more and more vulnerable to the exploits of hackers who gain unauthorized access to a broad array of sensitive personal information.

- Collection of information occurs every time a phone call or message is sent or received, whether over the cell system or internet/wi-fi connection. This information may include meta-data (time and numbers/addresses of the communication and participating individuals), content of the communication (may include user names and passwords), and even automatic updating of contact lists and the personal information of everyone listed as sender or recipient.

- Transmission of sensitive information occurs when data moves from one location to another; "location" may include a hard drive, cell phone internal memory or SD card, e-mail and attachment folder, server, or any other device in the data stream.

- Storage may be on a local hard drive, backup drive, flash drive or other USB device, remote server ("cloud"), or other means of holding electronic data.

- Distribution refers to the process of actively sending data or making it available for remote access; the content of the distribution process may include raw data, documents and attachments, user names and passwords, and other sensitive and personally identifiable information vulnerable to identity theft.

The two devices most used by consumers most vulnerable to identity thieves are the personal computer and the smartphone. Both have available security features in their native operating systems, but they are user options requiring selection in the "settings" menu. Both are used to connect to the internet, so employing good internet practices applies to both. Note that the following internet advice is illustrative, and does not cover every situation, especially in light of new tactics being used nearly every day by identity thieves.

At start-up or resuming from a period of not being used, a lock screen or similar protocol may be used to prevent the computer or phone from being accessed by unauthorized individuals. The lock-out feature may be launched by the consumer directly or set to apply after a specified time period. For instance, the device can be set to go to the lock-out screen after 5 minutes. Different devices have various means to re-open the device, such as a password or drawing a selected pattern on the screen.

Connections to the internet or specific servers may be accessed over the cell system or Wi-Fi for smartphones, and either hard-wired to a modem or over Wi-Fi for a computer. Using Wi-Fi requires a search of available Wi-Fi routers, and they may be open or secured. The device will usually show with an icon whether the Wi-Fi is secured, and which protocol is employed for security. Special care must be taken in connecting with an unsecured network, since other devices may be connected as well, and may be able to access the information and data store on the consumer's device.

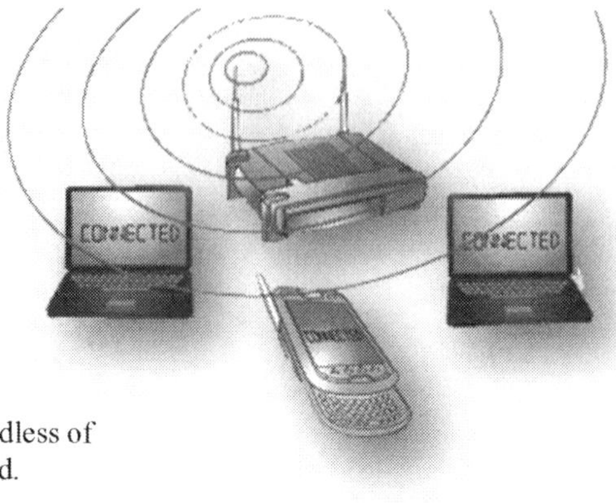

The first time the personal computer or smartphone connects to a secured wi-fi router, the router's password is required to complete the connection. Depending on the settings selected by the owner, the device may "remember" the password and connection requirements, and may even connect automatically when it comes into the operating range of the wi-fi router – regardless of whether the consumer is aware of the connection being completed.

Once connected, the issue becomes protection against unauthorized access to the data stored on the consumer's device and the information transmitted when the consumer carries out internet inquiries or conducts business on the internet. The most vulnerable aspects of this connection tend to be those requiring a sign-on procedure using a user name and password.

When signing into a web site to conduct business or transmit sensitive information, it's important to confirm the connection for transactions is secure. Currently, the "Transport Layer Security" (TLS) or its predecessor, "Secure Sockets Layer" (SSL), are the most common cryptographic protocols designed to provide communications security over a computer network. They are used in conjunction with
When the "Hypertext Transfer Protocol Secure" (HTTPS) the address in the internet browser's address bar will begin with https:// rather than http:// .

It is equally important to be aware that criminals may attempt to clone legitimate web sites and mask the real location's appearance in the address bar; an address that appears to begin with https:// may still be false. For this reason, it is recommended to avoid following links in e-mail messages, even to access a known web site of an organization with which the consumer has a relationship. If the e-mail is used to spoof a real web site, and the consumer logs in with the correct user name and password, the key to the account may just have been given to the identity thieves. Instead, it is recommended to log on by going to the main web site of the company, or a known log-in page, to access accounts or place online purchase orders.

Passwords

The use of passwords and additional means of authentication is a perfect example of making a conscious choice based on the "Security-Convenience Spectrum." A simple, easy to remember password is convenient, but not secure. Complicated (sometimes referred to as "strong") passwords are inconvenient, especially if a unique password is used for each of several, or many, web sites the consumers frequents. There is no single solution to this dilemma, which is the right one for everybody, but the following thoughts are intended to be helpful.

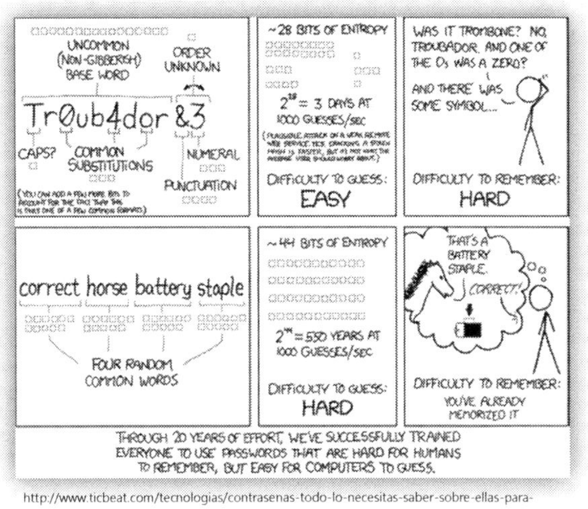

http://www.ticbeat.com/tecnologias/contrasenas-todo-lo-necesitas-saber-sobre-ellas-para-

Many web sites requiring passwords for access now have a utility that evaluates the password entered by the user and reports on its strength; some even show a red, yellow, or green graphic to grade the strength of the password. Many web sites will not accept a password of less than a certain number of characters (usually at least 8), or those without at least one number and one capital letter. Combinations of lower case and capital letters, numbers, and special symbols tend to be the strongest passwords.

Some web sites require "two-factor authentication," often using a second log-in screen asking for a personal identification number (PIN), response to previously established challenge questions, or other means of authenticating identity. At the time of this writing, more technologically advanced methods are used by highly secured servers; examples are finger print readers, facial recognition, and retinal (eye) security scanners, all of which employ additional hardware to interface with the computer. The time may come when these enhanced techniques become more widespread, most likely when the cost of the technology decreases.

Common practices resulting in the use of weak passwords include continuing to use an initial password assigned by the web site, using the word "password" (yes, it's a known habit), or selecting some other easily guessed combination, such as a date of birth, child's name, or other basic personal information. Passwords should be changed periodically. It is also recommended to use different passwords to log into different web sites. Although it is not well publicized, the user name as well as the password can be changed for the log-in on most web sites.

For obvious reasons, storing a list of passwords and their associated web sites or account information presents a vulnerability to identity thieves. Among other concerns, a list stored on a computer or smartphone may be vulnerable to hacking or the insertion of malware, such as keystroke logging programs, even if professional anti-virus programs are installed.

Writing down the list in a single place is also not fully secure, but a single physical list is generally safer than one in digital format. If the consumer is unable or unwilling to commit a long list of user names and passwords to memory, a hand-written list kept in a secure place may be a good solution.

Lost or forgotten passwords present another potential problem. Different web sites use different utilities to re-establish access. Among the more common are challenge questions, e-mail or text communications to provide a new temporary password, and proprietary password recovery tools. Each one of these is controlled by the individual organization or web site, so the consumer will have to be prepared to work with more than one type of utility.

The principal weakness of the use of challenge questions to re-set passwords is the relatively narrow range of questions offered. The answers tend to be information available elsewhere, and common to several locations used for authentication purposes. Information such as mother's maiden name, place of birth, and date of birth are constant, presumably posted in numerous other public or online records, and thus subject to the predations of identity thieves.

One response to the problem of secure storage of passwords is the creation of online utilities usually referred to as "password vaults." The intention is to allow the consumer to set up a single point of entry on the internet, and utilize that secure connection to access the web sites desired to conduct transactions. Such services employ encrypted data storage to foil identity thieves. However, a reported successful hack of a leading password vault service calls into question the efficacy of this kind of facility. [98]

It is not clear at this time what damage was done, but the discovery of the intrusion by hackers did result in users of this password vault facility to re-set their own master passwords and potentially require them to change the underlying passwords in the "vault." The cited blog from the company is updated from time to time, for the information of their existing and prospective users. The ICFE does not make any recommendation on the use of this or other password vault facilities, only that the CITRMS ® XV professional assist consumers in making informed choices.

Personal Computers

The consumer's own computer, whether it be a desktop system, laptop, notebook, tablet, or other computing device, contains a trove of data of interest to identity thieves. Section 4 elaborates on the ways in which these criminals operate to obtain this sensitive information. Here, the discussion centers on steps consumers can take to address this risk.

The most obvious action is to avoid letting identity thieves gain physical access to the device. Such access may involve stealing the computer itself or connecting a storage device, such as a flash drive or external hard drive to the computer to copy the stored information. The computer should be protected the same as any other item of value.

Other than a physical attack, the major threat to personal computers is from remote access. Hackers have developed many methods of accomplishing this. The principal ones are discussed in Section 4. From the risk management side, consumers can take several steps. The following are illustrative, not exhaustive, and the choice will depend on the degree of active participation the consumer wishes to take, and the risk the consumer is willing to assume.

Several national companies offer anti-virus software programs. They range in coverage from "complete" to "custom" protections. The most complete offerings include all-in-one features including internet scanning, detailed protection against known virus programs, near-constant updates of developing hacker exploits, and remote "fixes" for problems that may arise in the event a malware program is successfully launched. Those with fewer protective features, and lower costs, concentrate on solutions based on the expected behavior of the consumer, such as frequency and depth of internet usage, whether or not the consumer uses online financial services, and other features like automated backup to remote servers or external hardware. One thing these anti-virus programs have in common: they require a periodic (usually annual) subscription payment to keep the program updated to include all known threats.

Specific actions consumers can take to lessen the risk of computer-based identity theft also cover a wide range, and are dependent on the consumer's choices of whether to rely on third parties for support or to undertake such actions directly. The following are among the most widely recommended protective actions.

- Install and maintain firewalls and anti-virus software
- Update the computer's operating system and programs with the all the latest patches
- Launch anti-virus software regularly to scan the computer for any malware
- Watch for suspicious emails that may be phishing scams
- Be aware that connecting through an open wi-fi network, whether at home or a public place, may place the computer at risk of allowing others to access the hard drive
- Be careful about clicking on unknown links in e-mails or on web sites, and about downloading any suspicious material
- After logging on to a password-protected web site, close the browser; it is also recommended to clear the browser program's cache periodically to purge it of sensitive information that may be accessible to others
- Anyone else who uses the computer should understand these security procedures
- When the computer is replaced or sold, be sure to remove the hard drive or have a professional service delete all data; note that simply "deleting" the data from the hard drive may not effectively remove it to make it completely inaccessible (it may only delete the file names or locations)

Smartphone Security

Smartphones are discussed in detail in Section 5. The following suggestions on preventing identity thieves and other criminals from stealing information stored on or transmitted by smartphones should be considered a starting point. There is no doubt that development of new means of hacking into smartphones will continue.

- Smartphones are relatively small and easily misplaced or stolen. It's important to be aware of the phone's location and people who may be tempted to pick it up and walk away.

- "Shoulder surfing" can happen as easily with a smartphone as with an ATM. In public places, be careful in entering passcodes to open the phone or access passworded web sites. It is simple for someone nearby to record keystrokes, with the camera in another phone.
- In the "Settings" menu on the phone, it should be set to lock automatically after a short period of time or by setting a convenience button to do so. This not only prevents unintended outgoing calls ("butt-dialing"), but also prevents unauthorized use if the phone falls into someone else's hands.
- Be aware unsecured or public wi-fi connections may allow scammers to access data on smartphones. There are several ways they can accomplish this illicit access. Phone settings should be selected to connect only with networks trusted by the user.
- Keep all installed software updated, since patches for security flaws are usually included in software updates. Failure to maintain current versions of applications can leave the phone and its data contents vulnerable to identity thieves.
- GPS or other location applications may have positive or negative effects on security. On one hand, activating a location application may allow criminals to track the user's absence from home or office. On the other hand, if the device is lost or stolen, the location application may assist finding and retrieving it. Here, the suggested solution is to decide the value to the user of enabling the GPS or other location application, and turn it on when needed.
- In the event the phone is lost or stolen, the first notification should go to the cell phone service provider. If it's stolen, the police should be notified immediately as well. Notifying the provider will enable them to track the phone if it's being used through the cell system, or disable it entirely. In any case, the physical SIM card can be replaced if a new phone is required, and some of the stored information may be retrievable.

A current report on the Android operating system indicates a serious vulnerability exists in the Multimedia Messaging System (MMS). Until this has been patched, caution is advised in using MMS on Android phones. [99]

It is possible for malware to affect the phone even if the message or its attachment is automatically downloaded. One way to protect against this occurring is to turn off the auto-download or auto-retrieval feature on the phone's messaging application. This option is generally located in the Settings menu of the messaging application, and can be accessed from within each application. If you more than one application is installed on the phone, they should all be changed to disable automatic downloads.

This note is based in part on a news story appearing in the Arizona Republic:
http://www.azcentral.com/story/money/business/tech/2015/07/29/precautions-can-enhance-security-android-phone-users/30857359/

Consumer Actions to Minimize the Risk of Medical Identity Theft

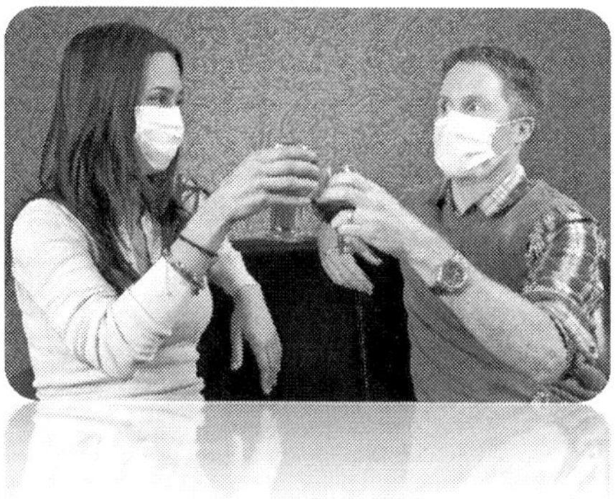

As discussed in more detail in Section 5, medical identity theft is among the fastest-growing types, due to the high cost of medical services and the corresponding high value of identity theft-prone personal health information.

There are several actions consumers can take to help prevent identity thieves from gaining access toand misusing their protected health information (PHI). Among the most effective and routine to conduct are the following, which should be considered exemplary but not exhaustive.

- Conduct a regular review of insurance statements, especially a statement of the annual health benefits paid for the consumer and family, to check for unauthorized or erroneous charges
- Review a copy of the electronic medical file, from the principal health care provider, primary attending physician, or hospital serving the consumer
- As part of the review of the credit report, check on any medical charges and payments
- Be sure the insurance card is kept in a safe place and only presented as required when checking in for medical services

As there have been numerous data breaches of medical records, both from health service providers and insurance carriers, it is imperative that any consumer notified of such a breach take prompt action to register with the identity theft service provider offered by the organization that suffered the data breach. Even if the consumer's information has been involved in more than one such breach, it is preferable to participate in overlapping identity theft service programs than to accept the possibility of a missed indication of misuse of the consumer's PHI.

Minimizing Vulnerable Information Held by Others

The proliferation of personally identifiable information (PII), the raw material of identity theft schemes, held by a broad array of businesses, government agencies, non-governmental organizations, and many others with relationships with the consumer is well known.

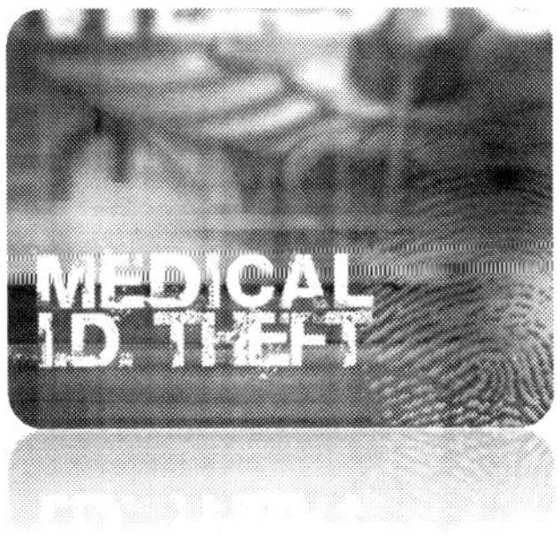

The magnitude and frequency of reported data breach incidents have increased exponentially in recent years. It is not uncommon for an individual to receive notifications from multiple organizations regarding the compromise of the confidentiality of the consumer's PII.

In the life of any given consumer, there are likely dozens of organizations with extensive identity theft-related information on file, in either hard copy or electronic format. Individually, or in combination, the data in these locations increase the vulnerability of the consumer to identity thieves.

It's important to recognize with some of these holders of PII, the horse is already out of the barn, and closing the barn door may be futile. However, that is not to abandon without further action restricting the collection and sharing of sensitive information on an unlimited basis. There are steps the informed consumer can take to restrict this proliferation. In so doing, the result may be avoiding situations in which third parties, with which the consumer has no direct relationship and which may have little or no duty to protect elements of the consumer's PII, have access to this information.

The following discussion lists the principal ways consumers can effectively minimize the spread of sensitive information. It is axiomatic that the less information the consumer allows to be collected, shared, maintained, or distributed, the lower the likelihood such information can be misappropriated by identity thieves.

There are two main ways a consumer can approach this exercise:

1. search out and take action to limit every known holder of PII;
2. methodically respond to communications (usually postal or e-mail) inviting the consumer to accept an offer of a service or product. There are advantages and disadvantages to each, and it may well be that a combination may be the best choice for many consumers.

The pro-active option (1) would be to set up a practice of reviewing all correspondence on file as well as current incoming offers. If there is an opt-out phone number or address for a response, use that contact information to make the request. The consumer may wish to keep a record of the companies and dates of the calls, in case the requested action is not taken, as a basis for filing a complaint with the appropriate government agency.

Examples of this kind of solicitation include, among others, the following:

- Pre-approved credit card or lending offers
- Convenience checks from existing credit card accounts
- Mortgage re-finance offers
- Credit repair or student loan modification assistance
- Reverse mortgages
- Insurance coverage of all types
- Phone solicitations

The opt-out arrangements are simpler with companies with which the consumer already has a relationship, such as a financial institution or credit card issuer. Under provisions of the Gramm-Leach-Bliley Law, they are required to provide periodic notices and opt-out instructions for consumers to restrict their sharing of information. In most cases, the contact information will also serve as a contact point for requests to cease sending pre-approved credit or convenience check offers.

Special consideration should be given regarding unsolicited communications from parties not known by the consumer. Responding to junk e-mails may result in the consumer's address being added to other lists, and actually increase the volume of spam arriving by e-mail. As mentioned elsewhere, care must be taken before opening any attachment or clicking on any link in e-mails from unknown senders, as they may launch malware attacks on the consumer's computer.

The first line of defense against unsolicited phone calls is to list the phone number on the National "Do Not Call" Registry, administered by the Federal Trade Commission (FTC). Online registration may be accomplished through the FTC's web site at https://www.ftc.gov/do-not-call or calling 1-888-382-1222 from the phone to be registered.

Unfortunately, criminals do not adhere to the Do Not Call requirements. One way to deal with unwanted phone calls appearing to be from the same number is available on many smartphones: the unwanted number can be added to the phone's "Reject List," effectively blocking the call from ringing on the consumer's phone. [100]
The FTC also offers this reminder: It's important to remember to not give out your personal or financial information over the telephone or Internet unless you're 100% confident to whom you're talking.

The second option may be referred to as "reactive," in that the consumer is reacting to incoming communications only, and only takes action when an unwanted communication is received. The consumer takes the same actions, but they only take effect on a prospective basis, and there may be long delays before the unwanted communications cease.

Well-informed consumers will likely choose a combination of the two approaches: use each offer or inquiry as a reminder to request to be removed from the solicitation list; and take further action as necessary to limit the number and kind of solicitations they receive.

One such action would be to contact the Direct Marketing Association (DMA), with a request to be deleted from the mailing lists maintained by the Association's members. This request can be made directly with the DMA through its online facility at https://www.dmachoice.org/ or the listed phone number: 212-768-7277, ext. 1888.

Some Thoughts on Consumer Responsibilities

In both the legal sense and in practical terms, the responsibilities of the consumer should be seen as a matter of individual choice, mainly choice about how much risk the consumer is willing to accept as opposed to how much effort the consumer is willing to expend to avoid becoming an identity theft victim.

Currently, there are developments in legislative, regulatory, and judicial arenas which will ultimately impact the consumer and the decisions to be made about risk assumed versus effort undertaken. Some of these developments insulate the consumer from the adverse effects of an identity theft incident – whether it be unauthorized use of a credit card or data breach involving the consumer's sensitive personal information.

To some degree, consumers have become lax in their protective practices. An example would be allowing a credit card to be taken out of the cardholder's presence, where it may be subject to skimming or cloning. Most consumers using credit cards are aware of the federal law protecting them from liability for more than $50 for unauthorized charges – and even that nearly every card issuer absorbs such losses rather than attempting to collect from the cardholder. But the consumer may adversely affect that protection if the card issuer sends a fraud alert (usually in the form of a text message to the phone listed on the account for the cardholder) and the cardholder fails to respond.

Another example is based on the recommendation of the Federal Trade Commission (FTC) to have checks sent to a post office box, or picking them up at the bank, rather than having the new checks mailed to the consumer's home. This option does reduce the risk of loss for both the bank and the customer through identity theft and misuse of the checks. Even though ultimately the bank may bear any loss due to impostors using the stolen checks, there will still be inconvenience and potentially loss of access to the missing funds to the account holder.

In the case of a data breach in which many consumers have received notice from the breached organization, where a credit monitoring and identity recovery service is provided at no charge to the consumer, it takes a positive action on the part of the consumer to register with the service provider in order to be covered by the benefit. It is not clear whether any consequent damage to the consumer is the liability of the breached company if the consumer fails to register for the service offered.

There is also an issue of whether a consumer whose personally identifiable information (PII) has been compromised in a data breach must demonstrate financial harm in order to recover money damages from the breached organization. In order to receive any potential recovery, it is imperative for the consumer to register for the credit monitoring and recovery service offered by the breached organization to mitigate damage from the data breach.

For the CITRMS® XV professional, these considerations should be an important aspect of counseling consumers in how best to minimize the risk of damage resulting from any aspect of identity theft or the compromise of confidentiality of sensitive information.

From Prevention to Recovery

Not all credit report or specialty report errors are the result of identity theft incidents. The cause may be human error, a typographical mistake, or some other accidental occurrence. The problem may come from a source outside the credit reporting agency, such as a payment inaccurately posted to a credit card or mortgage account. Not all situations in which criminals have accessed sensitive information illicitly result in any financial harm to the consumer. It helps to know what to look for when an error is discovered or news is received about a data breach that may have involved the consumer's personal information.

At a specific moment in time, the consumer learns there is a problem. It may come to light in many ways. Often, it is an inquiry from a creditor regarding a potentially fraudulent transaction. It may be when the consumer requests a free credit or specialty report and finds some unfamiliar activity. It may arise when a notice of denial of credit or employment or rental application is issued – and comes to the real person, not the one who has attempted to misuse the real person's identifying information. Regardless of how the news is received, there are several questions the affected individual should address in determining what steps to take next.

The Process of Recovery/Restoration/Remediation/Resolution

There are several common terms for restoring the integrity of the consumer's identity. The main ones used by Identity Theft Risk Management professionals are Remediation, Restoration, Resolution, and Recovery. These terms are often used interchangeably, or in conjunction with other phrases. Some of these expressions are "remediation of the problem," "restoration of the integrity of the identity," "resolution of the case," and "recovery of the victim's identity." For our purposes, and to accustom the CITRMS® XV professional to the various terms, no hairs will be split, but the terms will be used as appropriate.

Once the consumer has learned of a potential identity theft incident, the first step is control of possible damage, whether it be financial, medical, criminal impersonation, or of some other type. In most circumstances, the source of the notice will also disclose the nature, delay in discovery, and immediacy of the threat. These elements will guide the consumer in taking the most effective actions.

Warning Signs of Identity Theft

According to the Federal Trade Commission, the following are the most common warning signs that an identity theft has occurred:

- Unexplained withdrawals from a bank account
- Missing bills or other mail
- Merchants refuse to accept checks
- Debt collectors call about unrecognized debts
- Unfamiliar accounts or charges on the credit report
- Medical providers bills for services not received
- Health plan rejects a legitimate medical claim because the records show the benefits limit has been reached or exceeded
- A health plan won't extend coverage because medical records show a condition never before diagnosed
- The IRS sends notification of more than one tax return being filed in the consumer's name, or income from an employer the consumer doesn't work for
- Receipt of notice that sensitive information was compromised by a data breach at a company where the consumer does business or has an account

SOURCE: [101]

Immediate Actions

At the outset of dealing with an identity theft incident, it is important to set up a log or record of all actions taken. The record should include all phone calls and correspondence, especially the names and contact information of all individuals and their organizations, and the results of the communications. This record will help establish the facts and circumstances of the identity theft, and can expedite a resolution as well as supporting any claims of damages.

In each of these situations, the first step to minimize damage is to contact the company or organization where the fraud occurred. Whether it is the credit card issuer or medical insurer or government agency, it is imperative to give notice of the potential problem.

Next, place a fraud alert with each of the three major credit reporting agencies, especially of the apparent incident is financial in nature. In the event the situation involves medical or insurance claims, the medical facility involved as well as the Medical Information Bureau (now MIB Group, Inc.) should be notified. For identity theft involving employment, tenant history, insurance claims, academic records, or other specific data base entries, the appropriate organization listed above in this Section should be notified.

In early 2016, the FTC completely revamped its web site, to make it easier and more efficient for consumers and businesses to report incidents of identity theft at https://www.identitytheft.gov/

Accordingly, as soon as possible after making the two notifications above, the important **third step** for consumers is to get online and follow the FTC's "Report and Recovery" process. In short, this user-friendly facility helps the reporting individual do the following.

- Tell us what happened
- Get a recovery plan
- Put your plan into action

FEDERAL TRADE COMMISSION
IdentityTheft.gov

https://www.identitytheft.gov/

Options are to

- "**Get Started Now**" to create a personal recovery plan immediately or
- **"Browse a Complete List of Possible Recovery Steps"**

Additional information at the newly-launched FTC Identity Theft web site include:

- Know Your Rights
- Sample Letters
- Warning Signs of Identity Theft
- What to Do If Your Info Is Lost or Stolen
- Helpful Contact Info

Finally, in order to insulate against any potential criminal repercussions, the local police department should be contacted. It is not uncommon for a local police department to ask where the identity theft incident took place; this may be a way to deflect the law enforcement action to another jurisdiction. However, in most situations, the local police will take a report and issue a report number. In many cases, this report number, and the fact that the victim did make the report in a timely manner, can make the difference between a prompt resolution and a prolonged process of determining loss and liability.

Lost Wallet or Purse – Identification Documents and Credit Cards

The last option on the FTC's identity theft complaint questionnaire refers to a situation where reporting the incident is not only insufficient, but may give the consumer a false sense of security. In this case, unless the consumer is actually aware of the physical theft of the wallet or purse, the whereabouts and condition of the contents are simply not known.

The consumer is left with the choice of "wait and see," and maybe it will turn up as opposed to "cancel everything" before whoever has it ruins my life.

The cautious but perhaps choice that is more inconvenient is to notify the issuers of each and every piece of identification and financial account or credit card in the lost wallet or purse, have them deactivate the relevant account information and issue a replacement.

Many individuals make it a practice to place every item to be carried with them on a photocopier and keep a copy in a secure place, for precisely this reason.

As mentioned earlier, it's desirable to carry a minimum of cards and other documents. The Social Security card almost never needs to be carried. In the event of a lost wallet or purse, it's clear the fewer items on the consumer's person, the better.

Replacement documents such as the driver license may be easy to replace, though it may be time-consuming and inconvenient. Other important documents should be evaluated as to the necessity of keeping them close or just available at home as needed.

With credit cards, the copy of the reverse side usually has a toll-free number to contact the issuing financial institution. Otherwise, the issuing bank can be contacted using information from the monthly statement or the bank's web site. All credit card companies do maintain facilities to report fraudulent activity, both to support their card-issuing financial institutions and for other services they provide, such as travelers checks and other financial services.

Federal law offers protection if the consumer's credit, ATM, or debit card is lost or stolen. However, the consumer/cardholder is required to report the loss or misuse of the card. If the loss is reported before the card is used, the consumer has no liability for unauthorized use. If the card number and related information are stolen, the cardholder is also not liable for unauthorized use. In most cases, assuming the cardholder is not complicit in the misuse of the card, the card issuer or lender does not attempt to collect even the $50.00 maximum liability specified by law.

In order to assure the most favorable treatment by the card issuer of a lost or stolen card, the consumer should take the following steps:

- Call the card issuer to report the theft or loss of the card, and be sure to get a file or report number and, if possible, a contact name and direct phone number at the time of the call
- Confirm the call by letter or email, including the confirmation and contact information from the initial notification call
- Check online or on the next available card statement for any unrecognized transactions and report any unauthorized transactions to the card issuer immediately

If there is any continuing dispute about liability for unauthorized charges, homeowner's, or renter's insurance coverage may provide for reimbursement of any such losses. It is advisable to review in advance, whether the consumer's policy includes this coverage, and make an informed decision as to whether it is worthwhile to purchase it.

If the Credit Card Company Discovers an Unauthorized Charge before the Cardholder

The issue arises in the context of a lost wallet or purse, or perhaps just another case of credit card skimming. The consumer may know of the misplaced or stolen wallet or purse, but may still be deciding whether to notify the card issuer, when an alert is received on a cell phone by text or voice call, or even e-mail.

Such alerts are more and more common as credit card issuers collect and analyze spending and travel patterns of their cardholders. If the credit card is used in a place not usually frequented by the cardholder, or outside the cardholder's home State, or in an unusually large amount, the card issuer may contact the cardholder to confirm the charge was authorized.

Two concerns are at play here. First, of course, is the cardholder's responsibility to respond to the communication from the card issuer. Although most credit card agreements specify no such requirement on the part of the cardholder, the result of not responding will likely be suspension of the credit line and even rejection of recent legitimate charges.

The other concern is the possibility that the identity thief is pretending to be the card issuer, sending the message to the cardholder, and attempting to prolong the time to run up unauthorized charges.

In either case, it is advisable to contact the card issuer using the official phone number on the card or web site, to help determine whether the card is being misused and to help establish the authenticity of the cardholder's spending and travel patterns.

Medical Identity Theft Victims

Due to the interaction of the provision of health services and the payment arrangements for them, victims of medical identity theft need to protect both medical and financial information.

Illustrative warning signs of medical identity theft include the following notices coming to the attention of the consumer:

- A bill for medical services from a hospital or physician the victim has never visited. Such bills may be in someone else's name, but with the victim's Social Security number.
- A collection agency calls or sends a letter regarding overdue payment on a medical account not belonging to the victim.
- The victim's health insurance carrier sends a letter confirming a change of address when no such change has been made.
- Medical insurance coverage or payment is denied because an identity thief used the benefits.
- Notification from an insurer, hospital, or doctor that a data breach has occurred.
- Unpaid medical accounts appear in the victim's credit report, especially from doctors or hospitals that have never treated the victim. [102]

The adverse consequences of medical identity theft may go beyond corruption of medical or insurance files. Victims have been known to receive the wrong medical treatment, find that their health insurance benefits have been exhausted, and learn they have become uninsurable for both life and health insurance coverage.

Follow-Up Actions

Once the immediate damage control actions have been completed, the consumer can assess the threat of further problems, based on what is known about the identity theft incident. This is the time to consider questions like these:

- How long after the incident occurred was it discovered?
- Are there still opportunities for the identity thieves to misuse the victim's sensitive information?
- What additional misuses or unauthorized uses of the victim's identity might have occurred between the identity theft, the discovery, and the notifications?
- What steps should be taken to cancel and replace account information or other records, in order to complete the process of restoring the victim's identity?
- What further practices should be adopted in order to minimize the risk of identity theft in the future?

How long after the incident occurred was it discovered?

Tracking the passage of time between the identity theft and the discovery of the misuse of the victim's information can help determine whether additional steps should be either taken to protect against the compromise of the personally identifiable information being misused again or accessed by different identity thieves. Finding where the vulnerability occurred and preventing more effects that are adverse is a cornerstone of using experience to avoid repeat episodes.

Are there still opportunities for the identity thieves to misuse the victim's sensitive information?

The longer the delay between the compromise of the victim's sensitive information and the discovery of the identity theft, the more likely that more unauthorized use of the information may be taking place. This is particularly true in situations where the illicit use may be carried out multiple times and by more than one person. Examples would be identity theft to receive medical treatment, or for criminal or employment purposes, where the victim's personally identifiable information may be used in several locations by numerous individuals.

What additional misuses or unauthorized uses of the victim's identity might have occurred between the identity theft, the discovery, and the notifications?

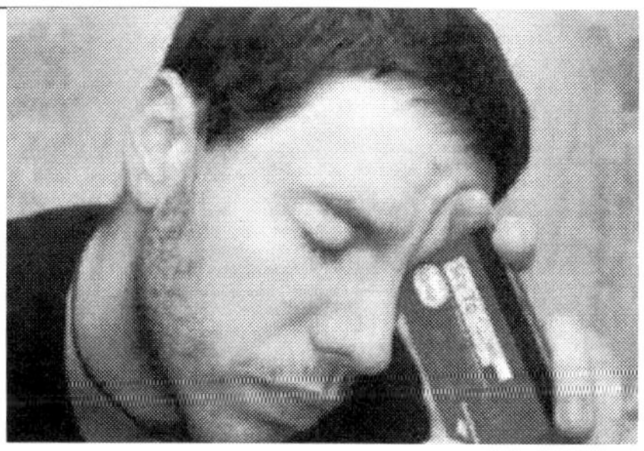

A pro-active search of data bases other than credit reports may disclose other abuses of the victim's personal information. Depending on whether the known identity theft incident appears to go beyond unauthorized use of a credit card, for instance, the cost involved may be justified if it enables the victim to delete erroneous, or even dangerous, information from relevant files on employment, tenant history, medical treatments and payments, and even criminal activities.

What steps should be taken to cancel and replace account information or other records, in order to complete the process of restoring the victim's identity?

It's prudent for someone known to be an identity theft victim to review all the relationships of a financial or business nature, to an extent commensurate with the victim's knowledge of the breadth of the identity theft incident.

Specific accounts that may have been affected are likely to require change in account numbers or other identifying features. A credit card that has been compromised, including the name, number, expiration date, and 3-digit security code, should be replaced immediately. The main inconvenience of such a replacement is making contact with any vendors or accounts with authorization to make charges automatically or periodically, so they won't be rejected when they attempt to charge to prior, closed card account.

What further practices should be adopted in order to minimize the risk of identity theft in the future?

CITRMS® XV professionals are advised to take this opportunity to review with their clients how they can evaluate the circumstances leading to the identity theft incident and decide whether there are additional steps they would like to take in order to prevent a reoccurrence or otherwise make adjustments in their Identity Theft Risk Management practices.

Image source: http://insurancethoughtleadership.com/a-holistic-approach-to-id-protection/ - IDT-Series_Article5_A-Holistic-Approach-to-Identity-Theft-Protection.png

8 Risk Management for Businesses

SECTION OVERVIEW

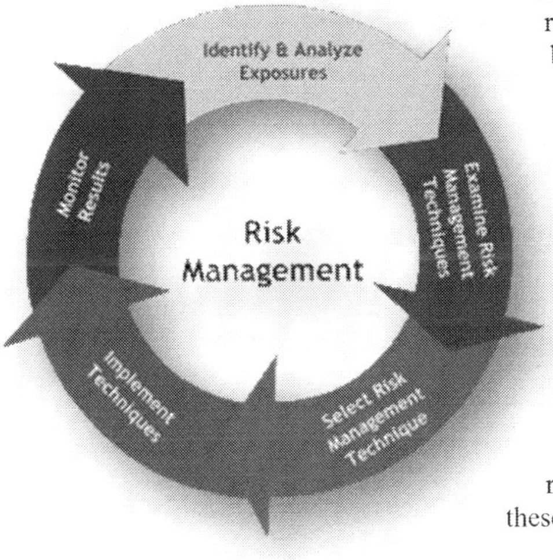

Businesses face two aspects of identity theft: as victims and as parties responsible for the protection of vulnerable data of others against a data breach by identity thieves. Either of these types of loss can be devastating, and it is possible to suffer both types in a single incident. This section identifies numerous risks faced by businesses, provides guidance on reducing these risks, and suggests both remedial actions and ways in which designated risks can be prevented or the consequences shifted to third parties.

Reports of data breaches have become commonplace, with hundreds of new incidents affecting millions of individuals each year. The actions of hackers have captured a great deal of attention in the media, and have effectively brought focus to this specific means of perpetrating identity theft. Bringing attention to data breaches and the preventive and remedial actions to deal with this risk is a positive stroke in the battle against identity theft. More detail on these trends is provided in Sections 2 and 3.

Viewed from another perspective, however, the concentration on data breaches, and the routine ways of responding to this threat, may take away from the less newsworthy activities of identity thieves. One of the objectives of this section is to broaden the ways businesses can strengthen the Identity Theft Risk Management practices of their organizations. Additional elaboration on compliance with the laws and regulations set out in Section 6 will also be covered in this section.

The Business as Identity Theft Victim

A business organization may experience identity theft in several ways. These include misuse of the personal information of the owners and employees of the company, its customers, as well as theft of the identity of the company itself.

Company owners and principals, such as officers and directors, face greater vulnerability than individuals with no such relationships. Accordingly, they are advised to take preventive actions beyond those described in Section 7 for all consumers. In addition to maintaining vigilance over credit reports and specialty data bases, their personal information may be collected and distributed by business credit reporting agencies, such as Dun & Bradstreet, and other publishers of internet-based company information.

There are many official and unofficial web sites with directory listings for businesses. Some of these are subscription services to advertise products and services; others are set up to receive and publish consumer reviews of the businesses. In either case, they can easily become targets of identity thieves. In many cases, this vulnerability is based on the way in which ownership of the business can be claimed by nearly anyone, and contact information such as phone numbers, web sites, and mailing addresses can be posted to lead consumers to the identity thieves rather than the victim company.

CASE IN POINT

– Company Identity

Identity thieves target a company and perform an internet search for the company name. Some of the search results lead to directory web sites with basic information on the company, and also ask "Is this your company?" If the real company has not claimed ownership, the identity thieves may do so. This sets up the possibility of consumers wishing to reach the company actually being directed to the fraudulent points of contact. Upon receiving an inquiry from the unsuspecting consumer, the identity thieves can take orders, receive payments, and otherwise gain access to bank account and credit card information of the consumers, all the while posing as the company whose identity they have stolen. Another adverse effect on the victim company is the negative reports consumers may then post regarding their unsatisfactory experience – even though the victim company was not involved at all.

Protective steps businesses can take to avoid this pattern of identity theft include conducting periodic internet searches for their own name, and the names of their officers and directors. Following the search results, they should review and contact any directory service where the company is listed, to make sure someone else has not claimed ownership.

Be aware these directory services may operate on a subscription basis, asking for payment to post the correct information for the company. Purchase of the directory listing is optional. At a minimum, the company should advise the directory service of the true ownership, and request this information be kept on file against the possibility of an identity theft event. At present, there is no specific law or regulation to require the directory service to comply. However, making a record of the communication could serve in the future as the basis for a claim against the directory service in the event of identity theft against the company.

CASE IN POINT

– Employee Identity Theft

Employees of businesses are also at heightened risk, with potential consequences to the company as well as to the damage they may sustain as a result of identity theft. The employer will no doubt suffer as well as the employee, though this effect may not be immediately recognized. The theft of an employee's identity can be devastating to the employer's business.

http://sarahgerdes.com/fraud-identity-theft-what-happens-in-between/

What are the potential costs to the business? They are not obvious at first. The employer probably won't write anybody a check directly, but there may be hidden costs such as:

- Lost time
- Reduced productivity
- Lower morale
- Deteriorating quality
- And more depending upon the individual business

If the employer does defense or national security work, or other manufacturing that requires employees to have security clearances, identity theft involving a key employee has the potential to be disastrous.

A valuable employee, through no fault of his own, becomes an identity theft victim. At best the victim is only distracted for a little while. At worst he's costing the employer business because of his legal problems, lost time, and deteriorating performance.

Depending on the size of the organization, appropriate actions may range from having a trained individual on staff who can support the affected employee in the event of identity theft, to obtaining coverage from a provider of identity restoration services, or other measures in between.

The important point of this discussion is to be aware and pro-active in taking risk management steps to insulate the business from the adverse effects of employee identity theft. [103]

Beyond theft of the identities of company principals and employees, a growing aspect of this crime is the theft of company's own identity. In this case, the identity thieves obtain sufficient information about the business enterprise to create business documents, web sites, e-mail accounts, and other elements of the victim company's identity to perpetrate crimes against the company and its suppliers and customers.

Although the data breach phenomenon has drawn most attention to large organizations with extensive data bases of personally identifiable information, small companies have also captured the attention of identity thieves. Information about the company itself can often be used more directly in targeted schemes, rather than the more complicated and diverse abuses of the data obtained in data breaches.

There are no reliable statistics to compare identity theft incidents in which customer information, such as credit card specifics or data base contents, may be the object of the crime, as opposed to situations where the scheme is to steal the information of the company itself. However, there are reported cases of using sensitive business information to steal money directly from the company or from third parties by assuming the identity of a customer or supplier of the victim company.

CASE IN POINT

Fraudulent Payment

Company scammed out of $53,900 by impersonator

PRESCOTT, AZ - An employee of a local company fell victim to a fraudulent email scheme and sent $53,900 to a scammer on July 8, according to a police report.

The man, who works for Agility Ventures, LLC, told police he received an email from someone he thought was his supervisor, telling him to wire $15,600 to an account in North Dakota, which he did.

The next day he got another email, directing him to send funds to an account in California, the report said.

That was when he realized the email address was misspelled: it was his supervisor's name, but at "agillityventures.com," with an extra "l."

The employee called police when he was requested to send $38,300 to a California account.

Police tried to stop the second transfer, but it had already gone through.

"We are working to identify where the scam may have originated so we can work with that agency (or) jurisdiction," Prescott Police Lt. Amy Bonney said. [104]

Preventive Steps

Steps businesses can take to prevent this kind of occurrence include the following:

- Adopt policies and procedures for control of payments
    - Include two-party signature requirements on checks for payments over a determined amount
    - Implement a confirmation process for approval of accounts payable
    - Institute a procedure for receipt and deposit of incoming payments
    - Conduct regular employee training sessions on identity theft and other fraud threats
    - CITRMS® XV professionals may wish to conduct training sessions
    - Coordinate with other professionals, such as information technology and security providers
- Integrate these steps in the audit and accounting process
    - Security and identity theft prevention should be an important part of the financial practices of the company
- Develop an incident response plan
    - Evaluate and minimize weaknesses in the control of internal and customer information
    - Utilize available internal resources
    - Supplement internal capability with outside providers of Identity Theft Risk Management and victim remediation services

Unsuspecting consumers are not the only ones vulnerable to schemes using stolen company information. Professionals can also easily become caught up in such identity theft practices.

CASE IN POINT

– Scams Against Third Parties

Company information can also be misused in scams against third parties. One pattern has emerged in which the identity thieves use a combination of victim company identity elements. The criminals send the same e-mail to many attorneys, purporting to be from the victim company. The e-mail claims the company has an account collection matter in the attorney's home state, and requests help. Upon engaging the attorney in a conversation, the identity thieves agree, on behalf of the company, to hire the attorney.
They then send a check to the attorney, apparently in the full amount of the delinquent customer account. The check appears to be on a valid bank account, in a real bank, in the name of the victim company. The identity thieves ask the attorney to deposit the check, keep the agreed-upon amount of the legal fees, and send a check back to them for the balance. The victim attorney only learns of the scam when the bogus check is returned by the bank.

In this scheme, the victim company is not only a tool of the criminals, but also suffers the loss of management time, potential bank fraud implications, and damage to corporate reputation due to the apparent adverse actions of the depository bank and consequent credit report entries.
The author followed an actual case of this type, including communication with the victim business. Apparently, there had been numerous repetitions of the use of victim company account information used by the identity thieves, even though the bank on which the bogus check was drawn had never had a relationship with the company. The company how many, if any, attorneys had actually been takin in by the scheme never established it. It was reported, however, the company had wasted many hours of management time dealing with the bank in question, removal of erroneous credit report entries, and responding to others who had been embroiled in the identity theft scheme.

Steps businesses can take to prevent this kind of occurrence include the following:

- Review all financial account statements promptly, to detect any problems, rather than waiting to learn from a third party, such as the financial institution involved.
- If there is a suspicious transaction, advise the credit card issuer or bank on which bogus check is drawn, to avoid it getting into your credit report
- Maintain regular contact with vendors and customers
- Even if Red Flags Rules, HIPAA, or other regulatory requirements in maintaining sensitive information of consumers do not cover the company, it is a good practice to follow the guidelines listed in Section 6.
- Conduct regular training for staff on identity theft issues

Small Businesses Targeted

One of the reported trends in this area concentrates on the vulnerabilities of small companies with retail operations. A recent article reported hackers are going local in their efforts to steal credit card information from United States customers, hitting small businesses with as much frequency as retail giants. The reported effects include disruption to the business, the extent of unanticipated costs and expenses, and the unwelcome frustration and concern caused upon customers.

Smaller businesses tend to have less sophisticated security defenses and are more vulnerable to hackers seeking to exploit weak spots in the point-of-sale systems used by companies to process credit card payments.
Many small businesses are lulled into thinking they are immune from hacking because they are too small to draw any attention.

Many attacks against small companies go unreported because the businesses are not publicly traded and are bound by fewer disclosure requirements.

Still, half of 675 small businesses surveyed by the National Small Business Association reported being victims of hackers' attacks last year, up from 44 percent in 2013. In addition, of those companies that reported being hacked last year, 68 percent said they had been victimized at least twice. [105]

Technology Issues and Mobility

In addition to the discussion in Section 5 on technological developments, and in Section 7 on individual consumer practices, further commentary on the use by businesses of these and other technological applications is warranted. Examples abound of business use of the convenience of mobile communications facilities, but the vulnerabilities extend beyond the business itself and into the realm of customer information as well.

CASE IN POINT

Mobile apps are becoming big business for businesses.
Many bank customers now check their account balances or transfer funds through an app on their cell phones. Savvy retail shoppers can use a favorite store's apps to learn about discounts, access coupons and find daily deals.

"The apps for financial institutions and retailers are getting greater use and that can be wonderful for business," says Gary Miliefsky, CEO of SnoopWall, a company that specializes in cyber security.

But as with so many things in the cyber world, caveats are connected. Even as companies provide additional services through those apps, they may be putting their customers at risk for fraud.

"Most companies don't realize just how vulnerable their apps are and what the potential is for leaking their customers' personal information," Miliefsky says. "And when that happens, it's bad for business."

He suggests a few reasons why most companies need better protection for their mobile apps:

- New forms of mobile malware are being widely deployed in the major app stores and can eavesdrop on a customer through a company's app. "These new forms of malware are undetected by anti-virus engines and are able to circumvent encryption, authentication, and tokenization," Miliefsky says. "That makes it easy for cyber criminals to exploit the personal information of a company's customers and commit fraud."
- The PCI Data Security Standard requires merchants to protect credit-card holder data. Likewise, mobile-commerce providers must protect any payment card information, whether it is printed, processed, transmitted, or stored, Miliefsky says. "Even though a customer has the breach on their mobile device, the retailer is responsible because it was their app that allowed the eavesdropping," he says. A breach of credit-card information potentially could result in fines for the retailer, Miliefsky says.
- The FDIC requires banks that are providing an ATM-like online or mobile-banking experience, to protect access to the confidential records of the consumer, the consumer's bank account information, user name and password credentials, and bill payment and check-deposit services. Just like with retailers, it doesn't matter that the breach happened on the customer's mobile device, Miliefsky says. The bank's app caused the problem because it allowed the eavesdropping, so "the risk and the responsibility is the bank's not the consumer's, he says. Moreover, as in the case with retailers, banks could face fines for a breach.
- "Businesses have become great at creating useful apps that their customers eventually feel they can't live without," Miliefsky says. "But the failure to secure that app is going to come back to haunt the business over the long haul." [106]

Another affirmative decision for businesses in the use of connectivity is whether to allow employees and others with access to the company's communications facilities to use their own devices or restrict them to using company-issued devices. The concept is generally referred to as "BYOD v. CYOD," meaning, "bring your own device" versus "choose your own device." The choice of device rules must reflect the current and future needs of the company. Due to the rapidly changing field of communications services, and the limited focus of this Identity Theft Risk Management course, no definitive solution is offered. However, a few guidelines are appropriate to include in this discussion.

- Start with an internal evaluation of the current and projected communications needs of the organization
- Incorporate standards and objectives, to support security considerations as well as ease of use by employees
- Consider whether it is more efficient to build in-house capability or to engage outside consultants to design and implement changes to the existing system and plan for future upgrades

- Include employee input in the process, since they are the ones who will be required to use the system and devices and their acceptance is required; consider whether BYOD or CYOD is the right choice for the enterprise
- Develop an implementation plan, including hardware and software choices best suited to these needs, and training for employees in security compliance
- Once the system is in place, conduct periodic reviews to assure the integration of hardware and software and security features are operating as planned

No doubt remains about the continued rapid pace of technological developments in applications for businesses. There will be for the foreseeable future a continuing necessity for business managers to make conscious decisions about the design, implementation, and control over the way they are incorporated into the company's operations. CITRMS® XV professionals are encouraged to stay current on news stories and industry publications on how these developments affect the challenges of and responses to identity theft.

Businesses as Holders of Personally Identifiable Information

This discussion should be studied in conjunction with the description of who holds the information in Section 3, and the law and regulation coverage in Section 6. The CITRMS® XV professional should recognize one size does <u>not</u> fit all in advising on the responsibilities of businesses to maintain the confidentiality of the personally identifiable information (PII) of consumers.
Many businesses are subject to specific requirements under relevant law and regulation to take mandated steps to protect the confidentiality of consumer PII. However, even if a specific business doesn't fall into one of these categories, the consequences of failing to protect this confidentiality can be disastrous to the company. What are some of the adverse effects on a business when it allows protected consumer information to be compromised and the consumers become victims of identity theft as a result? The following list is illustrative, not only because of the practices of identity thieves, but also because of the developing legal standards for what constitutes actionable harm.

Cost of Evaluation of the Loss

The most immediate cost to the business is usually the evaluation of the nature and extent of the compromised sensitive information, including the number of people affected and the specifics of the information itself. Initially, this will involve the time and efforts of internal personnel; in most cases, the next step requires the assistance of trained professionals prepared to address the magnitude of the loss and make recommendations on notification and remediation arrangements.

Cost of Notification and Remediation

Although there are exemptions from the federal and State notification requirements, principally based on the size of the company or the number of people whose personal information has been affected, in almost every case, the company will be required to make notification to those individuals affected. By its nature, the notification needs to inform the affected parties of the loss, the likelihood of the compromise of confidentiality resulting in the adverse effects of identity theft, and the steps taken by the company to offer a remediation service. Depending on the number of people who must be notified, this step can be costly in itself, since current practice is to complete the notification using the U. S. Postal Service.
Unless the company and its advisers are able to determine there is little or no likelihood of further identity theft adverse effects on the individuals whose sensitive information is involved, it is current practice to offer these parties a no-cost remediation service from a specialized provider. There are, at the time of this writing, several major providers of these after-the-fact services. It is a competitive business, both in terms of services and pricing. Nonetheless, the cost of providing this service should be expected to be substantial.

Consumer and Market Reactions

At this point, two occurrences happen in a short time period: affected consumers receive notification of the problem, and media coverage begins. The two can occur in either order, and may even become coordinated as consumer groups and the press often engage in close communication.

In the "micro" perspective, individual consumers may lose confidence in the company, resulting in customer abandonment. This can happen due to concerns over how the identity theft incident happened in the first place, the way the company handled the evaluation and remediation process, or any other aspect of the damage control exercise.

In the "macro" perspective, experience shows these events are subject to positive or negative responses from the press, consumer advocacy groups, and the marketplace. The marketplace in this context includes the way consumers perceive the conduct of the company as well as the potential effects on stock price and enterprise value for public companies.

Other Potential Legal Claims and Liabilities

The following commentary is not intended to offer any legal opinion. However there are currently several economic and judicial initiatives in development, and worthy of mention for purposes of this discussion. Two have been selected as illustrative of the changing landscape in business relationships and responsibility for losses to affected parties.

Liability Shifting from Financial Institutions

To an extensive degree, the cost of compromise of sensitive information occurring in retail settings has tended to fall on financial institutions and other issuers of credit and debit cards. This is due to the federal provisions holding the cardholders liable for a maximum of $50 in the event of an unauthorized charge appearing on the credit card account, as well as the nearly universal practice of the card issuers in absorbing even the $50 maximum, rather than pursuing cardholders for such amounts.

However, card issuers are reported to be re-evaluating the possibility of charging losses back against the retailers failing to protect sensitive consumer payment information. There are two aspects of this trend, one related to point-of-sale authentication and the other to data breaches.

With the adoption of the chip-and-pin technology using the chip embedded in the credit or debit card, card issuers are acting to encourage retailers to upgrade their card information capture systems (both hardware and software) to replace the magnetic strip reader with the more secure chip application. It has been reported Visa, MasterCard, Discover, American Express and their banking partners have set a government-enforced deadline of Oct. 15 for a "liability shift" that, for the first time, would make merchants liable for fraudulent charges that result from using point-of-service readers that can't read chip-and-pin EMV cards.

As similar development is under way in situations where the retailer is the victim of a data breach resulting in unauthorized card transactions. Rather than accept liability for these charges, the card issuers and card systems will analyze the nature and circumstances of the data breach in deciding whether to charge the breached company for the cost of these losses.

Note the greatest burden in the case of data breaches involving credit and debit card losses will likely fall on large retail companies with branded credit cards. In almost all cases, these branded cards use the name and trademarks of the retail company, but are actually issued by a separate financial institution. An example of this relationship would be the Target "Red Card," for which all outward appearances point to Target Credit Services as the corporate entity behind the card. However, the details demonstrate the actual card issuer is TD Bank, an affiliate of the original Toronto Dominion Bank. [107]

Consumer Claims for Financial and Other Damages

Due to the proliferation of incidents of data breaches and other events in which sensitive consumer information is compromised, attention has grown to the economic and other adverse effects suffered by the consumers whose information has been taken by identity thieves. It comes as no surprise for attorneys and other interested parties to initiate legal actions against the responsible companies, whether the problem stems from a data breach or a pattern of retail transactions subject to other identity theft schemes.

In the first instance, such claims have only been successful when the plaintiffs have been able to demonstrate actual financial damage. More recently, theories have been advanced to include non-financial considerations as measures of damages. For our purposes, it is more important to recognize these potential liabilities than to delve into the legal foundations for granting or denying compensation to the affected consumers. Suffice it to observe these developments will continue to occur and will have an increased impact on organizations holding sensitive consumer information.

Risk Management Actions for Businesses

As indicated in earlier discussion, the depth and breadth of protective and preventive actions for businesses reflect to a large extent the size and complexity of the organization. In most situations, there will already be an internal person or team responsible for Identity Theft Risk Management. The person or group may not carry that specific title; other terms, such as fraud, security, or information technology (IT) may be used. In any case, the place to start this exercise is within the business itself, by evaluating the capabilities of the internal resources.

Due care and attention should be given to the "institutional dynamics," which often demonstrate sensitivities about the internal capabilities and need, or lack of need, from outside experts. To be effective, management must initiate the adoption and implementation of Identity Theft Risk Management techniques and receive acceptance from the employees who will be most directly involved.

The following examples of 10 steps the Federal Trade Commission (FTC) suggests for businesses may not be necessary or appropriate for all enterprises, but they do represent a group of commonly applicable risk management techniques. Since these preventive steps are based on FTC's experience with both a broad array of known identity theft incidents and numerous actual compliance and enforcement actions, this guide is reproduced directly from the FTC's web site for businesses, edited to apply most closely to the purposes of this study guide.

1. *Start with security.*

From personal data on employment applications to network files with customers' credit card numbers, sensitive information pervades every part of many companies. Business executives often ask how to manage confidential information. Experts agree on the key first step: Start with security. Factor it into the decision-making in every department of your business – personnel, sales, accounting, information technology, etc. Collecting and maintaining information "just because" is no longer a sound business strategy. Savvy companies think through the implication of their data decisions. By making conscious choices about the kind of information you collect, how long you keep it, and who can access it, you can reduce the risk of a data compromise down the road. Of course, all of those decisions will depend on the nature of your business. Lessons from FTC cases illustrate the benefits of building security in from the start by going lean and mean in your data collection, retention, and use policies.

Don't collect personal information you don't need.

Here's a foundational principle to inform your initial decision-making: No one can steal what you don't have. When does your company ask people for sensitive information? Perhaps when they're registering online or setting up a new account. When was the last time you looked at that process to make sure you really need everything you ask for? That's the lesson to learn from a number of FTC cases. For example, the FTC's complaint in one case charged that the company collected lots of information during the site registration process, including the user's email address and email password. By collecting email passwords – not something the business needed – and then storing them in clear text, the FTC said the company created an unnecessary risk to people's email accounts. The business could have avoided that risk simply by not collecting sensitive information in the first place.

Hold on to information only as long as you have a legitimate business need.

Sometimes it's necessary to collect personal data as part of a transaction. But once the deal is done, it may be unwise to keep it. In another FTC case, the company collected customers' credit and debit card information to process transactions in its retail stores. But according to the complaint, it continued to store that data for up to 30 days – long after the sale was complete. Not only did that violate bank rules, but by holding on to the information without a legitimate business need, the FTC said the company created an unreasonable risk. By exploiting other weaknesses in the company's security practices, hackers stole the account data and used it to make counterfeit credit and debit cards. The business could have limited its risk by securely disposing of the financial information once it no longer had a legitimate need for it.

Don't use personal information when it's not necessary.

You wouldn't juggle with a Ming vase. Nor should businesses use personal information in contexts that create unnecessary risks. In one published case, the FTC alleged that the company used real people's personal information in employee training sessions, and then failed to remove the information from employees' computers after the sessions were over. In another, FTC charged that the company gave access to sensitive consumer data to service providers who were developing applications for the company. In both cases, the risk could have been avoided by using fictitious information for training or development purposes.

2. Control access to data sensibly.

Once you've decided you have a legitimate business need to hold on to sensitive data, take reasonable steps to keep it secure. You'll want to keep it from the prying eyes of outsiders, of course, but what about your own employees? Not everyone on your staff needs unrestricted access to your network and the information stored on it. Put controls in place to make sure employees have access only on a "need to know" basis. For your network, consider steps such as separate user accounts to limit access to the places where personal data is stored or to control who can use particular databases. For paper files, external drives, disks, etc., an access control could be as simple as a locked file cabinet. When thinking about how to control access to sensitive information in your possession, consider these lessons from FTC cases.

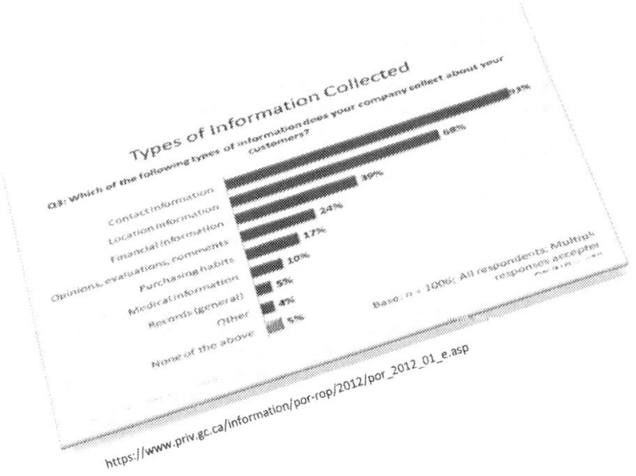

Restrict access to sensitive data.

If employees don't have to use personal information as part of their job, there's no need for them to have access to it. For example, the FTC alleged that one company failed to restrict employee access to personal information stored in paper files and on its network. As a result, a group of employees transferred more than 7,000 consumer files containing sensitive information to third parties without authorization. The company could have prevented that misstep by implementing proper controls and ensuring that only authorized employees with a business need had access to people's personal information.

Limit administrative access.

Administrative access, which allows a user to make system-wide changes to your system, should be limited to the employees tasked to do that job. In its action against a social network, for example, the FTC alleged that the company granted almost all of its employees' administrative control over its system, including the ability to reset user account passwords, view users' nonpublic entries, and send entries on users' behalf. According to the complaint, by providing administrative access to just about everybody in-house, the company increased the risk that a compromise of any of its employees' credentials could result in a serious breach. How could the company have reduced that risk? By ensuring that employees' access to the system's administrative controls was tailored to their job needs.

3. ***Require secure passwords and authentication.***

If you have personal information stored on your network, strong authentication procedures – including sensible password "hygiene" – can help ensure that only authorized individuals can access the data. When developing your company's policies, here are tips to take from FTC cases.

Insist on complex and unique passwords.

"Passwords" like 121212 or qwerty aren't much better than no passwords at all. That's why it's wise to give some thought to the password standards you implement. In another published case, for example, the company let employees use common dictionary words as administrative passwords, as well as passwords they were already using for other accounts. According to the FTC, those lax practices left the company's system vulnerable to hackers who used password-guessing tools, or tried passwords stolen from other services in the hope that employees used the same password to access the company's system. The company could have limited those risks by implementing a more secure password system – for example, by requiring employees to choose complex passwords and training them not to use the same or similar passwords for both business and personal accounts.

Store passwords securely.

Don't make it easy for interlopers to access passwords. The FTC alleged that one company stored network user credentials in clear, readable text that helped a hacker access customer credit card information on the network. Similarly, the FTC charged that another business allowed customers to store user credentials in a vulnerable format in cookies on their computers. The FTC said the company failed to establish policies that prohibited employees from storing administrative passwords in plain text in personal email accounts. In each of those cases, the risks could have been reduced if the companies had policies and procedures in place to store credentials securely. Businesses also may want to consider other protections – two-factor authentication, for example – that can help protect against password compromises.

Guard against brute force attacks.

Remember that adage about an infinite number of monkeys at an infinitive number of typewriters? Hackers use automated programs that perform a similar function. These brute force attacks work by typing endless combinations of characters until hackers luck into someone's password. In several cases, the FTC alleged that the businesses didn't suspend or disable user credentials after a certain number of unsuccessful login attempts. By not adequately restricting the number of tries, the companies placed their networks at risk. Implementing a policy to suspend or disable accounts after repeated login attempts would have helped to eliminate that risk.

Protect against authentication bypass.

Locking the front door doesn't offer much protection if the back door is left open. In one case, the FTC charged that the company failed to adequately test its web application for widely-known security flaws, including one called "predictable resource location." As a result, a hacker could easily predict patterns and manipulate URLs to bypass the web app's authentication screen and gain unauthorized access to the company's databases. The company could have improved the security of its authentication mechanism by testing for common vulnerabilities.

4. Store sensitive personal information securely and protect it during transmission.

For many companies, storing sensitive data is a business necessity. And even if you take appropriate steps to secure your network, sometimes you have to send that data elsewhere. Use strong cryptography to secure confidential material during storage and transmission. The method will depend on the types of information your business collects, how you collect it, and how you process it. Given the nature of your business, some possibilities may include Transport Layer Security/Secure Sockets Layer (TLS/SSL) encryption, data-at-rest encryption, or an iterative cryptographic hash. But regardless of the method, it's only as good as the personnel who implement it. Make sure the people you designate to do that job understand how your company uses sensitive data and have the know-how to determine what's appropriate for each situation. With that in mind, here are a few lessons from FTC cases to consider when securing sensitive information during storage and transmission.

Keep sensitive information secure throughout its lifecycle.

Data doesn't stay in one place. That's why it's important to consider security at all stages, if transmitting information is a necessity for your business. In a reported case, for example, the FTC alleged that the company used SSL encryption to secure the transmission of sensitive personal information between the customer's web browser and the business's website server. But once the information reached the server, the company's service provider decrypted it and emailed it in clear, readable text to the company's headquarters and branch offices. That risk could have been prevented by ensuring the data was secure throughout its lifecycle, and not just during the initial transmission.

Use industry-tested and accepted methods.

When considering what technical standards to follow, keep in mind that experts already may have developed effective standards that can apply to your business. Savvy companies don't start from scratch when it isn't necessary. Instead, they take advantage of that collected wisdom. According to the FTC, one company stored sensitive customer information collected through its e-commerce sites in a database that used a non-standard, proprietary form of encryption. Unlike widely-accepted encryption algorithms that are extensively tested, the complaint charged that the company's method used a simple alphabetic substitution system subject to significant vulnerabilities. The company could have avoided those weaknesses by using tried-and-true industry-tested and accepted methods for securing data.

Ensure proper configuration.

Encryption – even strong methods – won't protect your users if you don't configure it properly. That's one message businesses can take from reported FTC actions where the FTC alleged that the companies used SSL encryption in their mobile apps, but turned off a critical process known as SSL certificate validation without implementing other compensating security measures. That made the apps vulnerable to man-in-the-middle attacks, which could allow hackers to decrypt sensitive information the apps transmitted. Those risks could have been prevented if the companies' implementations of SSL had been properly configured.

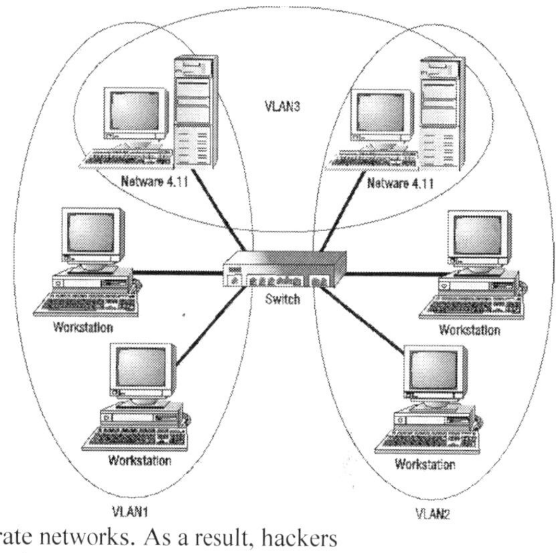

1. *Segment your network and monitor who's trying to get in and out.*
   When designing your network, consider using tools like firewalls to segment your network, thereby limiting access between computers on your network and between your computers and the internet. Another useful safeguard: intrusion detection and prevention tools to monitor your network for malicious activity. Here are some lessons from FTC cases to consider when designing your network.

Not every computer in your system needs to be able to communicate with every other one. You can help protect particularly sensitive data by housing it in a separate secure place on your network. The FTC alleged that a company didn't sufficiently limit computers from one in-store network from connecting to computers on other in-store and corporate networks. As a result, hackers could use one in-store network to connect to, and access personal information on, other in-store and corporate networks. The company could have reduced that risk by sufficiently segmenting its network.

Monitor activity on your network.

"Who's that knocking on my door?" That's what an effective intrusion detection tool asks when it detects unauthorized activity on your network. In an illustrative case, the FTC alleged that the company didn't use an intrusion detection system and didn't monitor system logs for suspicious activity. The FTC says something similar happened in another situation where the business didn't use sufficient measures to detect unauthorized access to its network. Hackers exploited weaknesses, installing programs on the company's network that collected stored sensitive data and sent it outside the network every four days. In each of these cases, the businesses could have reduced the risk of a data compromise or its breadth by using tools to monitor activity on their networks.

2. *Secure remote access to your network.*

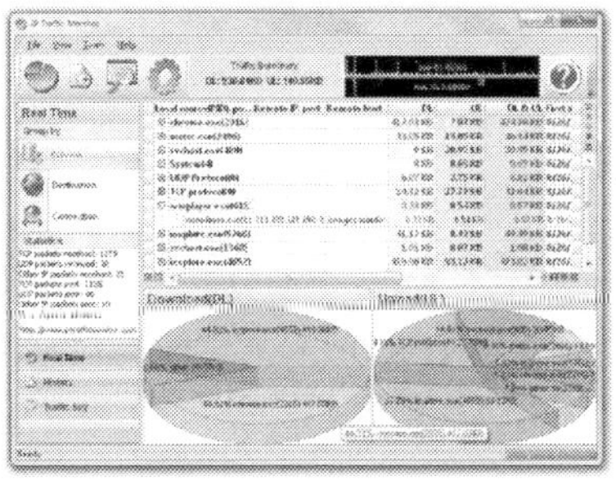

Business doesn't just happen in the office. While a mobile workforce can increase productivity, it also can pose new security challenges. If you give employees, clients, or service providers remote access to your network, have you taken steps to secure those access points? FTC cases suggest some factors to consider when developing your remote access policies.

Ensure endpoint security.

Just as a chain is only as strong as its weakest link, your network security is only as strong as the weakest security on a computer with remote access to it. That's the message of FTC cases in which companies failed to ensure that computers with remote access to their networks had appropriate endpoint security. For example, a company allegedly activated a remote login account for a business client to obtain consumer reports, without first assessing the business's security. When hackers accessed the client's system, they stole its remote login credentials and used them to grab consumers' personal information. According to the complaint in one case, the business allowed clients that didn't have basic security measures, like firewalls and updated antivirus software, to access consumer reports through its online portal. And in another, the FTC charged that the company failed to install antivirus programs on the computers that employees used to remotely access its network. These businesses could have reduced those risks by securing computers that had remote access to their networks.

Put sensible access limits in place.

Not everyone who might occasionally need to get on your network should have an all-access, backstage pass. That's why it's wise to limit access to what's needed to get the job done. In one case, for example, the FTC charged that the company failed to adequately restrict third-party access to its network. By exploiting security weaknesses in the third-party company's system, an intruder allegedly connected to the network numerous times and intercepted personal information. What could the company have done to reduce that risk? It could have placed limits on third-party access to its network – for example, by restricting connections to specified IP addresses or granting temporary, limited access.

3. ***Apply sound security practices when developing new products.***
   So you have a great new app or innovative software on the drawing board. Early in the development process, think through how customers will likely use the product. If they'll be storing or sending sensitive information, is your product up to the task of handling that data securely? Before going to market, consider the lessons from FTC cases involving product development, design, testing, and roll-out.

Train your engineers in secure coding.

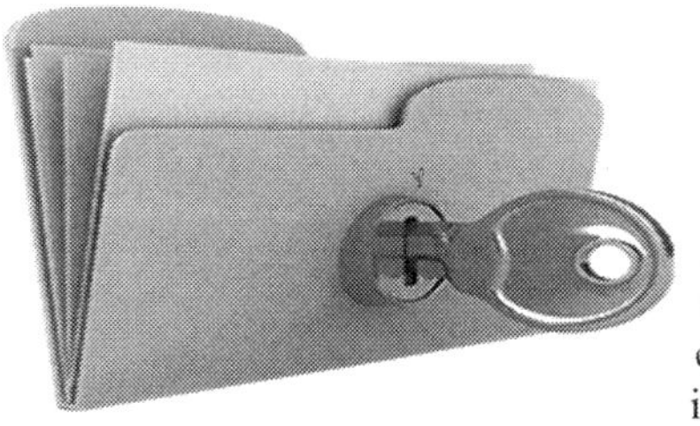

Have you explained to your developers the need to keep security at the forefront? In several cases, the FTC alleged that the companies failed to train their employees in secure coding practices. The upshot: questionable design decisions, including the introduction of vulnerabilities into the software. For example, according to one complaint, the company failed to implement readily available secure communications mechanisms in the logging applications it pre-installed on its mobile devices. As a result, malicious third-party apps could communicate with the logging applications, placing consumers' text messages, location data, and other sensitive information at risk. The company could have reduced the risk of vulnerabilities like that by adequately training its engineers in secure coding practices.

Follow platform guidelines for security.

When it comes to security, there may not be a need to reinvent the wheel. Sometimes the wisest course is to listen to the experts. In additional actions, the FTC alleged that the companies failed to follow explicit platform guidelines about secure development practices. For example, two of them turned off a critical process known as SSL certificate validation in their mobile apps, leaving the sensitive information consumers transmitted through those apps open to interception through man-in-the-middle attacks. The companies could have prevented this vulnerability by following the iOS and Android guidelines for developers, which explicitly warn against turning off SSL certificate validation.

Verify that privacy and security features work.

If your software offers a privacy or security feature, verify that the feature works as advertised. In one case, the FTC charged that the company failed to test that an option to make a consumer's camera feed private would, in fact, restrict access to that feed. As a result, hundreds of "private" camera feeds were publicly available. In another, the company advertised that messages would "disappear forever," but the FTC says it failed to ensure the accuracy of that claim. Among other things, the app saved video files to a location outside of the app's sandbox, making it easy to recover the video files with common file browsing tools. The lesson for other companies: When offering privacy and security features, ensure that your product lives up to your advertising claims.

Test for common vulnerabilities.

There is no way to anticipate every threat, but some vulnerabilities are commonly known and reasonably foreseeable. In more than a dozen FTC cases, businesses failed to adequately assess their applications for well-known vulnerabilities. For example, one case, the FTC alleged that the business failed to assess whether its web application was vulnerable to Structured Query Language (SQL) injection attacks. As a result, hackers were able to use SQL attacks to gain access to databases with consumers' credit card information. That's a risk that could have been avoided by testing for commonly-known vulnerabilities, either using internal resources or third-party providers.

4. ***Make sure your service providers implement reasonable security measures.***
   When it comes to security, keep a watchful eye on your service providers – for example, companies you hire to process personal information collected from customers or to develop apps. Before hiring someone, be candid about your security expectations. Take reasonable steps to select providers able to implement appropriate security measures and monitor that they're meeting your requirements. FTC cases offer advice on what to consider when hiring and overseeing service providers.

Put it in writing.

Insist that appropriate security standards are part of your contracts. In one case, the FTC alleged that the company hired service providers to transcribe sensitive audio files, but failed to require the service provider to take reasonable security measures. As a result, the files – many containing highly confidential health-related information – were widely exposed on the internet. For starters, the business could have included contract provisions that required service providers to adopt reasonable security precautions – for example, encryption.

Verify compliance.

Security can't be a "take our word for it" thing. Including security expectations in contracts with service providers is an important first step, but it's also important to build oversight into the process. In one case, the company hired a service provider to develop a browser toolbar. The company claimed to its users that the toolbar, which collected consumers' browsing information to provide personalized offers, would use a filter to "remove any personally identifiable information" before transmission. But, according to the FTC, the company failed to verify that the service provider had implemented the information collection program in a manner consistent with the company's privacy and security policies and the terms in the contract designed to protect consumer information. As a result, the toolbar collected sensitive personal information – including financial account numbers and security codes from secure web pages – and transmitted it in clear text. How could the company have reduced that risk? By asking questions and following up with the service provider during the development process.

5. ***Put procedures in place to keep your security current and address vulnerabilities that may arise.***
   Securing your software and networks isn't a one-and-done deal. An ongoing process requires you to keep your guard up. If you use third-party software on your networks, or you include third-party software libraries in your applications, apply updates as they're issued. If you develop your own software, how will people let you know if they spot a vulnerability, and how will you make things right? FTC cases offer points to consider in thinking through vulnerability management.

Update and patch third-party software.

Outdated software undermines security. The solution is to update it regularly and implement third-party patches. In one leading case, the FTC alleged that the company didn't update its anti-virus software, increasing the risk that hackers could exploit known vulnerabilities or overcome the business's defenses. Depending on the complexity of your network or software, you may need to prioritize patches by severity; nonetheless, having a reasonable process in place to update and patch third party software is an important step to reducing the risk of a compromise.

Heed credible security warnings and move quickly to fix them.

When vulnerabilities come to your attention, listen carefully and then get a move on. In one reported case, the FTC charged that the company didn't have a process for receiving and addressing reports about security vulnerabilities. HTC's alleged delay in responding to warnings meant that the vulnerabilities found their way onto even more devices across multiple operating system versions. Sometimes, companies receive security alerts, but they get lost in the shuffle. In another, the company relied on its general customer service system to respond to warnings about security risks. According to the complaint, when a researcher contacted the business about a vulnerability, the system incorrectly categorized the report as a password reset request, sent an automated response, and marked the message as "resolved" without flagging it for further review. As a result, Fandango didn't learn about the vulnerability until FTC staff contacted the company. The lesson for other businesses? Have an effective process in place to receive and address security vulnerability reports. Consider a clearly publicized and effective channel (for example, a dedicated email address like security(@)yourcompany.com) for receiving reports and flagging them for your security staff.

6. ***Secure paper, physical media, and devices.***
   Network security is a critical consideration, but many of the same lessons apply to paperwork and physical media like hard drives, laptops, flash drives, and disks. FTC cases offer some things to consider when evaluating physical security at your business.

Securely store sensitive files.

If it's necessary to retain important paperwork, take steps to keep it secure. In one case, the FTC alleged that the defendant maintained sensitive consumer information, collected by his former businesses, in boxes in his garage. In another, the complaint charged that the company left faxed documents that included consumers' personal information in an open and easily accessible area. In each case, the business could have reduced the risk to their customers by implementing policies to store documents securely.

Protect devices that process personal information.

Securing information stored on your network won't protect your customers if the data has already been stolen through the device that collects it. In a 2007 investigation, FTC staff said that the business's PIN entry devices were vulnerable to tampering and theft. As a result, unauthorized persons could capture consumer's payment card data, including the magnetic stripe data and PIN, through an attack known as "PED [pin entry device] skimming." Given the novelty of this type of attack at the time, and a number of other factors, staff closed the investigation. However, attacks targeting point-of-sale devices are now common and well-known, and businesses should take reasonable steps to protect such devices from compromise.

Keep safety standards in place when data is en-route.

Savvy businesses understand the importance of securing sensitive information when it's outside the office. In one case, the FTC alleged that an employee left a laptop containing more than 600 files, with 20 million pieces of information related to 23,000 patients, in the locked passenger compartment of a car, which was then stolen. Another case concerned alleged unencrypted backup tapes, a laptop, and an external hard drive – all of which contained sensitive information – that were lifted from an employee's car. In each case, the business could have reduced the risk to consumers' personal information by implementing reasonable security policies when data is en route. For example, when sending files, drives, disks, etc., use a mailing method that lets you track where the package is. Limit the instances when employees need to be out and about with sensitive data in their possession. But when there's a legitimate business need to travel with confidential information, employees should keep it out of sight and under lock and key whenever possible.

Dispose of sensitive data securely.

Paperwork or equipment you no longer need may look like trash, but it's treasure to identity thieves if it includes personal information about consumers or employees. For example, according to the FTC complaints in two related cases, the companies tossed sensitive personal information – like prescriptions – in dumpsters. In another, the FTC alleged that an employee sold surplus hard drives that contained the sensitive personal information of approximately 34,000 customers in clear text. The companies could have prevented the risk to consumers' personal information by shredding, burning, or pulverizing documents to make them unreadable and by using available technology to wipe devices that aren't in use.

SOURCE [108]

The CITRMS® XV professional is encouraged to explore with business managers the applicability of these actions to the subject organization, and to use this approach as a foundation for further discussion.

Following Rules as Guidelines, Even When They Don't Apply

Company management should be encouraged to learn, understand, and implement the standards applied to lenders under the FTC's Red Flags Rules, and to health care organizations under HIPAA regulations. Even if these requirements do not apply to the subject company, it is advisable to undertake an appropriate level of preventive steps.

There are two practical reasons for undertaking these actions:

1. They help avoid situations where the company may experience an identity theft incident and become liable for the consequences; there is no doubt of the wisdom of avoiding identity theft instead of curing it

2. In the event of a data breach or other identity theft occurrence, the ability to demonstrate preventive actions can help exonerate the company from further liability to either consumers or financial institutions

Preparing an Incident Response Plan

The unfortunate fact is identity theft incidents will happen regardless of the preventive and protective actions companies may implement to avoid them. The time to prepare for the eventuality of an identity theft incident is far in advance of its occurrence. That time is now.

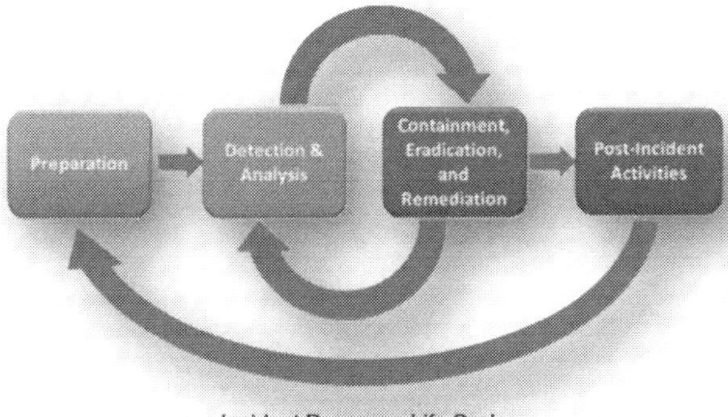

Incident Response Life Cycle

Whether the incident is a single occurrence involving only one other party or a major data breach involving thousands, preparation for an identity theft incident is imperative for any business. On one hand, the business may receive notification from a third party of its own sensitive information being abused by criminals. On the other, the company itself may discover it is the direct victim of a data breach or other type of identity theft attack. In either case, having an incident response plan in place in advance is the best choice.

Adopting and implementing an Identity Theft Incident Response Plan is not a stand-alone exercise. The Identity Theft Response Plan should constitute an integral part of an overall business continuity or incident response program. Whether the incident involves a fault or breakdown in systems supporting communications, transportation, power outage, or other type of threat, an incident of identity theft against the business should be a substantive aspect of proper business planning and administration.

As in prevention, one size does not fit all, but certain guiding principles and techniques in common will be instructive on how best to proceed. The limitations of time and space of this study guide preclude a comprehensive treatment of incident response plans. However, it is appropriate to provide an overview of the essential elements of a successful incident response plan, in order to help direct the business to make choices appropriate to its operations.

- Discovery and Notification.
  - The initiation of the process begins with the discovery of the event at the earliest possible moment, and the transmission of critical information to a designated point of contact for further action.
- Record of Facts.
  - All relevant facts as they become known should be maintained in a central incident facility. These facts should include the nature of the incident, the name and contact information of the person who reported it, the systems or equipment involved and its location, how and when the

incident was detected, and any other information that may help track the cause and potentially the basis for the resolution of the problem, as well as identifying the person or team with the capability and responsibility to resolve the problem.

- Locate and Isolate the Cause of the Problem.
  - Once the above facts are determined, and again in the shortest possible time frame, the person or team with capabilities to address the problem. This may involve only internal personnel or, depending on the circumstances, personnel from third parties on contract with the affected company to take action to resolve this type of event.
- Restore the integrity and operational capability of the affected system
  - This may involve shutting down or removing to another location the physical system, or other action to protect the integrity of the data as well as the system itself. These actions typically should protect against continuing illicit access and abuse of the data, and protect the system from similar attacks in the future.
- Assess the damage to the company and to any other parties potentially adversely affected by the data breach or other identity theft event.
  - It is the responsibility of the internal and third-party technical personnel to determine the extent of the damage to the systems, including the necessity of replacing or otherwise protecting them from further damage. This may include re-installation of systems, resetting passwords and other authentication routines, fully patching any observed flaws in security, and performing restoration from backup facilities.
  - It is the responsibility of other designated personnel to determine the nature and extent of potential damage to customers and other parties with business relationships with the company caused by access by criminals to the sensitive information involved in the breach. This may include coordination with insurers or other service providers under contract to respond to such incidents, as well as necessary notification procedures required by law.
- Documentation and Review of the Incident.
  - As a means of preventing a repetition of such an event, the company should assemble detailed documentation and carry out a full review of the causes, weaknesses, remedies, and future risk management procedures.
  - This may be viewed as an opportunity to strengthen the entire system and the processes for protecting sensitive information of the company, its business associates, and customers.

Looking again to the discussion of micro and macro effects of identity theft incidents, the manner in which a company suffering a data breach or other Identity Theft Incident deals with the problem is as important as the steps taken to prevent such a problem in the first place. Effective preparation for such an event can make the difference between the company's survival and failure. It's worth noting the risk management efforts and preparation for incidents also has a doubly positive effect: the likelihood and severity of such an incident is decreased, and the cost of dealing with the risk and resolution is also diminished.

Business Liability Insurance

Prior to the proliferation of large-scale data breaches and other identity theft incidents, insurance coverage for such liabilities as Director and Officer ("D&O) and Errors and Omissions ("E&O") normally included coverage for nearly all kinds of corporate acts or omissions. At least there were usually no specific exclusions for liabilities and claims arising out of electronic or digital hacks. As more and more data breaches occurred, the insurance carriers started making adjustments in the extent of coverage included in blanket or umbrella-type policies.

Within a few years, it became commonplace for renewal notices for major corporate insurance coverage to include a notice advising the company of the exclusion of coverage for liabilities arising out of these types of events.

Often, these notice documents included an invitation for the company to inquire about the availability of this extended coverage. Of course, underwriting this "new" coverage would involve assessments of the actions and plans the client company had in place to minimize the risk of loss due to identity theft and other data breach events.
The newly defined coverages are usually designed to apply regardless of whether a data breach or other intrusion event is caused by outside hackers, the company's own employees, or vendor relationships including those arising from malicious intent or accidental release of information.

The principal choices in insurance coverage for these types of risks include the following: (Note these are basic descriptions of available coverages, and the many insurance carriers offer different terms and conditions of liability insurance.)

- Coverage for legally enforceable damages and liabilities
- Coverage for regulatory action expenses
- Costs for victims whose personal data may have been compromised
- Coverage for events threatening business continuity
- Legal assistance in responding to regulatory actions and claims for damages
- Services to restore or recover the integrity of the identities of parties affected by a data breach

Businesses may also purchase corporate Identity Theft Protection Services for additional protection. These services may include restoration of the identity of the business itself and the defense of legal actions against the insured.

In evaluating alternatives for cyber insurance coverage, several recommendations are worthy of consideration:

- Start with an internal assessment of the vulnerabilities and potential costs of sustaining an identity theft event, such as a data breach, by considering questions such as these:
    - Is the company's business mostly oriented toward consumers or businesses?
    - What type and volume of data does the company collect, use, store, and distribute?
    - Are the company's technology and information security practices up to date?
    - Are mobile devices an integral part of the business?
    - Do outside business associates have access to the company's sensitive data?
    - Does the company have both an Identity Theft Risk Management plan and an incident response plan in place?

- Depending on the complexities and magnitude of the issues addressed in the internal evaluation, seek assistance from outside sources; examples would include:

    - Insurance agents who have experience with and understand cyber insurance, the nature and extent of liabilities covered, exclusions likely to come into play for the specific company, and alternatives among the insurance carriers offering such coverage
    - Outside professionals with experience and capabilities in assessing identity theft threats and risk management; they may assist in determining the level of risk the company wishes to maintain and comparing the cost and value of purchasing insurance to cover the risk exceeding the company's risk tolerance
    - Providers of monitoring and recovery services, both for the benefit of the company itself as a potential identity theft victim, and also as a potential victim of a data breach or other identity theft event; such providers may offer attractive pricing arrangements if the company sets up a relationship for

the service provider to offer identity restoration services to the parties whose sensitive information might be compromised in a future event.

- Make choices of the extent of coverage, cost of premiums, and provider of insurance based on informed decisions, such as:
    - Specific description of coverage points
    - Premiums and price points for "baskets" of coverage provisions
    - Exclusions and endorsements, which may be affected by State laws
    - Retroactive coverage for prior, but unknown, data breaches
    - Distinctions between "theft" of data and "loss" of data
    - Coverage to include actions or errors of business associates
    - Specific notification cost coverage and restoration benefits for affected parties
    - Defense against regulatory enforcement and penalties
    - To what extent is the company prepared to retain specific uninsured risks

By undertaking a thoughtful and in-depth approach to selecting cyber insurance coverage, the company, and especially the small business, can effectively use known risk management techniques in combination with laying off potentially costly remedial actions through the use of insurance coverage, to implement a successful Identity Theft Risk Management program.

Resources for Keeping Up to Date

As new developments take place in identity theft threats and methods, as well as legal and regulatory responses, numerous organizations provide educational programs at no cost to the participant. Compliance issues are among the featured topics, and the presentations are generally very informative and useful to the CITRMS® XV professional.

An internet search for webinars and similar presentations on identity theft will lead to some of the prominent providers of Identity Theft Risk Management services. Most of their web sites invite registration for these presentations and e-mail lists to be notified of new subjects as they are published. The ICFE does not endorse any specific company or educational program for this purpose. However, the ICFE does recommend taking advantage of these free resources to maintain currency in these trends and developments.

9 Identity Theft Risk Management Solutions

SECTION OVERVIEW

The ICFE has been active in the process of promulgating Identity Theft Risk Management standards, including participating in the Identity Theft Standards Panel (IDSP), an initiative of the American National Standards Institute. Contemporaneously, the ICFE also conducted a major survey of providers of Identity Theft Risk Management providers and their programs.

This section covers four aspects of Identity Theft Risk Management solutions:

1. The ICFE Identity Theft Risk Management Survey and Report
2. Features of Identity Theft Risk Management Services
3. How Identity Theft Risk Management Services are Marketed and Distributed
4. Decisions on Selecting an Identity Theft Risk Management Solution

The Identity Theft Risk Management Survey and Report – A Baseline

Similar to ICFE's disclaimer regarding legal opinions, with regard to Identity Theft Risk Management services, ICFE makes no recommendation on any individual provider. The specific needs of the consumer, and willingness to assume and deal with the risks of becoming a victim of identity theft, must be considered in evaluating and selecting an Identity Theft Risk Management solution. The CITRMS® XV professional and consumers in general should make informed decisions on which of the services, if any, is the right one for a particular individual, family, or business. [109]

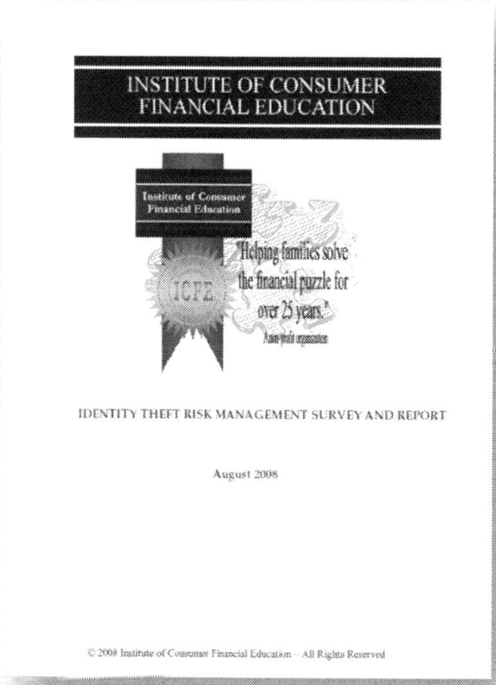

The complete survey and report are posted online at the ICFE web site:

http://www.financial-education-icfe.org/IDT_STUDY/media/aug_08_IDT_Study_report_final.pdf

While there have been some updates and adjustments to the results of the survey, it is appropriate to note that the bulk of the findings and conclusions of the report are still valid as of the date of this publication.

ICFE Identity Theft Risk Management Survey – Preface and Executive Summary

PREFACE

The purpose of this Report is to provide an objective analysis of participants in the marketplace of Identity Theft Risk Management programs.

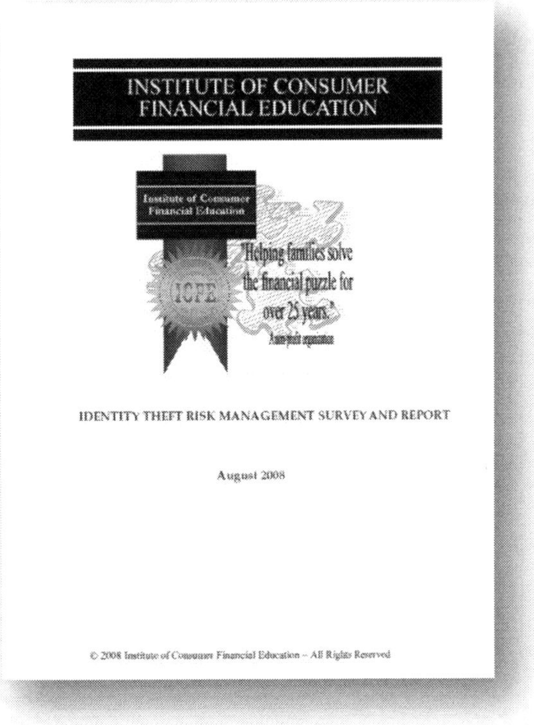

Through a comprehensive Survey and extensive research of publicly available materials, the Institute of Consumer Financial Education (ICFE) has compiled this Report for consumers and for organizations that hold personally identifiable confidential information; they have a duty to protect.

It is important to note that individual consumers have different needs and capabilities, just as not all holders of protected information face the same situation when a data breach occurs.

Accordingly, there is no single "best" provider for all purposes. Some plans are more comprehensive in their methods than others are; some are more or less costly.

Broad-based monitoring of databases that include personally identifiable information is generally the most effective starting point for preventing identity theft. Early notification of potential incidents and prompt follow-up are also essential.

Restoration or recovery services may require little input from the consumer – or it may require the consumer to do practically all the work.

Some plans offer guarantees with varying degrees of ability to fulfill them. The most valuable of such guarantees are those in which specialized third party providers or in-house licensed investigators carry out the restoration services.

Contrary to a common misperception, Identity Theft Risk Management that stops with monitoring or freezing the credit report cannot prevent nearly half of the reported incidents of identity theft, including such types as employment fraud, medical and benefit theft, driver's license issuance, and even criminal activity done in the name of the victim.

There is little regulatory oversight at either State or federal level. Identity Theft prevention programs that exist only in cyberspace are completely unregulated, and are only limited by the enactment and enforcement of anti-fraud laws.

The consumer or other user of these services needs to have access to information to make the best decisions on which is best for the current need.

To this end, ICFE offers this feature-by-feature analysis and comparison of thirty of the most prominent Identity Theft Risk Management programs available in the market today, in a form that is intended to be most readable and useful to those who are most in need of such services.

CONDENSED SUMMARY AND CONCLUSIONS

For Consumers:

It is important to understand the risk of becoming a victim of identity theft, so a good choice can be made. There are generally three types of programs that meet various needs:

- Broad-based monitoring and notification services
- Credit-report monitoring and "freeze" or "fraud alert" programs
- Restoration and Specialty programs (such as medical, employment, or criminal data)

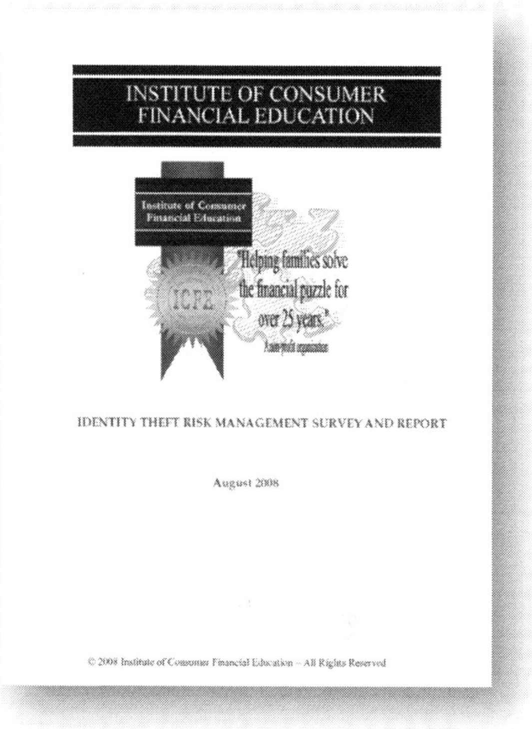
INSTITUTE OF CONSUMER FINANCIAL EDUCATION

Institute of Consumer Financial Education

ICFE

"Helping families solve the financial puzzle for over 25 years."

IDENTITY THEFT RISK MANAGEMENT SURVEY AND REPORT

August 2008

© 2008 Institute of Consumer Financial Education – All Rights Reserved

Broad-based monitoring and notification

Based on the ICFE's extensive research, the most effective means of preventing identity theft, and minimizing damage to the victim, is with a broad-based monitoring and notification service. These are the essential elements of such a service:

- Depth and breadth of databases monitored
- Immediate notification to the consumer of any anomalies
- Individualized risk assessment feature
- Means of predicting and stopping the misuse of personally identifiable information
- Restoration components can complete the safety net of coverage.

Credit-report monitoring and "freeze" programs

It is a common misconception that all incidents of identity theft are financial in nature, and can be prevented or avoided by taking actions on consumer credit files. In fact, official statistics indicate that one-third to one-half of all cases reported to the Federal Trade Commission (FTC) are of types that do not appear in credit reports.

Nonetheless, consumer-oriented Identity Theft Risk Management programs that couple credit report-related actions with restoration services can be effective, though not necessarily fully preventive.

In order to accomplish their risk management mission, the essential features of these programs include:

- Continuous monitoring of credit reports, preferably in all three of the major credit reporting agencies
- Prompt notification to the covered party in the event of any reportable event

- Capability to impose a credit freeze or fraud alert on behalf of the covered party, upon determination that such an action is appropriate and effective

- Pro-active search of other databases in the event that a covered party becomes a victim of identity theft

- Restoration/recovery service for identity theft incidents that are outside the purview of the credit report, such as employment, benefit, medical, drivers licenses, or criminal activities committed using the identifying information of the covered party

Restoration and Specialty Programs

Providers that do not fit neatly into either of the above two categories are assigned to this specialty group. They include providers of proprietary programs, private label services, and restoration specialists. Key features of their services include:

- Information and monitoring of specialized databases, such as medical and Criminal
- Restoration services only, based on insurance-premium type pricing scale
- Establishment of a Personal Identity Profile and monitoring of the elements of such individual profiles
- Direct expense reimbursement as an alternative to insurance
- Self-monitoring of selected databases, and proprietary systems for self-help by consumers

COMMENTS ON GUARANTEES AND INSURANCE

Guarantees

Several of the providers "guarantee" the effectiveness of their services in preventing identity theft. Like all guarantees, the value is no greater than the terms and conditions – and especially the limitations. In most cases, the "guarantee" provides for restoration services, but only if the incident of identity theft is a result of the failure of the underlying prevention program. The most valuable of such guarantees are those in which specialized third party providers or in-house licensed investigators carry out the restoration services.

Insurance

Several of the providers include an insurance component in their programs. The insurance feature typically covers reimbursement for out-of-pocket expenses incurred to restore the integrity of the victim's identity; most include a "lost work time" provision with a cap of $500 per week for 4 weeks. There are numerous limitations and conditions on the coverage. Deductibles range from zero to $250, with a common maximum coverage amount of $25,000.

Many insurance companies offer similar coverage as a rider to homeowners or renters insurance, at a nominal additional premium or even at no additional cost.

In general, the ICFE believes that the inclusion of an insurance feature in an identity theft risk management programs is not a sufficient consideration to make it a better choice than a program without insurance.

CONSIDERATIONS for CONSUMERS [110]

- Early discovery and notification of all types of identity theft-related incidents are paramount; most damage is done between time of the breach and the victim becoming aware of the problem
- Prompt action is required to minimize damages and to recover the integrity of the elements of the victim's identity
- Willingness to participate actively in the recovery and restoration process is an important consideration
- Make informed choices on the elements that are most important to the individual consumer -- and then act on them.

SPECIAL NOTE ON REVIEWS AND RANKINGS OF IDENTITY THEFT SERVICES

Consumers should be aware of many organizations and web sites offering reviews and rankings of Identity Theft Risk Management services. Some of these are public entities, some are non-profit educational organizations, and others are private operations offering advertising and marketing services for hire.

An internet search for terms like "identity theft" or "identity protection" will return many entries, including paid ads near the top and promoted links in favored position on the results page. In turn, companies who pay for preferential placement in the search engines tend to be the ones with monetary motivations rather than objective evaluations for the benefit of the consumer.

Before helping consumers select an Identity Theft Risk Management service based on a third-party review or ranking, the CITRMS® XV professional is advised to confirm the authenticity and objectivity of any such report.

For Holders of Protected Information:

Typically, the decision to select a provider of Identity Theft Risk Management services occurs when the organization responsible for maintaining the confidentiality of protected consumer information has experienced a breach and must take action to prevent or minimize the damage to potential identity theft victims whose personally identifiable information has been inadvertently captured by or released to unauthorized parties.

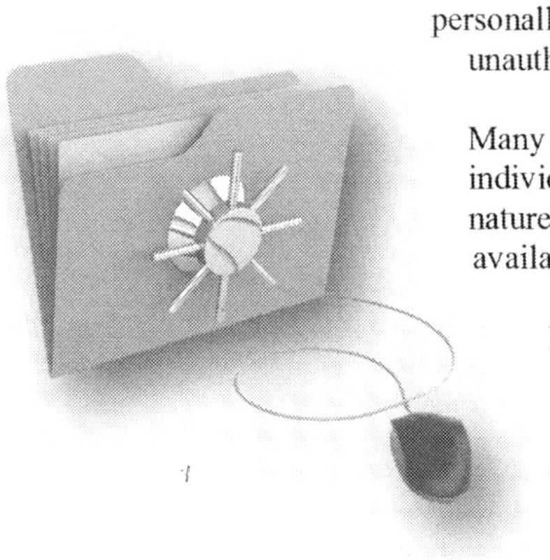

Many of the considerations for selecting such a service are similar to those for the individual consumer in managing this risk. Of special importance is an assessment of the nature of the risk, based on the type of information that has been compromised and any available knowledge about the unauthorized party in possession of the information.

In this context, it is critical to realize the expectation of the person whose information has been breached is not the determining factor about what choice should be made. If the breached information would give rise to the creation of false identity documents or perpetrating employment fraud, for instance, little effect would be accomplished by concentrating solely on prevention of new account fraud.

Of special interest in this regard is the national Identity Theft Standards Panel Initiative: [111]

First, the breached entity, whether it be a business, public or government agency, non-profit organization, or other holder of protected information, must evaluate the nature of the information that has been breached and vulnerabilities of the individuals whose information has been compromised.

In general, there are two categories of such information:

- Financial information, such as the specifics that are present in credit reports.
- Non-Financial information, of the type that does not appear in credit reports, such as employment histories, salary specifics, drivers licenses, criminal records, medical information such as health histories and drug-related items, and would typically be information on employees and receivers of benefits.

Once the determination is made as to type of information and the kinds of vulnerability to which the individuals might be subjected, the decision on the appropriate risk management and damage control program to employ can be made.

Common provisions of such programs are similar to those offered to consumers, as listed above.

Two important distinctions should be observed, based on needs of the parties:

- Consumers making a choice among the various risk management providers start from the assumption their identities have not been compromised, and they have an open choice as to which features best fit their needs.
- Holders of protected information who have suffered a breach of confidentiality need to control various types of potential damage that can result from the breach; beyond the damage to the affected individuals, the damage to the enterprise can include loss of public confidence, loss of customer base, damage to employee loyalty and retention, and other adverse consequences to the organization.

One recent phenomenon should be put into perspective is the claim consumers will be satisfied if their expectations are met in response to a breach of their protected information. Unfortunately, the expectations of the consumer are often based on either unrealistically high standards or unreasonably low standards under which the actual vulnerability of the breached information is simply not taken into account.

It does not help to give the consumer a false sense of security that no harm can befall him or her from the breach of personal information, in circumstances where the prevention program does not have the required depth or breadth.

The most direct example would be the case in which the compromised information is of the Non-Financial variety mentioned above. Securing the credit files to prevent the opening of new accounts in the victim's name does nothing to protect against misuse of personal information to commit employment fraud, medical and benefit abuse, get a drivers license, or engage in criminal activity to the detriment of the victim.

The ICFE's experience as well as information collected in the course of the Survey indicate the per-person costs of obtaining Identity Theft Risk Management coverage for the benefit of those whose information is compromised are variable and subject to negotiation. It is notable there are pricing break-points that can be applied to calculate upfront costs for a given number of individuals to have access to the program, and lesser per-activation charges payable at the time an individual actually enrolls.

Developments Since the ICFE Published the Survey and Report

Since the time of the 2008 survey, as might be expected, the market has undergone numerous changes in the methods of designing, selling, and delivering identity theft prevention and protection services. These include expanding the menu of features and price points for these services, the channels for delivering them, and education of consumers to make choices most appropriate for their specific needs.

More than ever, the application of the "One size does NOT fit all" rule has resulted in a proliferation of different plans and options to meet differing needs and respond to the market. The breadth of the offerings reflects the segmentation of the market. Those who perceive they have more at risk and are less willing to undertake protective and preventive measures themselves tend to require and purchase more robust plans.

Another shift in the marketplace is demonstrated by the growing field of wholesale purchases. In distinguishing wholesale from retail, the principal difference is who makes the purchase decision. Wholesale purchases are made by organizations wishing to provide Identity Theft Risk Management services for their customer or member base. The individuals themselves make retail purchases. In many cases, a hybrid approach is used, in which the basic coverage is provided at no charge to the customer or member, but an upgrade option is offered for individual purchase; these upgrades usually are priced below the charge offered to non-affiliated consumers.

Features of the Identity Theft Risk Management Plans

At present, there are over two dozen providers of Identity Theft Risk Management programs. Some are oriented toward the retail market, where consumers purchase plans directly or through a partnership channel. Some are focused on the wholesale market, providing coverage to large numbers of individuals and their families through bulk sales to businesses for their customers or other organizations for their members. Of course, there are providers addressing both markets.

An internet search for the term "Identity Theft" will return links to many of their web sites, where their specific offerings can be reviewed.

The following list of features represents a compendium of services collected from the Survey and Report, as well as various web sites of the providers. They tend to fall into three segments of bundles and prices: basic, mid-range, and expanded, but this menu is by no means consistent in the particular offerings of any specific provider.

Consumer-oriented Services (Retail)

Basic:

- Credit report monitoring (1 credit reporting agency)
- Address change verification
- Alerts of changes in credit or other personal information
- Guidance on opting out of pre-screened offers by mail and phone
- Identity restoration assistance
- Identity theft insurance

Mid-Range

- Basic services above
- Credit report monitoring (number of credit reporting agencies may vary)
- Social Security number monitoring
- Public record monitoring
- Monitoring employment and tenant records
- Identity vulnerability assessment
- Medical record monitoring
- Data breach notifications
- Alerts for deposit account and credit card activity
- Managed restoration services

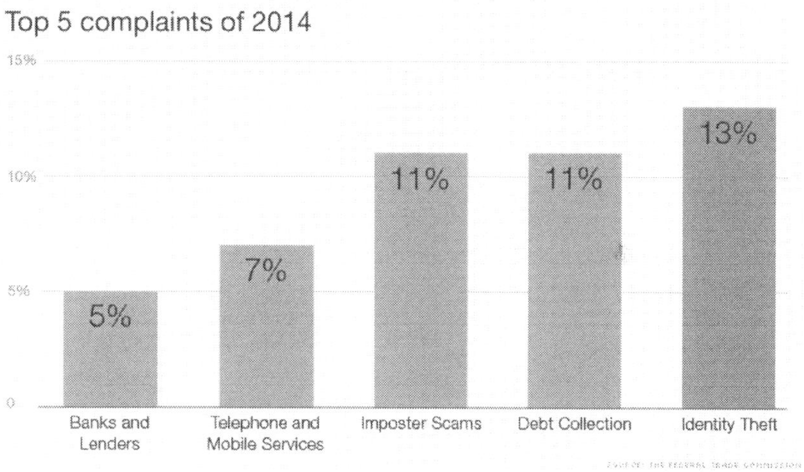

http://records.com/according-to-ftc-identity-theft-remains-top-complaint

Expanded

- Basic and Mid-Range services above
- Credit report monitoring (all 3 credit reporting agencies)
- Credit scores
- Public record monitoring
- Change of address alerts
- Computer protection software
- Credit analysis software
- Password protection software
- Internet black market monitoring for consumer's name and PII
- Customer assistance hotline
- Identity theft insurance
- Certified personnel to conduct identity restoration services

Note many of these terms are interchangeable; others are often used differently by the various service providers.

The important point in this listing is to enable the CITRMS® XV professional to help guide the consumer in selecting a plan, or no plan, to fulfill his or her individual needs.

Business or Organization-oriented Services (Wholesale)

There are three forces driving the Identity Theft Risk Management services toward the wholesale market:

1. Mitigation of damages and potential claims arising out of data breaches
2. Response to regulatory enforcement actions critical of the sale or delivery of these services
3. Economic decisions based on the relationship between the business and its customer.

It should be noted any of these three forces may be the reason for the trend change from retail to wholesale, or they may operate in combination. The important point is to recognize this trend and take appropriate action. From the consumer's perspective, the decision may be delayed in being presented until after an opportunity to try out the service.

CASE IN POINT

It is not unusual for an individual to receive notification from a company or other organization with a relationship with the consumer advising there has been a data breach. Such a notification often is accompanied by instructions on how the consumer can register or enroll for an Identity Theft Risk Management service paid for by the organization suffering the data breach.

Currently, depending on the severity of the breach and the nature and extent of the sensitive information involved, the most common service is to monitor the individual's credit report and provide a restoration service, usually for a period of one year.

Due to the large number of organizations having experienced massive data breaches, it is also common for a single individual to receive and be covered by more than one such service at a given point in time. There may be overlapping time periods of coverage, resulting in the individual being able to move from one service to another for extended periods without paying directly.

At the end of the monitoring and resolution period paid for by the breached organization, the consumer is usually offered the option of continuing the service at a reduced price. At that point, it is the consumer's decision to continue or not.

Remediation after Data Breach

For several years, the "default setting" for data breach remediation was for the breached organization to provide one year of credit report monitoring and restoration services to the individuals whose sensitive information was compromised in the breach.

Because of the complexity of the affected information and the statistical likelihood of identity thieves misusing it in ways that do not necessarily show up in credit reports, this solution has been reviewed with an eye toward broadening the monitoring services to match more closely the nature of the information in the specific breach.

> **Remediation after Data Breach**
>
> It now takes an average of 31 days at a cost of $20,000.00 per day to clean up and remediate after a cyber attack.
>
> - Ponemon Institute, 2014

Fortunately, the capabilities of the service providers have expanded as well, and the response to data breaches is in the process of becoming more effective for the benefit of the potentially affected individuals.

At the same time, it is becoming more incumbent on the affected consumer to participate more actively in preventing adverse effects resulting from the data breach. For instance, upon receiving the notification of the breach, with the offer of Identity Theft Risk Management services, the consumer must take action to enroll in the service. This enrollment usually requires the consumer to authenticate his or her identity, and pay attention and respond appropriately to any communications from the service provider.

Once enrolled, the consumer should cooperate in pursuing both the remedy and the perpetrator, if so requested, as a means of mitigating any potential damage. As observed in Section 6, any claim for damages the consumer may pursue would be undercut if the consumer were to fail to take such mitigating actions.

Overall, the impact of data breaches on the Identity Theft Risk Management service market has been to offer and register tens of millions of consumers in plans they would likely not have purchased on a retail basis.

Response to Regulatory Enforcement Actions

For several years, starting in the late 1990s, a substantial number of financial institutions and membership organizations set up arrangements with providers of Identity Theft Risk Management services. These alliances or partnerships involved having the company with the customer or member relationship offering the identity theft plan on a retail basis to their customers or members. The pricing was usually set up to provide a discount to the consumer and a revenue share to the participating organization. For some time, it appeared to benefit all concerned.

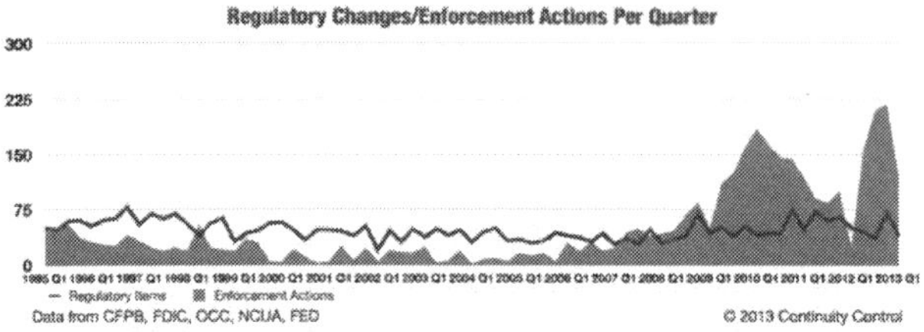

http://www.continuity.net/knowledge-center/press-releases/54-first-regulatory-index-launched-to-gauge-burden-on-

However, the systems for enrollment, payment, and delivery of services was not always free of troubles and disputes. As detailed in Section 6, the Federal Trade Commission (FTC) in recent years has brought numerous enforcement actions against companies, which have offered these identity theft services to their existing customers. The principal stated reasons for these actions include the following:

- Failure to provide the services as described
- Incomplete or inaccurate sign-up procedures, resulting in "unauthorized charges"
- Charges continuing after the customer requested termination of the service

State Attorneys General joined some of these enforcement actions in, under provisions of State law. This is important due to the charges and penalties assessed against the companies involved.

Typically, these cases were settled rather than proceeding to further administrative hearings or judicial actions. The settlement terms often included a statement of no culpability, but also a statement the offending practices would not be used in the future. The financial penalties often covered three payments:

1. Costs and additional payment to the FTC
2. Costs and additional payment to the participating State Attorneys General
3. Reimbursements to the consumers affected by the offending practices

In practical terms, these enforcement actions resulted in the affected companies, and many of their competitors, abandoning the retail sale of identity theft plans to their customers. That left a vacuum in the marketplace.

Economic Decisions [112]

Although the following analysis is anecdotal, not statistical, it appears there is a trend toward a new pattern of providing consumers with Identity Theft Risk Management services based on strengthening the business or organizational relationship rather than simply maximizing immediate revenues.

At the time of this writing, there has been a move away from the optional add-on service model for the consumer to make a stand-alone retail buying decision. In its place, the provision of a basic identity theft service at no cost to the consumer appears to be growing as a way to gain the consumer's loyalty and continued relationship.

There are several models for this trend. They may be seen as replacements for the customer/member discount retail offering, or as follow-ons when coverage pursuant to a data breach expires, or filling another business purpose.

For current purposes, three of these models bear further elaboration:

- Free basic service with an upgrade option
- Free restoration-only service
- Specialized proprietary services

Developments in How Identity Theft Risk Management Services are Marketed and Distributed

Free basic service with an upgrade option

In this arrangement, the company or organization contracts with a service provider to extend the basic coverage package to all customers/members at no cost to the consumer. The consumer must enroll or register with the service provider to receive this service.

The sponsoring company or organization also offers the consumer an expanded or upgraded service, usually at a discount from the retail price advertised by the service provider to non-affiliated individuals. There may or may not be a share of the revenue paid back to the sponsoring company or organization from the sale of upgraded services.

There are no publicly available reports on the take-up rate for either the non-cost basic service or upgrade options for any of the companies or organizations participating in this arrangement.

Presumably, the success of these arrangements will determine how long they continue or how they are modified or replaced by other programs.

CASE IN POINT

AAA of Arizona for several years offered a discounted Identity Theft Risk Management service to members. For undisclosed reasons, this organization changed to an offering of "free identity theft monitoring" with a discounted upgrade option.

The free service offers features common to those listed above as "Basic," and the upgraded service features are in the "Mid-Range" to "Expanded" type.

Detailed information is posted at the organization's web site:

https://www.az.aaa.com/financial/identity-theft-monitoring

Free restoration-only service

This approach has gained acceptance as a benefit for large-scale membership organizations and employment-related groups. It tends to be considered when a periodic review is conducted on the utilization and cost-effectiveness of competing benefits of all kinds.

Since the restoration-only service is similar to insurance against a damage event, the cost to the provider only comes into play when the covered party becomes aware of an identity theft event. As with any other application of large numbers, the rate of claims against the numbers of covered parties results in a very reasonable per-person "premium" cost.

Given the undisputed growth in the number and severity of identity theft incidents, and the likelihood of identity theft needs growing in comparison with other common membership and employment benefits, continuation of this trend can be extrapolated.

CASE IN POINT

The Indiana Farm Bureau provides all of its paying members with free Identity Fraud Resolution Service from a recognized national identity theft service provider. In addition to long-standing mainstream membership benefits, such as financial, medical, travel, and general insurance features, it is becoming more common to include a free restoration-only identity theft benefit as an attractive and valuable part of the membership experience.

Detailed information is posted at the organization's web site: http://www.infarmbureau.com/membership/

Specialized proprietary services

In some cases, large umbrella service organizations use an identity theft service offered through its participating businesses to strengthen their brands and relationship values. These relationships exist on two levels: the organization with its business customer and the organization with the retail customer of the business.

In this arrangement, emphasizing the brand of the umbrella organization as well as its business customer go hand in hand. The apportioning of payment for the service is not generally disclosed, but to the consumer it is free.

Prominent participants in this kind of arrangement include financial institutions, which formerly offered a retail purchase option to their customers, but decided for regulatory or other economic reasons to terminate that offering.

Nonetheless, the perceived need and value involved in identity theft protection and prevention led them to replace the optional coverage with a cost-free customer benefit.

Note the consumer may retain an extensive responsibility in resolving an identity theft incident, unlike the full-service restoration benefits in which the provider interacts directly with the credit reporting agencies, businesses, law enforcement, and public repositories of complaints such as the FTC.

In this case, economies of scale come into play, and the purchasing power combined with the application of large number effects, as in loss/damage insurance, permit the participating companies to provide this benefit on a very cost-effective basis.

CASE IN POINT

MasterCard offers proprietary "Identity Theft Resolution Services" through participating credit card issuers. Following is a summary of the description of this service in a release from MasterCard:
Program Description: Personal Identity Theft Resolution Services provides you with access to a number of Identity Theft resolution services, should you believe you are a victim of Identity Theft.

Eligibility: To be eligible for this coverage, you must be a valid MasterCard cardholder issued by a U.S. financial institution.

Services provided - Services provided are on a 24-hour basis, 365 days a year. They include:

- Providing the cardholder with a uniform Identity Theft Affidavit and providing assistance with completion of the Affidavit. It is the responsibility of the cardholder to submit the Affidavit to the proper authorities, credit bureaus, and creditors.
- Assistance in notifying all three major credit-reporting agencies to obtain a free credit report for the cardholder and placing an alert on the cardholder's record with the agencies.
- Assisting the cardholder with debit, credit, and/or charge card replacement.
- Assisting cardholder with membership/affinity card replacement.
- Educating the cardholder on how Identity Theft can occur and of protective measures to avoid further occurrences.
- Providing the cardholder with the Identity Theft Resolution Kit.
- Providing the cardholder with sample letters for use in canceling checks, ATM cards, and other accounts.

Identity Theft Alerts: MasterCard is offering Cardholders cyber security through Identity Theft Alerts, a proprietary Internet surveillance technology that proactively detects the illegal trading and selling of personally identifiable information (PII) online. At any point in time, Identity Theft Alerts is tracking thousands of websites and millions of data points, and alerting Cardholders whose personal information they find has been compromised online. This information is being gathered in real-time so that Cardholders have the opportunity to react quickly and take the necessary steps to protect themselves.

The Alerts service includes monitoring specific bank and credit accounts of covered cardholders as well as phone numbers, Social Security, driver license and passport numbers, e-mail addresses and medical identification numbers. The cardholder to activate each of these items must fill in the specific information.

This legend appears on the enrollment page: "MasterCard is the only payment brand that provides its U.S. cardholders with services—at no extra cost—to help them detect and resolve identity theft." [113]

CAVEAT: The cardholder is encouraged to inquire and confirm coverage for identity theft involving business, as well as personal information, especially regarding the use of a business account credit card.

Although MasterCard offers this service at no cost to the cardholder, it is not alone in providing Identity Theft Risk Management support through its financial institution network. The Visa system concentrates on monitoring use of its branded credit cards and provides its own security program to assist Visa cardholders. Visa advises the cardholder must still notify the card issuer of any unauthorized transaction. Visa also offers access to confidential assistance for help recovering from identity theft, through a telephone hotline to reach trained volunteers. [114]

To round out discussion of Identity Theft Risk Management practices of the major credit card systems, both American Express and Discover offer online educational resources and monitoring of their own card accounts. They have instituted enhanced authentication facilities, as well as ways to receive alerts to confirm transactions. At the time of this writing, neither one offered a general identity theft monitoring or resolution service. [115]

Decisions on Selecting an Identity Theft Risk Management Solution

As stated by the ICFE on numerous occasions, including earlier in this course guide, the ICFE does not make specific recommendations on the most appropriate choice, if any, of an identity theft service plan for any given individual or group.

The ICFE does encourage CITRMS® XV professionals to be sufficiently knowledgeable about the range of services offered by various service providers. To assist consumers and businesses in determining the best steps they can take in responding to the threat of identity theft, as well as how much of the risk they are comfortable keeping themselves, and what level of peace of mind they require, by keeping current with these marketplace developments.

Future Developments

It is too early to tell whether the changes in retail and wholesale marketing of Identity Theft Risk Management services represent a sea change or only an intermediate development on the way to yet another emerging pattern.

There is no indication the retail offerings to consumers will ever be discontinued. On the contrary, it should be expected to see more refined packages of services closely fitting the perceived needs of specific consumer demographics.

The ICFE and the author stand ready to respond to inquiries by CITRMS® XV professionals and to help consumers, businesses and other organizations manage the risk of identity theft in the most appropriate way for each individual situation.

APPENDIX

The ICFE and the author expect all CITRMS® XV professionals to have access to the internet. Unlike the prior course, this Appendix does not include the extensive list of postal addresses and phone numbers for government agencies and other relevant organizations.

Detailed contact information for many holders of sensitive information appears in Section 4, including the three major consumer reporting agencies, specialty reporting agencies, and other holders of PII and PHI.

For practical reasons, this Appendix includes only information and forms for illustrative purposes. Extensive identity theft prevention and reporting facilities are now available online.

For example, there is an interactive "Consumer Complaint" report program hosted by the Federal Trade Commission at http://www.consumerfinance.gov/complaint/ . The first step is to select "Identity Theft," the first item on the navigation bar on the left. The eight following steps lead the consumer through a complete reporting routine to complete the filing.

Similarly, the Consumer Financial Protection Bureau hosts an interactive complaint center, online at http://www.consumerfinance.gov/ . The "Submit a Complaint" box leads to a choice of financial product involved in the problem, and the consumer can either post a specific report on the complaint or write a narrative of the problem.

The following documents may be found online; as they are of exemplary importance, they are printed out here for easy access.

Average time to complete: 10 minutes

Identity Theft Victim's Complaint and Affidavit

A voluntary form for filing a report with law enforcement, and disputes with credit reporting agencies and creditors about identity theft-related problems. Visit identitytheft.gov to use a secure online version that you can print for your records.

Before completing this form:
1. Place a fraud alert on your credit reports, and review the reports for signs of fraud.
2. Close the accounts that you know, or believe, have been tampered with or opened fraudulently.

About You *(the victim)*

Now

Leave (3) blank until you provide this form to someone with a legitimate business need, like when you are filing your report at the police station or sending the form to a credit reporting agency to correct your credit report.

(1) My full legal name: ______________________
First Middle Last Suffix

(2) My date of birth: ______________
mm/dd/yyyy

(3) My Social Security number: ______-_____-______

(4) My driver's license: ________ ______________
State Number

(5) My current street address:

____
Number & Street Name Apartment, Suite, etc.

____
City State Zip Code Country

(6) I have lived at this address since ______________
mm/yyyy

(7) My daytime phone: (___)______________
My evening phone: (___)______________
My email: ______________________

At the Time of the Fraud

Skip (8) - (10) if your information has not changed since the fraud.

(8) My full legal name was: ______________________
First Middle Last Suffix

(9) My address was: ______________________
Number & Street Name Apartment, Suite, etc.

____
City State Zip Code Country

(10) My daytime phone: (___)______________ My evening phone: (___)______________
My email: ______________________

The Paperwork Reduction Act requires the FTC to display a valid control number (in this case, OMB control #3084-0047) before we can collect – or sponsor the collection of – your information, or require you to provide it.

Victim's Name ______________________ *Phone number* (___)__________ *Page 2*

About You *(the victim) (Continued)*

Declarations

(11) I ☐ did OR ☐ did not authorize anyone to use my name or personal information to obtain money, credit, loans, goods, or services — or for any other purpose — as described in this report.

(12) I ☐ did OR ☐ did not receive any money, goods, services, or other benefit as a result of the events described in this report.

(13) I ☐ am OR ☐ am not willing to work with law enforcement if charges are brought against the person(s) who committed the fraud.

About the Fraud

(14) I believe the following person used my information or identification documents to open new accounts, use my existing accounts, or commit other fraud.

(14): Enter what you know about anyone you believe was involved (even if you don't have complete information).

Name: ______________________________
First Middle Last Suffix

Address: ______________________________
Number & Street Name Apartment, Suite, etc.

____
City State Zip Code Country

Phone Numbers: (___)__________ (___)__________

Additional information about this person: ______________________________

____

____

____

____

____

____

____

____

____

____

Victim's Name ______________________ *Phone number* (___)__________ *Page 3*

(15) Additional information about the crime (for example, how the identity thief gained access to your information or which documents or information were used):

____
____
____
____
____
____
____

(14) and (15): Attach additional sheets as needed.

Documentation

(16) I can verify my identity with these documents:

☐ A valid government-issued photo identification card (for example, my driver's license, state-issued ID card, or my passport).
If you are under 16 and don't have a photo-ID, a copy of your birth certificate or a copy of your official school record showing your enrollment and legal address is acceptable.

☐ Proof of residency during the time the disputed charges occurred, the loan was made, or the other event took place (for example, a copy of a rental/lease agreement in my name, a utility bill, or an insurance bill).

(16): Reminder: Attach copies of your identity documents when sending this form to creditors and credit reporting agencies.

About the Information or Accounts

(17) The following personal information (like my name, address, Social Security number, or date of birth) in my credit report is inaccurate as a result of this identity theft:

(A) ____
(B) ____
(C) ____

(18) Credit inquiries from these companies appear on my credit report as a result of this identity theft:

Company Name: ______________________________________
Company Name: ______________________________________
Company Name: ______________________________________

Victim's Name ______________________ *Phone number* (____)______________ *Page 4*

(19) Below are details about the different frauds committed using my personal information.

Name of Institution   Contact Person   Phone   Extension

Account Number   Routing Number   Affected Check Number(s)

Account Type: ☐ Credit ☐ Bank ☐ Phone/Utilities ☐ Loan
☐ Government Benefits ☐ Internet or Email ☐ Other

Select ONE:
☐ This account was opened fraudulently.
☐ This was an existing account that someone tampered with.

Date Opened or Misused (mm/yyyy)   Date Discovered (mm/yyyy)   Total Amount Obtained ($)

Name of Institution   Contact Person   Phone   Extension

Account Number   Routing Number   Affected Check Number(s)

Account Type: ☐ Credit ☐ Bank ☐ Phone/Utilities ☐ Loan
☐ Government Benefits ☐ Internet or Email ☐ Other

Select ONE:
☐ This account was opened fraudulently.
☐ This was an existing account that someone tampered with.

Date Opened or Misused (mm/yyyy)   Date Discovered (mm/yyyy)   Total Amount Obtained ($)

Name of Institution   Contact Person   Phone   Extension

Account Number   Routing Number   Affected Check Number(s)

Account Type: ☐ Credit ☐ Bank ☐ Phone/Utilities ☐ Loan
☐ Government Benefits ☐ Internet or Email ☐ Other

Select ONE:
☐ This account was opened fraudulently.
☐ This was an existing account that someone tampered with.

Date Opened or Misused (mm/yyyy)   Date Discovered (mm/yyyy)   Total Amount Obtained ($)

---

(19):
If there were more than three frauds, copy this page blank, and attach as many additional copies as necessary.

Enter any applicable information that you have, even if it is incomplete or an estimate.

If the thief committed two types of fraud at one company, list the company twice, giving the information about the two frauds separately.

Contact Person: Someone you dealt with, whom an investigator can call about this fraud.

Account Number: The number of the credit or debit card, bank account, loan, or other account that was misused.

Dates: Indicate when the thief began to misuse your information and when you discovered the problem.

Amount Obtained: For instance, the total amount purchased with the card or withdrawn from the account.

Victim's Name ______________________ *Phone number* (___)________________ *Page 5*

Your Law Enforcement Report

(20) One way to get a credit reporting agency to quickly block identity theft-related information from appearing on your credit report is to submit a detailed law enforcement report ("Identity Theft Report"). You can obtain an Identity Theft Report by taking this form to your local law enforcement office, along with your supporting documentation. Ask an officer to witness your signature and complete the rest of the information in this section. It's important to get your report number, whether or not you are able to file in person or get a copy of the official law enforcement report. Attach a copy of any confirmation letter or official law enforcement report you receive when sending this form to credit reporting agencies.

Select ONE:

- ☐ I have not filed a law enforcement report.
- ☐ I was unable to file any law enforcement report.
- ☐ I filed an automated report with the law enforcement agency listed below.
- ☐ I filed my report in person with the law enforcement officer and agency listed below.

(20): Check "I have not..." if you have not yet filed a report with law enforcement or you have chosen not to. Check "I was unable..." if you tried to file a report but law enforcement refused to take it.

Automated report: A law enforcement report filed through an automated system, for example, by telephone, mail, or the Internet, instead of a face-to-face interview with a law enforcement officer.

____
Law Enforcement Department State

______________________ ______________________
Report Number Filing Date (mm/dd/yyyy)

______________________ ______________________
Officer's Name (please print) Officer's Signature

______________________ (___)__________
Badge Number Phone Number

Did the victim receive a copy of the report from the law enforcement officer? ☐ Yes OR ☐ No

Victim's FTC complaint number (if available): ______________________

Victim's Name ______________________ *Phone number* (___)______________ *Page 6*

Signature

As applicable, sign and date *IN THE PRESENCE OF* a law enforcement officer, a notary, or a witness.

(21) I certify that, to the best of my knowledge and belief, all of the information on and attached to this complaint is true, correct, and complete and made in good faith. I understand that this complaint or the information it contains may be made available to federal, state, and/or local law enforcement agencies for such action within their jurisdiction as they deem appropriate. I understand that knowingly making any false or fraudulent statement or representation to the government may violate federal, state, or local criminal statutes, and may result in a fine, imprisonment, or both.

______________________ ______________________
Signature Date Signed (mm/dd/yyyy)

Your Affidavit

(22) If you do not choose to file a report with law enforcement, you may use this form as an Identity Theft Affidavit to prove to each of the companies where the thief misused your information that you are not responsible for the fraud. While many companies accept this affidavit, others require that you submit different forms. Check with each company to see if it accepts this form. You should also check to see if it requires notarization. If so, sign in the presence of a notary. If it does not, please have one witness (non-relative) sign that you completed and signed this Affidavit. If someone has used your Social Security number (SSN) to get a tax refund or a job, or you suspect your SSN has been stolen, alert the IRS using Form 14039 at **www.irs.gov/pub/irs-pdf/f14039.pdf**.

____
Notary

Witness:

______________________ ______________________
Signature Printed Name

______________________ ______________________
Date Telephone Number

Located at http://www.ftc.gov/bcp/edu/resources/forms/affidavit.pdf

EQUIFAX experian TransUnion

Annual Credit Report Request Form

You have the right to get a free copy of your credit file disclosure, commonly called a credit report, once every 12 months, from each of the nationwide consumer credit reporting companies - Equifax, Experian and TransUnion.

For instant access to your free credit report, visit www.annualcreditreport.com.

For more information on obtaining your free credit report, visit www.annualcreditreport.com or call 877-322-8228.

Use this form if you prefer to write to request your credit report from any, or all, of the nationwide consumer credit reporting companies. The following information is required to process your request. **Omission of any information may delay your request.**

Once complete, fold (do not staple or tape), place into a #10 envelope, affix required postage and mail to:
Annual Credit Report Request Service P.O. Box 105281 Atlanta, GA 30348-5281.

Please use a Black or Blue Pen and write your responses in PRINTED CAPITAL LETTERS without touching the sides of the boxes like the examples listed below:

A B C D E F G H I J K L M N O P Q R S T U V W X Y Z 0 1 2 3 4 5 6 7 8 9

Social Security Number: ___ - __ - ____

Date of Birth: __ / __ / ____
Month Day Year

Fold Here Fold Here

First Name M.I.

Last Name JR, SR, III, etc.

Current Mailing Address:

House Number Street Name

Apartment Number / Private Mailbox For Puerto Rico Only: Print Urbanization Name

City State ZipCode

Previous Mailing Address (complete only if at current mailing address for less than two years):

House Number Street Name

Fold Here Fold Here

Apartment Number / Private Mailbox For Puerto Rico Only: Print Urbanization Name

City State ZipCode

Shade Circle Like This → ●

Not Like This → ⊗ ✓

I want a credit report from (shade each that you would like to receive):
○ Equifax
○ Experian
○ TransUnion

○ Shade here if, for security reasons, you want your credit report to include no more than the last four digits of your Social Security Number.

If additional information is needed to process your request, the consumer credit reporting company will contact you by mail.

Your request will be processed within 15 days of receipt and then mailed to you.

31238

G-1

Source: http://www.consumer.ftc.gov/articles/pdf-0093-annual-report-request-form.pdf

LexisNexis®

Instructions for Requesting Free C.L.U.E. Inc. Consumer File Disclosure

Thank you for your interest in receiving your free C.L.U.E. Inc. consumer file disclosure under the FACT Act.

You may request C.L.U.E. Inc. consumer file disclosure only on yourself or your minor child. Please submit a separate request for each individual and complete all the appropriate items on the request form.

Please provide the following proof of identity along with your request.

Required: Submit one item from Category A below.
Required: Submit one item from Category B below for your primary mailing address.
Conditional: Submit one item from Category B below if the report requested is for a second home or rental property (provide this when the property is not your primary mailing address).

Category A – Photocopy of one of these items, in your name:

1. Social Security Card
2. State Drivers License.
3. State Issued ID Card: Must be in effect (expiration date has not passed).
4. Canadian Issued Drivers License: Must be in effect (expiration date has not passed)

Category B – Photocopy of one of these documents, dated within the preceding two months, or as noted:
(Must Reference Your Name and Mailing Address or Secondary/Rental Property Address):

1. Major Credit Card Billing Statement
2. Utility Bill
3. Telephone Bill
4. Insurance Declaration Page: Must be in effect (expiration date has not passed).
5. Property Tax Bill: Must be for most current year or year immediately preceding.
6. Property Deed: No date requirement.

Send the completed order form to:

LexisNexis Consumer Center
C.L.U.E. Inc.
P.O. Box 105295
Atlanta, GA 30348-5295

You should receive your file disclosure(s) in the mail approximately 15 business days after we receive your request.

CD041m-11-14f

LexisNexis

C.L.U.E. Auto/Property Request Form

Order Options: C.L.U.E. Auto Report ☐ C.L.U.E. Property Report ☐ Both Reports ☐

Shaded information is required – please print clearly

First Name (required) | Middle Name (required unless none)

Last Name (required) | Suffix (Sr., Jr., III, etc.)

Social Security Number (required) ___-___-___ | Date of Birth (Month-Day-Year – required) ___-___-___ | Gender (M/F)

Current physical address

Current Street Address (required) | Apt. #

City (required) | State (required) | ZIP (required)

Phone Number ___-___-___

Complete this section if you have lived at your current address for less than six (6) months

Previous Street Address | Apt. #

Previous City | Previous State | Previous ZIP

Page 1 CD105m-06-12e

LexisNexis

C.L.U.E. Auto/Property Request Form

Complete this section if your mailing address is different from your current address

Mailing Address — Apt. #

City — State — ZIP

Complete this section if you are requesting C.L.U.E. property reports on a residential property or vacation home

Street Address — Apt. #

City — State — ZIP

Complete this section if you are requesting a C.L.U.E. auto report

Driver's License Number — Driver's License State

Previous Driver's License Number — Previous Driver's License State

Signature (required) — Date (required)

Page 2 CD105m-06-12e

source: https://personalreports.lexisnexis.com/pdfs/clue-order-by-mail.pdf

Sample Certificate

ENDNOTES 1-115

[1] The use of similar terms in physical health advice provides an apt analogy: proper diet and regular exercise are important elements in preventing and protecting against disease and ill health, but they cannot assure a long and healthy life.

[2] The **Data Security and Breach Notification Act of 2015** has been pending in the U. S. House of Representatives since April 2015. Arguments for and against have been advanced by various parties, including business interests claiming it is too broad and burdensome, and privacy advocates who are concerned that it may weaken stronger State laws. *This ENDNOTE will be updated in the online version of this ISG as appropriate.*

[3] http://www.consumer.ftc.gov/articles/0005-identity-theft

[4] http://www.justice.gov/criminal/fraud/websites/idtheft.html

[5] http://www.consumerfinance.gov/askcfpb/1243/what-identity-theft.html

[6] https://en.wikipedia.org/wiki/Identity_theft

[7] **For more on this distinction, see the article posted at** http://it.med.miami.edu/x718.xml

[8] For further discussion of this concept, see Arvind Narayanan and Vitaly Shmatikov, in "Myths and Fallacies of Personally Identifiable Information"
https://www.cs.utexas.edu/~shmat/shmat_cacm10.pdf

[9] http://www.hhs.gov/ocr/privacy/hipaa/understanding/training/udmn.pdf

[10] http://www.hhs.gov/ocr/privacy/hipaa/understanding/coveredentities/De-identification/guidance.html

[11] SOURCE:
http://www.hhs.gov/ocr/privacy/hipaa/understanding/coveredentities/index.html
HHS provides via this web site a question and answer decision tool, to help organizations determine whether or not it appears they are covered entities for this purpose.

[12] http://www.hhs.gov/ocr/privacy/hipaa/understanding/coveredentities/businessassociates.html

[13] For more on synthetic identity theft, see, for example http://securityintelligence.com/synthetic-identity-theft-three-ways-synthetic-identities-are-created/#.VYCPnUanGbQ

[14] For a broader perspective, try searching **"Right to be Forgotten"**

[15] A chronology of data breaches is maintained by the Privacy Rights Clearinghouse and is posted online at: http://www.privacy information.org/articles/chronology_of_data_breaches

[16] The respective reports can be found via the following links:
http://www.privacyrights.org/data-breach and
http://www.idtheftcenter.org/ITRC-Surveys-Studies/2014databreaches.html
Each one shows links to access additional information about the methodologies they use to compile their reports.

[17] http://www.privacyrights.org/data-breach

[18] http://www.idtheftcenter.org/images/breach/DataBreachReports_2014.pdf

[19] https://www.javelinstrategy.com/news/1556/92/16-Billion-Stolen-from-12-7-Million-Identity-Fraud-Victims-in-2014-According-to-Javelin-Strategy-Research/

[20] http://www.bankinfosecurity.com/blogs/will-sony-settle-cyber-attack-lawsuit-p-1880

[21] http://www-03.ibm.com/security/data-breach/

[22] http://www-03.ibm.com/security/data-breach/

[23] http://blogs.findlaw.com/free_enterprise/2013/09/cost-of-a-small-business-cyberattack-9k.html and http://www.nsba.biz/wp-content/uploads/2013/09/Technology-Survey-2013.pdf
Overall, it is fair to observe that while an organization may be smaller in size, and suffer a less extensive data breach, the result may be more threatening to the its continuation as a going concern and future sustainability.

[24] http://medidfraud.org/2014-fifth-annual-study-on-medical-identity-theft/ Used by permission from the Medical Identity Fraud Alliance ("MIFA").

[25] http://medidfraud.org/about/

[26] http://www.healthcareitnews.com/news/medical-identity-theft-hits-all-time-high?single-page=true Used by permission from the Medical Identity Fraud Alliance ("MIFA").

[27] http://www.foia.gov

[28] http://www.census.gov/history/www/genealogy/decennial_census_records/census_records_2.html

[29] Lists of such services appear in various places on the internet. A few are the following (there are many others, and they change from time to time): *www.privacyrights.org/ar/infobrokers.htm* *http://www.publicrecordsreviews.com/Drivers-License-Records* and *www.napbs.com*

[30] http://www.washingtonpost.com/blogs/federal-eye/wp/2015/06/07/after-the-latest-hack-attack-can-feds-trust-uncle-sam-with-their-personal-information/?tid=hpModule_ba0d4c2a-86a2-11e2-9d71-f0feafdd1394&hpid=z10 and http://www.gao.gov/products/GAO-15-573T

[31] https://servicearizona.com/webapp/vehicle/renewal/step2Plate.do

[32] See the periodically updated list from Consumer Financial Protection Bureau (CFPB), an independent federal agency: http://files.consumerfinance.gov/f/201501_cfpb_list-consumer-reporting-agencies.pdf
Note the CFPB uses the more-inclusive designation "Consumer Reporting Agencies" in its listing; accordingly, some of the listings and discussion below on "Specialty Reports" also refer to the CFPB listings and descriptions.

[33] Source, Federal Trade Commission Complaint, February 2008.

[34] http://www.king5.com/story/news/local/2015/05/30/thousands-targeted-by-credit-card-skimmer-in-seatac/28202255/

[35] This case discussion is based on several public sources, primarily the following:

- https://communities.usaa.com/t5/USAA-News/Insta-Scam-Fraudsters-Target-USAA-Members-with-Card-Cracking/ba-p/64486?EID=corp_cc_15_06_EANEWS3-05
- http://www.usatoday.com/story/money/columnist/tompor/2015/05/24/cracking-cards-scam-fbi-aba-warning/27726127/

[36] For more information on "Rachel" and this scheme, see http://www.nbcnews.com/business/consumer/robocall-credit-card-interest-scam-continues-plague-consumers-n387676

[37] http://nypost.com/2015/05/23/bogus-credit-card-alerts-a-new-concern-for-consumers/

[38] http://www.azcentral.com/story/money/business/2015/06/25/phone-scammers-reinvent-ruse/29294207/

[39] http://www.makeuseof.com/tag/anatomy-scam-windows-tech-support-con-examined/

[40] http://whatis.techtarget.com/definition/de-anonymization-deanonymization

[41] https://privacyassociation.org/news/a/why-director-comey-cant-have-his-cake-and-eat-it-too/

[42] Representative current reports appear online at http://mobile.reuters.com/article/idUSKCN0PJ2M420150709?irpc=932 and https://privacyassociation.org/news/a/21-5-million-breached-in-second-opm-hack/

[43] https://www.mastercardconnect.com/mol/molbe/public/login/ebusiness/smart_cards/one_smart_card/biz_opportunity/cap/index.jsp

[44] http://www.visa.gr/media/images/dynamicpasscodeauthentication-42-6506.pdf

[45] http://blogs.wsj.com/cmo/2015/06/05/fraudsters-use-amazons-cloud-to-create-fake-web-traffic/

[46] https://privacyassociation.org/news/a/why-director-comey-cant-have-his-cake-and-eat-it-too/

[47] See the information posted at www.icfe.org and also ICFE's Certified Credit Report Reviewer® (CCRR) course.

[48] These common definitions are based on the information posted on Wikipedia.

[49] http://www.theverge.com/2015/7/14/8956945/google-photos-collecting-pictures-android-after-delete-app

[50] http://www.sciencedaily.com/releases/2015/07/150701152319.htm and The above post is reprinted from materials provided by **The Optical Society.**

[51] http://money.cnn.com/2015/06/17/technology/samsung-galaxy-hack/index.html

[52] http://www.usatoday.com/story/tech/columnist/komando/2015/07/03/komando car-rental-mistakes/29614165/

[53] Hayden's comments in an exclusive interview were reported in detail at http://www.wsj.com/articles/michael-hayden-says-u-s-is-easy-prey-for-hackers-1434924058?KEYWORDS=michael+hayden

[54] http://www.pcmag.com/article2/0,2817,2487023,00.asp

[55] http://www.google.com/policies/faq/ and https://cse.google.com/cse/docs/tos

[56] https://en.wikipedia.org/wiki/Big_data

[57] http://www.pcworld.com/article/2948332/most-google-delisting-requests-are-from-everyday-folk-leaked-data-shows.html and http://www.pcworld.com/article/2922012/a-year-after-the-right-to-be-forgotten-ruling-google-is-not-very-likely-to-forget-about-you.html

[58] http://www.cnet.com/news/amazon-discloses-transparency-report-for-first-time/ and http://www.cnet.com/news/facebook-governments-still-clamoring-for-user-data/

[59] http://www.washingtonpost.com/world/national-security/as-encryption-spreads-us-worries-about-access-to-data-for-investigations/2015/04/10/7c1c7518-d401-11e4-a62f-ee745911a4ff_story.html?hpid=z3

[60] https://fortune.com/2015/06/12/cytech-product-demo-opm-breach/

[61] http://www.reuters.com/article/2014/09/24/us-cybersecurity-hospitals-idUSKCN0HJ21I20140924

[62] http://www.irs.gov/uac/Examples-of-Identity-Theft-Schemes-Fiscal-Year-2014

[63]http://files.consumerfinance.gov/f/201207_cfpb_bulletin_marketing_of_credit_card_addon_products.pdf and http://www.consumerfinance.gov/newsroom/cfpb-orders-chase-and-jpmorgan-chase-to-pay-309-million-refund-for-illegal-credit-card-practices/

[64] http://www.washingtonpost.com/blogs/federal-eye/wp/2015/05/26/hackers-stole-personal-information-from-104000-taxpayers-irs-says/?hpid=z1

[65] The IRS "Identity Verification Service" website is the most efficient way to complete the task. See: https://idverify.irs.gov/IE/e-authenticate/welcome.do

[66] Taxpayers can also access ID Verify through www.IRS.gov on the Understanding Your 5071C Letter or the Understanding Your IRS Notice or Letter page. The service is also available in Spanish.

[67] DISCLAIMER: http://www.ovc.gov/disclaimer.html

Links to Other Sites
OVC provides links to other Web sites as a convenience to its visitors and tries to ensure that the links are current. The inclusion of a link on this Web site does not constitute an official endorsement, guarantee, or approval by OVC. OVC neither endorses, has any responsibility for, nor exercises any control over the organizations' views or the accuracy of the information contained in those pages outside of OVC's Web site.

[68] https://www.ftc.gov/tips-advice/business-center/privacy-and-security/red-flags-rule

[69] The specificity with which the FTC has reduced this analysis to writing makes it a preferred source for the interpretation of the provisions. See more at: https://www.ftc.gov/tips-advice/business-center/guidance/fighting-identity-theft-red-flags-rule-how-guide-business#who

Several useful FAQs appear at this same URL, and CITRMS® XV Certificants are encouraged to review this information from time to time.

[70] Full listing appears in the lower portion of the FTC's URL at https://www.ftc.gov/tips-advice/business-center/guidance/fighting-identity-theft-red-flags-rule-how-guide-business#who

[71] Detailed information is posted at the CFPB web site: http://www.consumerfinance.gov/

[72] http://www.consumerfinance.gov/newsroom/cfpb-takes-action-against-companies-for-unfair-billing-of-credit-card-add-on-products-and-services/

[73] http://www.consumerfinance.gov/newsroom/cfpb-orders-bank-of-america-to-pay-727-million-in-consumer-relief-for-illegal-credit-card-practices/

[74] http://www.consumerfinance.gov/newsroom/cfpb-orders-american-express-to-pay-59-5-million-for-illegal-credit-card-practices/

[75] http://www.consumerfinance.gov/newsroom/cfpb-orders-chase-and-jpmorgan-chase-to-pay-309-million-refund-for-illegal-credit-card-practices/

[76] http://www.consumerfinance.gov/newsroom/discover-consent-order/

[77] This material was sourced directly from the U. S. Department of Health and Human Services web site. More detailed discussion for further study is posted at this URL:
http://www.hhs.gov/ocr/privacy/hipaa/understanding/training/udmn.pdf

[78] This material was sourced directly from the U. S. Department of Health and Human Services web site. More detailed discussion for further study is posted at this URL:
http://www.hhs.gov/ocr/privacy/hipaa/understanding/srsummary.html

[79] This graphic comes directly from the HHS web site at
http://www.hhs.gov/ocr/privacy/hipaa/enforcement/process/index.html

[80] This material was sourced directly from the U. S. Department of Health and Human Services web site. More detailed discussion for further study is posted at these URLs:
http://www.hhs.gov/ocr/privacy/hipaa/enforcement/highlights/index.html
http://www.hhs.gov/ocr/privacy/hipaa/administrative/enforcementrule/index.html
http://www.hhs.gov/ocr/privacy/hipaa/enforcement/examples/allcases.html#case16#case13

[81] This material was sourced directly from the U. S. Department of Health and Human Services web site. More detailed discussion for further study is posted at these URLs:
http://www.hhs.gov/ocr/privacy/hipaa/administrative/enforcementrule/hitechenforcementifr.html
http://www.hhs.gov/ocr/privacy/hipaa/administrative/enforcementrule/enfifr.pdf

[82] Detailed information can be accessed online at http://www2.ed.gov/policy/gen/guid/fpco/ferpa/index.html

[83] https://www.ftc.gov/tips-advice/business-center/privacy-and-security/children%27s-privacy is the original source for the above information. The full text of the COPPA Rule is posted at http://www.ecfr.gov/cgi-bin/text- idx?SID=4939e77c77a1a1a08c1cbf905fc4b409&node=16%3A1.0.1.3.36&rgn=div5

[84] http://www.consumer.ftc.gov/articles/0497-credit-freeze-faqs

[85] For more detailed information on DPPA, see http://www.gpo.gov/fdsys/granule/USCODE-2011-title18/USCODE-2011-title18-partI-chap123-sec2721/content-detail.html

[86] The Arizona Title and Registration form includes a check-off box with this language:

"I consent to the release of personal information contained in my driver license and vehicle record. I understand that this is not a one-time consent that applies only to a specific individual or organization, but is instead a general consent that applies to all requests from any and all individuals or organizations for any purpose, until revoked by me in writing. Consent for a vehicle record applies to all owners."

[87] See the discussion in Section 2 of the magnitude and trends in data breaches.

[88] http://www.leginfo.ca.gov/cgi-bin/displaycode?section=civ&group=01001-02000&file=1798.25-1798.29 and http://fas.org/sgp/crs/misc/R42475.pdf Report by the Congressional Research Service.

[89] As of the time of this writing, current provisions are listed at http://www.ncsl.org/research/telecommunications-and-information-technology/security-breach-notification-laws.aspx
"States with no security breach law: Alabama, New Mexico, and South Dakota."

[90] http://www.hhs.gov/ocr/privacy/hipaa/enforcement/sag/index.html

[91] An interesting synopsis of the historical changes to the features of the Social Security card appears on the official web site at http://www.ssa.gov/history/ssn/ssnversions.html

[92] This list is posted at https://www.annualcreditreport.com/protectYourIdentity.action

[93] Be aware that many web sites with similar sounding names are being used by private companies to offer their services, and even by identity thieves attempting to gain access to sensitive consumer information. Even those claiming to be free are actually selling something, usually credit monitoring services or credit scores. The *only* official web site authorized by federal law is www.annualcreditreport.com

[94] As indicated in Section 6, these legal requirements are subject to periodic legislative modification, and should not be relied upon for a definitive statement of current law.

[95] For more information visit the Federal Trade Commission's website at www.consumer.ftc.gov/articles/0058-credit-repair-how-help-yourself or the Consumer Finance Protection Bureau's website at www.consumerfinance.gov/askcfpb/315/what-is-my-credit-score.html

[96] For more information on earning these certifications, please see the ICFE's main web site at www.icfe.org

[97] The bulletin is posted online at http://files.consumerfinance.gov/f/201211_cfpb_NSCRA_Bulletin.pdf

[98] https://blog.lastpass.com/2015/06/lastpass-security-notice.html/

[99] It has been reported that several newly discovered vulnerabilities in a central Android software component called Stage fright (which is used to play, process or record multimedia files) could affect up to 95 percent of Android users. If the user opens a malicious Multimedia Messaging Service (MMS) message, it may provide complete access to the phone to hackers, allowing them to access anything on the phone or wipe everything out. Caution should be exercised with MMS messages, especially if the sender is unknown.

[100] The Federal Trade Commission recently issued the following "scam alert":
Scammers have been making phone calls claiming to represent the National Do Not Call Registry. The calls claim to provide an opportunity to sign up for the Registry. These calls are not coming from the Registry or the Federal Trade Commission, and you should not respond to these calls.

[101] https://www.identitytheft.gov/warning-signs-of-identity-theft.html

[102] A recent regulatory action by the Consumer Financial Protection Bureau requires credit reporting agencies to delay reporting delinquent consumer payments for health services for 180 days, on account of the delays in payment by health insurance companies.

[103] This discussion is adapted from an article published by the author **"When the Victim of Identity Theft is Your Employee"** http://www.alllaw.com/articles/employment/article51.asp